WHO KILLED EMMETT TILL?

WHO KILLED EMMETT TILL?

By Susan Klopfer

New Background on the Continuing Story of a Chicago School Boy Whose Murder Inspired the Modern Civil Rights Movement

Published by Susan Klopfer at Lulu
Edited by Jay Mattsson

Copyright © 2010 by Susan Klopfer

All rights reserved. No part of this book may be reproduced, stored, or transmitted by any means—whether auditory, graphic, mechanical, or electronic—without written permission of both publisher and author, except in the case of brief excerpts used in critical articles and reviews. Unauthorized reproduction of any part of this work is illegal and is punishable by law.

Lulu Edition
Susan Klopfer

ISBN 10 - 0-9826049-1-2
ISBN 13 - 9780982604915

Mount Pleasant, Iowa 52641
sklopfer@gmail.com
web: http://susanklopfer.com
Delta Photo Gallery http://mygalleryplace.com/delta

This book is dedicated to Eight Mississippi Delta Civil Rights Martyrs – Joe Pullen, Rev. George Lee, Lamar Smith, Emmett Till, Birdia Keglar, Adlena Hamlett, Jo Etha Collier and Cleveland McDowell. Written Especially For My Granddaughter, Grace Sophia Klopfer.

Table of Contents

This book was first written as a blog. All chapters are "posts" which have been reversed so that the book reads in chronological order.

Prologue	xi
Introduction: The Delta	1
Post #1: Early Life in the Yazoo-Mississippi Delta; a Land of 'Runaway Slaves Horribly Disfigured By Their Cruel Masters'	7
Post #2: African American Enslaved Built Mississippi; 'Maroons' Found Asylum in a Swamp Community Known as 'Africa'	13
Post #3: Delta Rife With Violence During Reconstruction	23
Post #4: Mississippi Lynching Becomes 'Theatrical Spectacular'	37
Post #5: The Marcus Garvey Movement Awakened Race Consciousness: The Delta Would Have Changed For Better, Had Garvey Succeeded	47
Post #6: I was in the middle of posting to this blogbook when ...	57

Post #7:	Murder of Joe Pullen, "Another Civil Rights Movement Watershed — Like the Elaine Massacre"	59
Post #8:	Emmett Till's Casket Acquired By Smithsonian and My Reaction, Thursday, August 27, 2009	67
Post #9:	Mississippi flood of 1927, Continued Violence and Government Failure Disrupt the Delta; Scientists, Theologians, Journalists, Communists Try to Help	69
Post #10	U.S. Rep. Benjamin Thompson Seeks Attorney General's Probe in Sumner	81
Post #11	"Emmett, Down In My Heart" — the 1955 Lynching of 14-year-old Emmett Till in the Mississippi Delta	83
Post #12	Remembering and Honoring Memories of Emmett Till and Dr. Martin Luther King, Jr.	85
Post #13:	Mississippi Mau Mau; Veterans Return Home From World War II	87
Post #14	Tallahatchie County: Long Known For Civil Rights Violence and Frequent Klan Encounters	105
Post #15	"A Child Shouldn't Have To Be Scared."	109
Post #16:	Tallahatchie Manhunt, Booze, Guns, Dogs and More	117
Post #17	Brown I, Brown II and Three Mississippi Murders	119
Post #18	Update: Manhunt Rumors Haunt Mississippi Town With Troubled Past	125

Post #19	"Negroes Up North Have No Respect For People" — "It's a Shame Emmett Till Had To Die So Soon"	129
Post #20	Sumner, Miss., Milam/Bryant Murder Trial; 'First Great Media Event of the Civil Rights Movement'	139
Post #21	Sumner 'a Good Place to Raise a Boy': The Emmett Till Murder Trial	145
Post #22	Cemetery Where Emmett Till Buried; Handed Back to Owners	159
Post #23	Still Another Unsolved Mississippi Murder? Cleve McDowell Investigated Delta Murder Victims, Including Emmett Till	161
Post #24	The Autopsy of Cleveland McDowell	171
Post #25	Mississippi Reporter Fought Racism; Jerry Mitchell, Wins MacArthur Award	189
Post #26	Burr Oak, New Overseers; Emmett Till's Grave Unharmed	191
Post #27	Sick and Tired of Being Sick and Tired of Racist Remarks By Glenn Beck	193
Post #28	Final Post: The Beginning or the End?	195
Epilogue		225
Afterword		229
Questions & Answers		231
Acknowledgements		243
About the author		245
End Notes		247
Extended Bibliography		265
Index		281

Prologue

"I think that every time a man stands for an ideal or speaks out against injustice, he sends out a tiny ripple of hope."

Aaron Henry, Mississippi civil rights leader

IN THE HOT SUMMER before the cold winter in which our nation entered the second world war to end all wars, two boys were born two weeks apart; one in Illinois and the other in Mississippi.

They would never meet but both were murdered at different times in their lives, in and near the cotton-ginning town of Drew in Sunflower County, the heart of the Mississippi Delta. Each would have his place in this country's civil rights movement.

Fourteen-year-old Emmett Till of Chicago was kidnapped in the early morning hours of August 28 in 1955. The young man was visiting Mississippi relatives in a small cotton hamlet known as Money, a tiny community spread out on a patch of dirt under very old oak trees with several homes, a few businesses and a red brick church house with a humble graveyard near it.

Accused of whistling at a white store owner's wife, Emmett Till was kidnapped and taken to a plantation owner's tool shed at the edge of Drew where he was tortured and possibly killed. His body was hauled by truck to the edges of another small town, Glendora, anchored with barbed wire to a 75-pound metal, cotton gin fan and thrown into the Tallahatchie River.

The sight of Till's brutalized body in an open pine box casket was shown to thousands of mourners in Chicago a week later, after being returned home from the Delta. And this display pushed many who had been content to stay on the civil rights sidelines directly into the fight.

Young Emmett Till's body showed the world the racial problems belonging to the United States, and gave a new voice for victims of racial injustice.

Among those moved to action was civil rights activist Rosa Parks of Montgomery, Alabama who, at the age of 42, refused to obey a city bus driver's order that she give up a forward seat to make room for a white passenger.

Her action came twelve weeks after an all-white Mississippi jury, after sixty-seven minutes of deliberation, acquitted J.W. Milam and Roy Bryant of the murder of Emmett Till. She was not the first activist to make this move. There had been other attempts. But Parks had been planning her personal protest, and along with the NAACP knew the right time had arrived.

Some 42 years later, Cleveland McDowell of Drew, a life-long Mississippi attorney and a minister, whose career was unquestionably defined by Till's brutal murder, was shot to death in his home. As a foot soldier in the modern civil rights movement, sparked by the death of Emmett Till, McDowell became a friend to hosts of civil rights leaders including Rev. Martin Luther King, Jr. , Rev. Jesse Jackson, Fannie Lou Hamer and Medgar Evers.

In 1963, McDowell became the first black student admitted to the University of Mississippi law school, following in the footsteps of his mentor, James Meredith. All of his professional life, McDowell secretly tracked details of race-based murders, including Till's lynching, while keeping in touch with Emmett's mother in Chicago. McDowell was only fifty-six years old when he was gunned down.

Introduction: The Delta

A river is a living soul that flows along, continually picking up and dropping off tiny pieces of rock and dirt from its bed throughout its length. Where the river slows, more are dropped than picked up and this becomes a place of alluvial soil or a flood plain. Such regions are the stuff of agricultural wealth — at least for the landowners who make their riches from healthy crops and the physical labor of others.

Nearly 18,000 years ago a continental glacier covered North America. As the frozen waters melted, the Mississippi River and its tributaries carved valleys and created flood plains giving birth to what is technically the Yazoo-Mississippi Delta, an agricultural flood plain so filled with rich alluvial soil that you can smell the money through the morning mist.

"Yazoo" is of Native American origin, meaning "River of Death." As evening comes to the Yazoo-Mississippi Delta, there is dampness in the air. When cotton is at its peak, if you take a deep breath, there is a smell that comes from just below the damp topsoil, an unsettling scent for those who know the region's history of enslavement and inhumanity. It fills one's nostrils as if cruelty has no trouble finding a direct pathway to the brain. Some who have spent time in the Delta, and who know its stories, say that ghosts of martyrs rise from the rich dirt's faint mist.

THE MISSISSIPPI DELTA is not a place I would have picked to live and if you had asked me a few years ago what I knew about the region, it would have been a puzzle since I knew nothing of its history or culture — I'd never even heard of the Delta Blues.

My husband, Fred, was hired by a private group to be the mental health director for inmates in Mississippi's state-run prisons, and so our lives took on a new dimension as we made a small, red-brick house on the grounds of Parchman Penitentiary our new Sunflower County home, in the heart of the Delta.

Eventually, I would enjoying smelling the richness of the alluvial soil and appreciate where we had been dropped. But not the afternoon of my arrival.

The air conditioning was broken and the house had not been cleaned by maintenance crews. There were cobwebs in every corner, dirt on the floor and it was at least 100 degrees plus beastly humid in the shade.

I was madder than hell when I arrived because the car broke down in Oklahoma, putting our three cats and myself into a dilemma. Fred had been living in Jackson, the state capitol, for a month and could only help problem solve by telephone as we drove in from Nevada.

One thing I learned following my self-serving fit of anger was that prisoners don't ever have air conditioning at Parchman, except in the hospital unit. All of the historic brick and buildings were replaced years ago by metal construction and the prisoners were living in what amounted to bake ovens. They were living in hell.

Summer left and on cooler fall mornings, I watched out the front window of our new home through the leaves of mature pecan trees as several prisoners at a time trotted rescue and misfit horses into the ripe cotton fields. They earned this privilege, working with a unique horse-care program, and I wondered how much it would hurt to enjoy and then relinquish such freedom when evening came.

One year before we arrived, Mississippi's Department of Archives and History, upon court order, made its second release of an online full-text version of the state's secret Sovereignty Commission records. The commission operated as a private spy agency from 1956 to 1972 within the state government, with a mission to investigate and halt all integration attempts. The commission's second goal was to make Mississippi look good to the world, despite the frequent beatings and murders of its black citizens and outsiders who came into the state, trying to end racial violence and discrimination, and reinstate voting rights.

The year we moved to Mississippi, the FBI began re-examining the murder of Emmett Till and would exhume his body the following summer as one of more than 100 unsolved civil rights cold cases that occurred prior to 1969.

Fred came from a liberal, big-city family and could recall hearing his parents talk about Till when he was a child growing up in Oregon. Raised in a small eastern Oregon town, in a more conservative family, I had never heard the story. But even Fred did not recognize that we were living in the epicenter of the Land of Emmett Till.

The story of this young man murdered in a small, nearby cotton hamlet began to resurface when his body was exhumed and examined in June of 2005 by the Cook County medical examiner's office. While eating catfish and greens in Drew's Main Street restaurant, we listened in as some Delta people, black and white, talked quietly about what was happening.

Who would not be interested in this story? Soon, I was spending more and more hours in Walter Scurlock's restaurant listening and then driving around the Delta, trying to piece together the stories I was gathering. Many older black people quickly warmed to my questions and soon shared their secrets of relatives and others who were brutalized and sometimes killed over the years.

And as they told their stories, it was as if these crimes had just taken place. Most white people, on the other hand, didn't seem to want to share what they knew unless they had been actively involved in the movement. Or they simply didn't know the history.

Mississippi's William Faulkner once wrote "The past is never dead, in fact, it's not even past."

And in true Faulknerian spirit, the people who wanted to talk to me were soon sharing their stories as though it were yesterday. Some had kept lists of up to thirty names, passed through their families, of people who had "disappeared." Others told stories of their own involvement in trying to bring change.

I spent time looking through yellowed files in small-town libraries, museums and newspaper offices seeking records of any kind to expand my knowledge; some records were so delicate and uncared for, they crumbled in my hands and I had to quickly put them down so they would not be ruined.

But the best history came directly from the people who talked to me — men and women wanting to examine what they experienced or had heard during some of the worst years of Mississippi's civil wrongs.

Who Killed Emmett Till?

Emmett Till's story has its roots in Mississippi's early history, when kidnapped and enslaved Africans were brought into the Delta, forced to clear swamps, and plant and harvest cotton under the vilest conditions.

In 1975 Professor James Loewen tried to help his Tougaloo College students go to these roots for understanding the Till story, and other history, when he co-wrote the first revisionist state-history textbook in America, winning the Lillian Smith Award for "best nonfiction about the South."

But Loewen had to sue the state to make *Mississippi: Conflict and Change* even available to public schools. We can hope that today's Mississippi historical gatekeepers won't let this happen again.

From Loewen and others, there appear to be three major themes surrounding Mississippi's civil rights history. First, few of Mississippi's thousands of race-based murders can be seen as isolated events, including the slaying of Till. These atrocities fit into a larger pattern reflective of the region's brutal society formed even before statehood.

Secondly, there were powerful forces outside of Mississippi contributing money and other resources to keep the evil flowing — from Northern people who had always profited from enslavement and discrimination in one way or another.

More than three fourths of the cotton consumed by British mills during antebellum years came from the American South via New England mills and New York businesses that marketed and shipped the cotton overseas.

Northern banking interests supported the slave trade. Slave ships built and outfitted in New England sailed to Africa right up to the Civil War. Twelve million Africans would be shipped to the Americas from the 16th to the 19th centuries; with an estimated 645,000 enslaved brought to what is now the United States.

Interestingly, Mississippi state records show most money collected and spent by Mississippians to fund and sustain the fight against the 1964 Civil Rights Act and to develop Mississippi's private, segregated academies or schools, came from outside of Mississippi. Money came from Northern business concerns and was moved through a Northern bank. Significant help came from a famous publisher, William "Bill" Loeb III, publisher of the *Manchester Union Leader* newspaper in New Hampshire and from Morgan Guaranty Trust.

Thirdly, some of the people involved in bringing change to their state have simply been forgotten or still undiscovered by historians. Cleve McDowell, Jo Etha Collier, Birdia Keglar and Adlena Hamlett, Lamar Smith, Rev. George Lee, Joe Pullen, and so many others unnamed, have earned their place in history.

Why does Mississippi's history matter today?

Some believe the modern civil rights movement began with Rosa Parks and the Montgomery bus boycott. Others mark this date as the murder of Emmett Till. But no mass movement starts all of a sudden. Before the Civil War began and well into the 1940s and early '50s, many years before the modern civil rights movement made the pages of the white press and then television, there were brave souls trying to right wrongs. They worked in the North and they tried their best from inside "the belly of the beast"—Mississippi.

With today's increased racism and discrimination, especially following the election of this country's first black president, we would all be well served to watch closely as Mississippi attempts to transcend from a state denying some of the worst mental and physical atrocities against kidnapped Africans and African Americans in this nation, to a state accepting its history and seeking clues that explain the functions of racism and discrimination.

Mississippi's newly announced History in the Classroom program is the outgrowth of a state law passed in 2006. Statewide implementation is planned for the 2010-2011 school year, following an unsuccessful legislative effort to eliminate the plan entirely in 2009.

It will be an interesting journey to follow as Mississippi moves along, and a process from which to learn.

Note: This book was first written as a blog. All chapters are "posts" which have been reversed so that the book reads in chronological order.

Post #1:

Early Life in the Yazoo-Mississippi Delta; a Land of 'Runaway Slaves Horribly Disfigured By Their Cruel Masters'

Delta attorney Cleve McDowell's father and his grandmother loved to tell family stories, and as a child McDowell learned early family history and how his kin survived as enslaved Africans. He eventually inherited the role as his family's record-keeper and was so thorough, he was often asked by unrelated friends and neighbors in his hometown of Drew, in Sunflower County, to help sort out their own family roots, his sister said.

"They knew everybody, their families and everything that had happened to them. My father's own mother, a former slave, lived to be near 100, too. She could remember back to the Civil War. Her name was Sally McDowell and she hid in the chimney when the Yankees liberated that area. I think they were in Arkansas at the time," Cleve McDowell said in an oral interview given in 1997, one year before he was murdered.[1]

What was life like for those who picked the cotton? For McDowell's relatives and others, a glimpse comes from the writings of Charles Dickens who visited Mississippi at the age of 29.

In January of 1842 Dickens sailed from Liverpool on the Steamship Britannia bound for America. At the height of his popularity in both countries, Dickens had taken a year off from writing, determined to visit the young nation "to see for himself this haven for the oppressed which had righted all the wrongs of the Old World."[2]

Dickens was soon disenchanted as he traveled down the Mississippi River viewing the cotton fields from the deck. In *American Notes*, the book he wrote after returning home to England, Dickens made scathing comments about the institution of slavery, citing newspaper accounts of "runaway slaves horribly disfigured by their cruel masters."

The famous English writer would later observe: "This is not the Republic I came to see ... This is not the Republic of my imagination ... The more I think of its youth and strength, the poorer and more trifling in a thousand respects, it appears in my eyes. In everything of which it has made a boast ... it sinks immeasurably below the level I had placed it upon."

As the visiting writer made his trip from Memphis, Tenn., down the Mississippi River, it was the Yazoo-Mississippi Delta where he could so closely see the inhumanity of slavery.

MOST MISSISSIPPIANS KNOW that saying "the Delta" refers to Mississippi's region of flat farming lands, reaching from the Chickasaw Bluffs below Memphis to the Walnut Hills above Vicksburg, Miss., a unique expanse of great wealth and greater poverty. It is common to hear a person from Mississippi say they are from "the Delta." The word "Yazoo" is left out.

Few could describe *the Delta* more eloquently than David Cohn, a popular white writer coming from the region who wrote, "The Mississippi Delta begins in the lobby of the Peabody Hotel in Memphis and ends on Catfish Row in Vicksburg."

Cohn painted the Delta as a land of excess: "The hot sun, the torrential rains, the savage caprices of the unpredictable river. The fecund earth, the startling rapid growth of vegetation, the illimitable flat plains, and the vast dome of heaven arching over all of them: these environmental influences almost seemed to breed in the people a tendency toward the excessive."[3]

Even with a century of clearing, cultivating, draining and land leveling, the Delta's earthy beauty stands out at sunset when the sun's burnt orange rays press into murky waters of swamps, bayous, and oxbow lakes. Ripe cotton fields blanket the Delta like soft snow. Wheat, rice and sorghum crops are separated by large and very shallow catfish farm ponds, often outlined by flocks of dinner-seeking and protected snow-white egrets.

The handsome birds were once imported to the Delta for their perfect hat feathers, but now irritate pond owners with their "pound-a-day" fish-eating habits. Mississippi is now the largest catfish producing state, despite the egrets.

Driving a car around the Delta seems one of the best ways to get in touch with the region's rich history. The intensity of the Delta's unforgiving past runs through miles of kudzu vine-covered railroad tracks and sweeps across small country bridges spanning innumerable muddy rivers and streams, small lakes, cane breaks and mossy tree-silhouetted bayous.

Evil still courses through abandoned cotton gins rusting in the centers of nearly ghost towns where their tales are etched into crumbling red brick that once gave structure to active retail stores, cafes, movie houses, Masonic halls, Baptist churches and "colored" and white schools.

Today's Delta countryside remains dotted with white one-room churches that served sharecroppers as schools and houses of worship, some later morphing into freedom schools, NAACP meeting halls or unsafe quarters for "outside agitators." Along most back roads near the small churches or along the edges of cotton fields are occasional run-down sharecropper houses, some abandoned while others still in use. Nearby are small cemeteries, some overgrown by the kudzu.

When seeking formal historical accounts of three definite civil rights time periods, the Delta has its dedicated gatekeepers. Some represent old-line aristocratic families trying to keep their spin on the past. Others may believe that hiding embarrassing Mississippi moments is their inherent responsibility, and good for state economics and better for national politicians.

One Delta blues historian, when preparing a brochure on the history of the Drew Blues Tradition, said he was told to remove a pivotal story involving a gunfight in the town's blues alley that influenced the movement of prominent bluesmen to Chicago. The story was too gruesome.

What is the Delta? Geographically, the entire Mississippi River drainage basin is massive. Stretching north into Canada and south to the Gulf of Mexico, east to New York and west to New Mexico, the total watershed covers 41 percent of the continental United States.

But the much smaller Yazoo-Mississippi Delta (or "the Delta") is one of the region's many smaller basins or flood plains. Once called "the most Southern place on Earth," by historian James C. Cobb, because of its cotton-rich history and defined culture, this flat triangle of fertile land is about two hundred miles long, and at its greatest width stretches between 60 and 70 miles. The surface slopes toward the gulf. At Memphis, the altitude is 217 feet and at Vicksburg it is 94 feet above sea level. The area is about 8,600 square miles.

On a map, the Delta looks like half a football with its western edge following along the mighty Mississippi River's path, but it was a mean-spirited ballgame that was played on this field. With a reputation for harboring a sweltering summer heat, the Delta became an endless supplier of cheap black labor beginning in the 1800s, enabling thousands of white families to become rich and forcing generations of black families to work their entire lives for nothing — to live and die in poverty, illness and despair.

IN THE YEARS from 1820 to 1860, antebellum, or pre-Civil War, slavery was developing throughout the South as thousands of enslaved people, including hundreds still coming directly from Africa, were taken not only into Mississippi but Alabama, Louisiana and Tennessee as well.

In Mississippi, the first counties were organizing in 1820 with Delta counties created later; the last two Delta counties, Issaquena and Sunflower, were not carved out of the others until well after the Civil War, in 1884.

A Vicksburg correspondent to the *National Intelligencer* of Washington, D.C. in 1855 described an ideal plantation. The size would be about 1,600 acres with 1,000 under cultivation. To work 750 acres of cotton and 250 acres of food crops, such as corn, sweet potatoes and peas, required 75 "effective hands."[4]

The total number of enslaved workers, including those not working in the fields, would be about 135 or 140. Draft animals would include 50 mules and 12 yokes of oxen, with 100 cattle and 300 hogs as livestock. Wagons, gins and other required equipment (like a press, or blacksmith tools) would put the estimated cost of the establishment at $150,000 "if there were no steam engines."

Properly managed, such an enterprise would produce "eight bales to the hand and a bale to the acre." With an estimate of expenses running "$100 to the hand," the reporter calculated a net return of about $12,000.

Post #2:

African American Enslaved Built Mississippi; 'Maroons' Found Asylum in a Swamp Community Known as 'Africa'

"Drive down Highway 61 from Memphis, Tennessee, into Mississippi, through 70 miles of mostly cotton fields into the town of Clarksdale. As you cross the Sunflower River Bridge on the highway, there is a road sign reading New Africa Road. Turn parallel to the river and drive a mile or two, then, at the cotton gin of a late-come plantation, turn right to remain on the New Africa Road, and you will enter Africa."

John Hatch, author of *Africa Love* [5]

There is no doubt that African American enslaved built Mississippi. State historian Bradley G. Bond gathered many first-hand accounts of enslaved who maintained roads, constructed levees, drained swamplands, washed, cooked, cleaned, tended livestock and worked at various jobs that required skilled labor.

"The vast majority of slaves cultivated cotton and other raw crops on plantations and farms," Bond wrote. "Whether they lived on a vast plantation or a small farm, the lives of slaves consisted largely of work, short rations, and fear of arbitrary violence, cruel taskmasters, and forced separation from their families."[6]

The enslaved often constructed worlds of their own, worlds invisible to whites. Those enslaved built not only the wealth of Mississippi through their labor, but they also built a dynamic culture that celebrated family and religion.

Poor health was a serious reality and kept many enslaved blacks from reaching old age. Men, women and children were often driven to dirt eating, practicing Caehixia Africana, a specific class of dietary-deficiency diseases relating to a lack of minerals. Many adult slaves suffered from mental and nervous disorders, and most had tooth decay.

Too often, their white owners and others used the words "lazy" and "shiftless" to describe enslaved people who were physically, and sometimes mentally, ill due to horrid treatment and living conditions.

Historians like Bond point out that childbearing resulted in high incidences of infant mortality from spontaneous abortions, stillbirths, and womb diseases. Death in childbirth occurred two to three times as frequently among enslaved women as among white women.

Pregnant enslaved women were not allowed to see a doctor, and depended upon midwives during birthing. New mothers were sent out to work in the fields the next day; there are accounts of new mothers going back to the fields even on the same day or giving birth in the fields and continuing to work.

While the Delta clearly was an unhealthy place to live and work, with its jungle-like vegetation and mosquito-hosting climate, this did not slow the region's growth or its appetite for enslaved laborers. Kidnapped Africans did not have an end to their term of service as indentured servants did but some still tried to leave.

Leaving Enslavement by Means of Escape

Since settlements in Mississippi were quite isolated, running away was only a temporary means of resistance for most who tried. According to historian Jaime Boler, flight was dangerous, and male slaves were more likely to flee than female slaves. "Runaway slaves encountered slave patrols, slave catchers, dogs, wild animals, and unfamiliar surroundings. Desperation, starvation, and fear led many runaways to return to their masters."[7]

Yet escape proved more successful than direct conflict, and secret runaway swamp communities emerged in the Great Mississippi Swamp north of Vicksburg in the heart of the Delta. Native American Choctaw often helped runaway African Americans, at times becoming part of their secret communities and intermarrying.

Following the theft of Choctaw tribal lands in the 1830 Treaty of Dancing Rabbit Creek (a treaty that pledged "peace and perpetual friendship"), many affected Native Americans remained behind, wandering throughout the vast Mississippi swamplands, as had their ancestors.

One early shared Delta community located near the later developed city of Clarksdale was known as Africa. The enslaved, as well as indigenous people who sought its wilderness sanctuary and other safe havens all over the Americas, were called Maroons.

Dr. L.C. Dorsey, retired associate director of the Delta Research and Cultural Institute at Mississippi Valley State University in Itta Bena, grew up in the Delta. She places this early hidden asylum of Africa "somewhere south of Clarksdale, between Alligator and Clarksdale."

A second black community, New Africa, was formed years later, perhaps in the early 1940s. Dorsey said, "When you realized how violent the Delta was, it's amazing New Africa was allowed to exist ... and it is sort of overshadowed ... almost like it was just quietly kept there. Nobody talked about it. Mound Bayou got all the publicity. Winstonville, another all-black community, also got publicity. I'd never heard about New Africa until 1968 [when]

Amzie Moore took me there." Moore was a black leader in the Delta.[8]

Leaving Enslavement by Returning to Native Africa

Well before emancipation took place, even before the Civil War began, some blacks left the country entirely, returning by choice to their native African continent.

Following earlier revolts in Louisiana and Virginia, the American Colonization Society was founded in 1816. Advocating repatriation, the society created a Liberian colony in 1820, following the British example of Sierra Leone, founded thirty years earlier as a home for freed British and some American slaves who fought for Great Britain during the American Revolution.

In 1836, Isaac Wade Ross, a Revolutionary War hero and a wealthy Mississippi cotton planter, willed that proceeds from the sale of his plantation be used to pay passage of his enslaved to a newly created abolitionist colony in Western Africa. Like many abolitionists, Ross believed freed blacks would harm society, thus making it better for everyone that they return to their native lands. Nevertheless, Ross gave his slaves a chance at opportunity in Africa.

As Ross drafted his will, memories were fresh of the Nat Turner slave revolt of 1831. Since then, many states were passing new and more restrictive slave laws. Meanwhile, there were increased challenges to sending blacks to Liberia as some free blacks were now arguing that repatriation was the same as deportation.

In 1834 the Mississippi Colonization Society sent out two African men "by the names of Moore and Simpson" to look over Liberia and report back. Ignoring the obvious and pervasive hunger and illness, they gave Liberia a thumbs up. Later in 1846, Liberia became an independent nation under the paternalistic motto, "The

Love of Liberty Brought Us Here." The U.S. government at first had doubts about entertaining black diplomats and did not recognize the new nation. Yet, over several decades, thousands of former enslaved left for Africa.[9]

Leaving Enslavement by Going North Via the Underground Railroad

A THIRD ESCAPE option was to use the services of the Underground Railroad. Ser Seshs Ab Heter of Natchez, coordinator of the Friends of the Forks of the Roads, broadens the definition of Underground Railroad or UGR, defining it as "any form of resistance to chattel enslavement."

"You must not view UGR activity in Mississippi the same as it has been viewed in the traditional sense ... with safe houses, tunnels, lamps in windows, hidden passages," said Heter, who assisted the National Park Service with its National Underground Railroad Network to Freedom Program, which focused on the Mississippi River as a major Uhuru or Freedom Route from Memphis to the Gulf of Mexico.[10]

Escapees and others, to hide themselves and live as maroons while seeking freedom, relied on protection from the Delta's secretive bayous and swamps, caves, canebrakes, cotton towns, and plantation outskirts.

A smaller river, the Tombigbee, also played an important role for escapees. Where this river ends in northeastern Mississippi, near the Alabama state line, as one legend goes, those fleeing were told to continue north, to follow the drinking gourd, a code name for the Big Dipper star formation that looks like the hollowed out gourd used by slaves as a water dipper.

From 1831 to 1841, few if any black labor insurrections were formally reported in the South. Then, in 1841, the crew of the slave ship Creole was overpowered off the coast of Alabama by its cargo of slaves and the ship diverted to the British West Indies. England refused to return the enslaved, having abolished slavery in 1833. The issue of slavery in America was so contentious between the two countries that this incident prompted Secretary of State Daniel Webster to encourage congressmen to openly talk about war against England.

In 1859, white abolitionist John Brown and an army of five black and 13 thirteen white supporters seized the Federal arsenal at Harper's Ferry, Virginia, hoping to launch a populist rebellion.

Brown was convinced that local slaves would rise up behind him and hoped to establish a new republic of fugitives in the Appalachian Mountains. Eventually, Brown was surrounded and his men were all killed or captured.

Brown's raid sent shockwaves throughout the country as whites "assumed that Brown represented the violent sentiment of every Northern man and woman" Convicted of criminal conspiracy and treason, Brown was hanged. Ralph Waldo Emerson honoring the executed Brown, wrote, "He will make the gallows as holy as the cross."[11]

The Civil War

While there are dozens of theories of how and why the Civil War began, historian Howard Zinn offered a unique proposal. The United States had become a system agitated by slave rebellion, or at least the threat of such. To prevent popular insurrection would now require an immediate end to slavery — an end to the system that had made the United States the most successful capitalist economy in the world.

Enslavement had been supported all along "based on an overpowering practicality." By 1790, Southern states were producing a thousand tons of cotton every year. This figure became a million tons by 1860 — as 500,000 enslaved grew to 4 four million in the same period.

Yet the system was aggravated by rebellions and conspiracies, such as Turner's and Brown's efforts, bringing on "a network of controls" in the Southern states that were backed by the legal system, the military, and racial prejudice of most political leaders. Slavery would have to end but this would be no simple task.

Zinn compared 1860 views of two possibilities: If a slave rebellion occurred, this could get out of hand, with a "returned ferocity beyond slavery" and against the United States. However, if a war occurred, those who made the war would also organize its consequences — and so it would be Abraham Lincoln who freed the slaves, and not John Brown.

Following Lincoln's election, Mississippi — on an 84-15 vote — was the second Southern state to secede. In Montgomery, Alabama on February 4, 1861, the six seceding states formed a provisional government of the Confederate States of American and five days later elected Mississippi's Jefferson Davis as its president.

John Anthony Quitman, a Delta planter and U.S. Representative in the 34th and 35th Congresses, has been called the "father of secession in Mississippi" for his early role as "an advocate of secession in 1832 at the state constitutional convention, in 1850 as governor, and finally as a congressman in the late 1850s."

Quitman served in Congress until his death in 1858 on his plantation, Monmouth, near Natchez. Africans who worked on his plantation poisoned Quitman by secretly doctoring his food.

Some Southern male enslaved accompanied their masters to war as servants, and received Confederate pensions and laudatory words from whites in later years. Boat Deggins of southern Mississippi, the great-grandfather of modern Delta civil rights activists Sam Block and Margaret Block, was forced to follow his master into the Battle of Shiloh.

But Deggins helped Union soldiers by passing secrets that he overheard as the Confederates made their plans. "They talked in front of him because they thought he couldn't understand what they were saying — well, he did," Margaret Block said.[12]

Those who knew her great-grandfather said he had an old sword that he would take out and wave wildly while telling his Civil War stories. "It was kind of funny, but sad, too." Block's great-grandfather was probably kidnapped from French Senegal, she believes. "The name 'Boat' is a clue and he spoke some French."

As the Union swept through the South, Jefferson Davis ordered that black Union soldiers and their officers captured by Confederate troops were not to be treated as Prisoners of War but would be given no quarter, meaning no clemency or mercy would be given upon surrender and no lives would be spared. The most vengeful fighting took place when black soldiers were involved, and white officers sometimes paid the price with them.

In all, an estimated 200,000 black soldiers and sailors served in the Union Army and Navy. As the ultimate mark of valor, 16 black soldiers had been awarded the Medal of Honor by the end of the Civil War. Black soldiers from Mississippi numbered about 18,000 while some 50 Mississippi whites reportedly fought for the Union.[13] As Union soldiers entered the South, thousands of Africans fled from their owners to Union camps. Some Union officers first returned slaves to their owners, but others kept the blacks within their lines, nicknaming them "contraband of war."

Slavery is seen in the Constitution in a few key places. First is in the Enumeration Clause, where representatives are apportioned. Each state is given a number of representatives based on its population. Slaves, called "other persons," are counted as three-fifths of a whole person. The three-fifths number was a ratio used by the Congress in contemporary legislation and was agreed upon with little debate.

In Article 1, Section 9, Congress is limited, expressly, from prohibiting the "Importation" of slaves, before 1808. The slave trade was a bone of contention for many, with some who supported slavery abhorring the slave trade. The 1808 date, a compromise of 20 years, allowed the slave trade to continue, but placed a date-certain on its survival. Congress eventually passed a law outlawing the slave trade that became effective on January 1, 1808.

The Fugitive Slave Clause is the last mention. In it, a problem that slave states had with extradition of escaped slaves was resolved. The laws of one state, the clause says, cannot excuse a person from "Service or Labour" in another state. The clause expressly requires that the state in which an escapee is found deliver the slave to the state he escaped from "on Claim of the Party."[14]

Post #3:

Delta Rife With Violence During Reconstruction

"I think God intended the niggers to be slaves. Now since man has deranged God's plan, I think the best we can do is keep 'em as near to a state of bondage as possible. My theory is, feed 'em well, clothe 'em well, and then, if they don't work, whip 'em well."

An unnamed Yazoo-Mississippi Delta planter, 1866[15]

At the end of the Civil War, freed Africans suffered severe food and related shortages. Many who had led secret underground organizations were tracked down and massacred. To bring them aid, Congress quickly established a Bureau of Refugees, Freedmen, and Abandoned Lands or the "Freedmen's Bureau."[16]

The bureau head, former Union Army General Oliver O. Howard, believed that education, citizenship rights and self-help would make freedmen full members of American society, and he soon established over 3,000 Southern schools.

Meanwhile, planters, struggling to keep control of black labor, tried bringing foreign labor to the Delta rather than employ former enslaved. They also encouraged threats against blacks by the Ku Klux Klan, a white terrorist organization founded in 1865 by Tennessee veterans of the Confederate Army.

Besides losing the African Americans they had enslaved, Delta planters lost legal and social status. For the first time in their lives, many planters had to deal and bargain with their laborers. Blacks who had worked for them for twenty years were simply walking away.

A disgruntled Delta planter wrote to Governor William Sharkey in the summer of 1865, suggesting "some form of punishment" and help from physicians in determining if workers' illnesses were feigned.[17]

For the first time in their lives, there were many freed African Americans who found ways to purchase their own land in the Delta and begin new lives.

Some landowners seeking labor to clear their plantations and to increase cotton production, rented land to blacks for cash; many renters, black and white, became part-time backwoodsmen.

The Freedman's Bureau encouraged freedmen to seek employment with local white planters and agents did check into some reported cases of severe mistreatment by planters. One Bureau agent found that Greenwood planter W.P. Atkins beat a former enslaved woman and tied her up by the thumbs after she attempted to board a boat from Vicksburg. In Issaquena County, another bureau agent observed freedmen "with cheeks pounded, eyes badly injured, with teeth knocked out" and other evidences of brutal mistreatment.[18]

Freed men and women faced unspeakable horrors during this post-Civil War era, ranging from lack of food and shelter, to aggressive attempts to keep them under white control as long as possible.

One Delta planter would not furnish clothing for his laborers and they were forced to work naked in the cotton fields. When federal troops left the region, whites set up roadblocks outside of

Yazoo City to stop black laborers from leaving, forcing them to work for their former masters.

On still another Delta plantation, former enslaved were made to live on rations of cornmeal, pork, and a pint of molasses each week. But many black Deltans fought back and began demanding more time off and other concessions, even if they were rarely successful.

To regain control over black laborers, Mississippi led several Southern states in implementing the South's notorious Black Codes regulating anything from marriage and the right to hold, sell, and lease property to the right of mobility, speech and thought. Freedmen were defined as agricultural laborers and kept away from other potential employment when possible.

The federal government responded to Black Codes by threatening to prosecute under the Civil Rights Act of 1866, a piece of legislation that gave further rights to the freed slaves after the end of the Civil War. Any power once held in Black Codes was quickly overturned within a year of Mississippi's passage. But this really did not matter since Mississippi took Reconstruction to another level.

Presidential Reconstruction

By 1866, considerable racial violence had occurred in Southern states forcing Congress to divide the ten unreconstructed states into five military districts, making federal generals their governors. To be readmitted to the Union, a state was required to hold a constitutional convention.

Most of the ten states under surveillance soon qualified, but Mississippi held out until 1870.

Once elected, President Ulysses S. Grant sent federal troops to restore law and order to many of the most violent areas in the South afflicted by the Ku Klux Klan. Grant's disruptions of Klan activities bought him both friends and foes since most states had either advocated Klan interests or were too intimidated to confront Klansmen.

The Delta was rife with racial violence during Reconstruction. William T. Combash, a controversial black political leader, led a small protest in Sunflower and Carroll counties in early November 1869, with twenty blacks marching into Greenwood. Local whites held them back and Combash threatened to return, bringing an additional five hundred men.

The sheriff organized a posse, and along with a squad of troops sent by Mississippi Governor Adelbert Ames to bring order to the region, attacked the marchers, killing Combash.[19]

After 13 thirteen blacks were reported killed in Sunflower County, the realities of black voting and Republican influence on local politics resulted in as cooperative an attitude toward blacks as white leaders could muster.[20]

Blacks protesting after the shooting of a black girl in Tunica County in 1874 were not tracked down — in contrast to a "wave of white vigilantism" that left thirty blacks dead in Meridian, south of the Delta, following a similar incident.

DESPITE THE TERRORISM going on around them, three black Mississippi men became the first African Americans to serve in the U.S. Congress. All worked to pass ambitious civil rights and public education laws during the post-Civil War occupation of the South.

Prior to the passage of the 17th Amendment in 1913, U.S. senators were chosen by state legislatures rather than a popular vote. U.S. Senator Blanche K. Bruce, the first black person to serve a full U.S. Senate term, had already been a county sheriff, tax collector, and education official in Bolivar County before his election to the state legislature in 1874.

But Mississippi was also setting set new records for lynching more black people than any other state. Freelance journalist Earnest McBride reported that in just two days alone — December 7 and 8, 1874 — in the same year Bruce was elected to serve in the Senate, over 26 black citizens of Vicksburg were slaughtered by whites seeking to push black elected officials from office.[21]

Led by former confederates, the extermination of black Republicans and the restoration of white, Democratic Party rule were carried out with precision.

Charles Caldwell, born enslaved and later elected to the state senate, was blamed for killing the son of a white Mississippi judge in 1868. Caldwell argued self-defense in front of an all-white jury and, surprisingly, was acquitted. He was the first black, charged with killing a white in Mississippi, who was able to go free after a trial. But seven years later, on Christmas Day of 1875, a white gang, the Redeemers, shot Caldwell to death[22] in the western Hinds County town of Bolton.

Most lynching was by hanging or shooting, or both. Many events were more hideous and included burning at the stake, maiming, dismemberment, castration, and other brutal methods of physical torture — such as boiling two men to death in Sunflower County.

While Reconstruction quickly unraveled in Mississippi, this short period of history, despite the possibilities of being lynched or murdered, still had its positive moments for the former enslaved, as some Mississippians worked their best to improve government services and protection of the rights of blacks.

Historians Dale Krane and Stephen D. Shaffer point out that a state civil rights act was passed in 1870 outlawing discrimination in public places and on public vehicles. Railroads, bridges, and public facilities were rebuilt, levees were repaired, and hospitals and insane asylums were built.

In their book, *Mississippi Government and Politics: Modernizers Versus Traditionalists*, these historians observed: "One of the most controversial Reconstruction measures was a public school law, opposed by many whites, which significantly increased student enrollment. Some whites resented having to pay property taxes to educate black children, whose parents often did not pay such taxes because they generally did not own land."[23]

Segregated schools were maintained in Southern states, and the schools attended by black children were targeted by the Ku Klux

Klan, which often intimidated teachers and destroyed school buildings.

Even as life was becoming somewhat better for some black citizens, the old times were not forgotten by Southern plantation owners, who were facing low cotton prices. In response, production at capacity was demanded of black laborers, no matter the cost to human lives.

As the 1875 campaign season in Mississippi entered its final phase, political and racial violence prompted Mississippi's Governor Ames to appeal to President Grant for troops. Grant refused the governor's request and although thousands of black voters came to the polls, braving White League threats, the Democratic-Conservatives achieved an overwhelming victory in the November 1875 elections and then dismantled the Republican order, forcing Governor Ames and others to resign from office. One could say that Mississippi's confederacy had finally won the Civil War, courtesy of Grant.

After 1875, every aspect of Mississippi daily life was increasingly segregated, even though for every white in the Delta there were seven blacks. To maintain subjugation over the growing population of blacks required incessant abuse, most planters believed. Historian Clyde Woods of Pennsylvania State University described a state "gripped by fear."[24]

"Mississippi led the nation in lynching, tar-and-featherings, whippings, and human burnings. There is no way to estimate accurately the thousands upon thousands of African American community leaders and members who were murdered during this period. One can only speculate on the impact of this pogrom upon the younger generation."[25]

As federal troops were removed from Southern states, white ex-confederates took back the state of Mississippi. There still was greater mobility than under slavery, and there was greater communication among African Americans. Uniting this censored but mobile generation was the blues, coming straight from the heart of the Delta, with the guitar and harmonica as the major instruments, and vocal styles ranging from soulful to fiery.

With increased homelessness, lack of food and jobs, and increased numbers of children left to fend for themselves, the anguish of these times was tendered by this musical form.

Levee hollers and cries of the cotton fields, prisons, docks, and streets were returning as music that comforted and united many African Americans. Black people were managing their destinies and using their own artistic tools to do so.

Carrollton Massacre

ON MARCH 17, 1886, twenty-three people, all black, were killed in a courthouse massacre in Carrollton, Mississippi when sixty armed white men charged in and opened fire in a court room. Two black brothers, Ed and Charley Brown, accused Jim Lidell, Jr. of attempted murder. Both brothers were killed and no one was indicted for their murders.

T.E. Marshal would later tell a WPA oral histories interviewer that descriptions of the "Carrollton Courthouse Riot" were not true. He said many who died that day were "peaceable but curious" men who were in the wrong place at the wrong time, adding that the massacre seemed well planned and executed.[26]

What had been lost by the white South during the Civil War and during Reconstruction was largely retaken as "Jim Crow" laws expanded, affecting all classes and ages. Jim Crow laws reached far and wide, requiring such absurdities as separate Bibles used in court for swearing in black witnesses.

Years later, additional Jim Crow practices required separate telephone booths, separate bank windows for black and white depositors, and even Jim Crow elevator rules requiring blacks to use freight elevators instead of the regular elevators reserved for whites, only.

Every village and town had its own version of Jim Crow laws and black people would have to learn what the "rules" were or pay the ultimate price. Seventy years later, in the summer of 1955, ignorance of this grim fact resulted in the horrific murder of 14-year-old Emmett Till.

Life on the Other Side of the Tracks, the Henry Waring Ball Diary Entries, February 1887

While most living in the Cotton South experienced lives of extreme hardship and poverty after the Civil War, there were others who only lived the good life, as shown in the 1887 diary entries of Henry Waring Ball, a Greenville lawyer, journalist, and planter:[27]

Sat. 19. Went last night with Miss Carrie Yerger to "speculation party" at W.G. Yerger's. Girls all elegantly dressed. House and tables all decorated with flowers in great profusion. Drew Mrs. George Alexander for a partner "speculated" until about 12. First prize Miss Lelia, others Miss Lady Percy, Mrs. Geo. Alexander, Hal Rucks and Harry Johnson. After cards most lavish and elegant supper, and dancing until 3.

Mon. 21. At night went to Ball at the theatre. Everybody's a little tired. Quite a successful affair however, danced until 3.

Tues. 22. Hard rain. Paperers at work.

Wed. 23. Threatened to be Ash Wednesday in earnest, for just after breakfast a sudden quarrel sprung up between the servants, and increased until each avowed loudly his and her intention of no longer living together; whereupon Father got exasperated and ordered the whole tribe to pack up and leave immediately, and half an hour afterwards there was not an African on the lot, to my blank dismay.

We consulted together, and Willy and I rolled up our sleeves and went into the kitchen, with all the confidence of complacent ignorance and by five o'clock had a pretty good dinner, and felt independent of the evilly necessary colored gentry.

Thur. 24. I got up tolerably early, went to market, played ostler, routed out Willy, and we went into the kitchen together, to such good purpose that a first rate breakfast was the result... About 12 one Miss Winny something or other appeared and applied for the position, which was at once tendered her, and she got dinner... Our cooking has made us all three deathly sick.

Land of Jim Crow

IN THE SUMMER of 1964, Fanny Lou Hamer, a farmer and passionate civil rights activists from Ruleville of Sunflower County, stunned America when she told a television newscaster during the Democratic National Convention of her severe beating and rape by police officers in the small town of Winona after using a "white" restroom at a bus stop on her way home from a civil rights training camp. Hamer, a child polio victim, never fully recovered from the abuse.

Over the years, there would be some African Americans like Hamer who bravely boycotted Jim Crow laws while others tried going to court, risking jail or injuries, savage beatings or lynching, as they refused to comply. Still others prided themselves on their practical approach of staying away from any place that was segregated.

"We didn't ride the streetcar; we did not go to the theater. And any place where it was segregated, we didn't go," an older Drew resident explained.

Some bluesmen courageously mocked the ludicrous workings of Jim Crow, as described by author Leon F. Litwack:

"W.C. Handy, in his frequent sojourns through the South, recalled more than once passing though towns with signs warning, 'Nigger don't let the sun go down on you here.' In the all-black town of Mound Bayou, in the Mississippi Delta, however, 'the boot was on the other foot,' as Handy noted, and 'sentiment' among the townspeople applied the same exclusionist rule to 'rednecks' and 'peckerwoods.'"[28]

By this time, veterans of the Abolitionist and Reconstruction movements were nearly gone. Frederick Douglass, known for his elegant orations on the condition of the black race and on other issues, such as abolition, died in 1895, a sad leader who told friends he could not shut his eyes "to the ugly facts" before him. So many earlier achievements were now devastated, leaving this brave leader to pass on in despair.

IN THE YEARS following the overthrow of Reconstruction, some resistant blacks who did not leave the South tried to organize and their stories are too often filled with anguish.

Minter City Massacre

One Mississippi black Populist leader, probably from Leflore County, (described in the press as "the notoriously bad negro") and named after the famous English zealot Oliver Cromwell, organized the Colored Farmers Alliance (CFA) in Leflore County in 1889, at a time when the population was 14,276 black and 2,597 white residents[29].

Meetings grew from small groups to large rallies, and Cromwell encouraged African American farmers to buy their supplies at Southern Farmers Alliance cooperative stores, posing a threat to the food/debt dependency created by the planter/merchant monopolies.

Planters threatened Cromwell with death and demanded that he leave Mississippi. Seventy CFA members marched through the tiny village of Shell Mound, not far from the Tallahatchie River where Emmett Till's body was tossed years later, protesting intimidation and announcing their resolve.[30]

Some Delta planters feared a race war and, in September of 1889, the Governor sent three regiments to Minter City to ensure that the CFA members were unarmed. Completing their assignment, the state regiments withdrew and allowed a massacre of CFA members and families to proceed. There were no reports of blacks being armed or of whites being shot; estimates of African Americans murdered reached as high as one hundred.

From his research on the massacre, historian William F. Holmes discovered several first-hand accounts recorded by travelers who happened to be in the region, including the observations of J.C. Engle, an agent for a New York textile company, who was in and about Greenwood during the trouble.

When he arrived at New Orleans several days later, Engle described how Negroes "were shot down like dogs." Members of the posse not only killed people in the swamps, he wrote, but they even invaded homes and murdered men, women and children. Engle told how a sixteen-year-old white boy "beat out the brains of a little colored girl while a bigger brother, with a gun, kept the little one's parents off."

Several sources reported that the posse singled out four well-known leaders of the Colored Farmers Alliance whom they shot to death: Adolph Horton, Scot Morris, Jack Dial and J.M. Dial. "A black undercover reporter sent to the region stated that the truth may never be known because terrified blacks dare not speak of the matter, even to each other."[31]

The lack of coverage of this massacre by the Mississippi press, and the failure of state and federal officials to lead investigations, left researcher Holmes asking how many other instances of violence of a "greater and lesser magnitude" happened in Mississippi during this era.

One informant, who grew up in Minter City long after this incident took place, told Holmes that he had never heard of the massacre but did report of folk lore from his youth about dead bodies in the "Singing River," who could sometimes be heard at night.

QUITE CONVENIENTLY throughout the Delta, a green vine called kudzu creeps along the ground silently and slowly strangles the life out of a tree or bush. While it looks so innocent and its purple flowers smell so good, be reminded it is the plant that eats Mississippi, digesting much of the state's historical reminders as it roams.

Traveling into Minter City, the quiet, nearly vacant town centers on a small brick church that is carefully maintained. But kudzu vines have started to overtake an enormous cotton-ginning operation nearby that no longer functions. No singing came from the river on this day I traveled to Minter City, not to my ears, at least.

As the kudzu story goes, during the 1930's when the economy was so poor, the federal government encouraged Southern farmers to plant kudzu, claiming it to be the savior of Southern soil that was worn out through poor management and too much planting of cotton. The government provided the kudzu seedlings free of charge and paid farmers to plant it.

Kudzu is not native to this country and with no natural enemies and a warm, humid climate, kudzu quickly took root in Mississippi and in the rest of the South. The Asian plant is almost impossible to get rid of once it has taken root; kudzu roots may go more than twelve feet deep and its vines can grow a foot in length a day and more than sixty feet over the course of the summer. Kudzu is said to cover over 250,000 acres in Mississippi, alone.

Kudzu actually has some benefits. Vines are good for basket making and there is something in the kudzu root that reduces the craving for alcohol as much as 90 percent, current researchers find. As kudzu snakes across fields, creeping over roads and worn down buildings, this plant is by far the best for aiding and abetting Mississippi's cover up of its history, perhaps even better than some of its native historians.

BY THE LATE 1880s, a 75 percent fall in cotton prices meant that even the ruling caste was failing, and it was in such an environment that Delta planters quickly moved to stop new activist blacks from voting and, again, restrict their mobility through violence. This time, rebellious white Populists were also kept from voting.

Mound Bayou, a Small Town Lost in Time

In an area surrounded by white-controlled cotton plantations and at a time of increased racial violence, the small town of Mound Bayou in Bolivar County — halfway from Vicksburg to Memphis — was carved out of the wilderness in 1887, becoming an important all-black community. In its heyday, residents had access to a railroad station where the "colored" waiting room was larger than the "white" waiting room.

With a newspaper, numerous churches, schools, a bank, a telephone exchange, and many other black-owned businesses and industries, this unique Delta town impressed President Theodore Roosevelt so much that he once described it as "an object lesson full of hope for colored people."

Nearly everyone in and around Mound Bayou could read and, early on, Mound Bayou was a center of black separatism. Even as brutalities occurred throughout the Delta, Mound Bayou reportedly remained safer for blacks. The town's history actually began with the birth of Isaiah Montgomery, born a slave at Hurricane, a large plantation on the Mississippi River, on May 21st, 1847 and was the property of Joseph Davis, the older brother of Jefferson Davis.[32]

In 1866, Joseph Davis sold the plantation to Isaiah's father, Benjamin Montgomery, and Benjamin's sons, who turned it into a cooperative community of freed slaves. Isaiah Montgomery went on to establish Mound Bayou and became its mayor where he advocated the educational theories that had been promoted by his friend, Booker T. Washington. Schools provided technical training and scientific agriculture. Girls were taught homemaking skills so they could provide better care for their families. Montgomery also imposed a ban on the sale of alcoholic beverages as a means to keep down crime.

Montgomery later lost the support of many civil rights leaders when he became the only black delegate at the 1890 Constitutional Convention in Mississippi by supporting disfranchisement of black voters. He believed this controversial action would build a bridge between the races that threatened further destruction between them.

In 1926, the Mound Bayou community became headquarters to the Knights and Daughters of Tabor, a black fraternal organization named for a mountain in Galilee and founded by black Civil War veterans. Taborians touched the lives of most Delta blacks through their low-cost medical insurance program, providing health care to blacks who could not avail themselves of services used by white people.

Years later, a beloved civil rights leader, Medgar Evers, later took his first job out of college to work in this small town, selling and maintaining insurance policies for black families. He was employed by Dr. T.R.M. Howard, a wealthy and admired community leader.

In 1963, Evers, by then the field secretary for the National Association for the Advancement of Colored People or NAACP, would be killed in the driveway of his Jackson, Mississippi home by a member of Mississippi's White Citizens Councils, Byron De La Beckwith of Greenwood, as racist insanity mounted.

Post #4:

Mississippi Lynching Becomes 'Theatrical Spectacular'

"In the years following the Civil War, lynching eventually came to be presented differently—a theatrical spectacle that said, 'The community has come together in a spontaneous outpouring of outrage against an African-American who committed an atrocity.' Rather than receiving a secretive visit from the KKK at night, victims of terrorism were lynched in public by a mob. Often the victims were taken from a jail where they awaited legal punishment."

Eliza Steelwater, *The Hangman's Knot: Lynching, Legal Execution, and America's Struggle with the Death Penalty*

Early Mississippi's horrifying history must factor in when trying to figure out what happened in this state leading into and during the modern civil rights movement, says a Native American sociologist who co-led the Jackson Movement of the early 1960s.

Hunter Bear is a former Tougaloo College sociology professor and civil rights activist who then went by the name of John R. Salter. He was injured several times while participating in downtown Jackson's lunch counter sit-ins and again, more seriously, when his car was broadsided by the son of a white Mississippi politician on the day of Medgar Evers funeral.

Around 1890, as Mississippi took the lead in a massive and successful campaign to disenfranchise or remove voting rights from Southern blacks, is a good place to start — a period when lynching became the most popular method used by whites to reinforce white supremacy, said Hunter Bear.[33]

Data support the sociologist's assertion. During the end of the 19th century and the beginning of the 20th century, two or three black Southerners were lynched nearly every week. Frequently, the killings were well-attended entertainment events, and photos often show cheerful, complacent faces of the onlookers.

Modern-day photographer Jacob Jacoby sought a better sense of history through the eyes of onlookers as he produced a book of lynching photography.

"Neither crazed fiends nor the dregs of white society, the bulk of the lynchers tended to be ordinary and respectable people," historian Leon Litwack wrote in his introduction to Jacoby's stunning pictorial book, *Without Sanctuary.*

Following one memorable Delta lynching in Charleston, one of Tallahatchie County's two governing seats, the local newspaper praised "prominent citizens" involved for having carried it out in the "most approved and up-to-date fashion."

Most of those lynched were innocent of any crime and "all were denied due process, an impartial judge and jury, an able defense, the right to appeal. Their executions were acts of revenge and hate," Litwack observed.[34]

Not surprisingly, lynching often followed arguments about money due sharecroppers and laborers by planters. In 1905, Federal courts tried to ease such conflicts by outlawing debt peonage and allowing for guilty landlords to be heavily fined.

Officially, laborers could now leave in the middle of a crop to search for better contracts, creating shortages for landlords. Desperate for help, some planters lured men, women and children under false promises, and then held them at gunpoint to work the fields with no pay. Other planters crossed state lines to track down and bring back sharecroppers who left their plantations.

Reports of farm-labor entrapment continued as late as the 1970s, with some farm workers being held at gunpoint or whipped for various reasons, including staying at home when they were sick. Escaping from a plantation in the middle of the night was not uncommon.

Files of civil rights leader Aaron Henry of Clarksdale include a report written in the early 1970s from The Box Project describing aid given to a farming couple in Coahoma County seeking to flee the plantation on which they resided. The escape took place in early morning hours, because the family feared they would be shot and killed by the planter, who forbade them to leave.

SPEAKING OUT AGAINST the racist tyranny was taboo in the daily life of black Mississippians, even in jukes, a name for popular entertainment clubs. Yet, it wasn't uncommon for blues musicians to cloak their feelings about what was going on around them by using metaphors that described conflicts between the sexes. Lyrics were often coded for any messages deemed too unsafe to talk about.

> *You know they'll jump you up and down*
> *They'll carry you all 'round and 'round*
> *Just as soon as your back is turned*
> *They'll be trying to crush you down*
>
> – Delta bluesman Son House, "Grinnin' in Your Face"

Researcher Ethan Crosby, studying post-Civil War Delta blues, found structures of this music close to earlier work songs and field hollers of antebellum slaves. "When the labor was hard, workers sang to make themselves feel better and to work their brain as they worked their bodies."[35]

Delta-Born Journalist Crusaded Against Lynching

Ida B. Wells, a daughter of Mississippi Delta enslaved, wrote and published in 1895, *A Red Record*, a historical paper that tabulated statistics and alleged causes of lynching in the United States. It was a significant work demanding federal intervention to stop this practice and it began:

"Not all nor nearly all of the murders done by white men, during the past thirty years in the South, have come to light, but the statistics as gathered and preserved by white men, and which have not been questioned, show that during these years more than ten thousand Negroes have been killed in cold blood, without the formality of judicial trial and legal execution...."

"The first excuse given to the civilized world for the murder of unoffending Negroes was the necessity of the white man to repress and stamp out alleged "race riots." For years immediately succeeding the war there was an appalling slaughter of colored people, and the wires usually conveyed to Northern people and the world the intelligence, first, that an insurrection was being planned by Negroes, which, a few hours later, would prove to have been vigorously resisted by white men, and controlled with a resulting loss of several killed and wounded. It was always a remarkable feature in these insurrections and riots that only Negroes were killed during the rioting, and that all the white men escaped unharmed..."[36]

Wells was born in Holly Springs, a wealthy and unique town set outside of the Delta between Oxford, Miss. and Memphis, Tenn. in the northeastern part of the state. Rich cotton planters often brought their families to live in this hilly region, building elegant mansions where they could enjoy the cooler air, removed from the steamy and mosquito-infested swamplands of the Delta.

With its 64 antebellum mansions, Holly Springs was once the site of a key Civil War battle and over the years would be home to thirteen generals, one admiral, six U.S. senators, ten U.S. congressmen and several famous artists and writers, including Wells.

Several months before Lincoln signed the Emancipation Proclamation, Lynching and the Excuse For It, written by Wells, stressed that, "Nowhere in the civilized worlds save the United States of America, do men, possessing all civil and political power, go out in bands of 50 to 5,000 to hunt down, shoot, hang or burn to death an individual unarmed and absolutely powerless."

Wells was the oldest of eight children. When her parents died in 1880 during a yellow fever plague, she taught in Holly Springs to support her younger siblings, where she also completed her studies at Rust College, in the heart of this small town. She later moved to nearby Memphis to own and edit a local black newspaper, *The Free Speech and Headlight,* building her reputation for writing strong, anti-lynching editorials under the pen name "Iola."

In 1890, Wells printed the first statistical record of lynching in the South. Two years later, when three of her good friends were lynched in Memphis, she used her power of the press to attack the treatment of blacks as less than human. Wells let others know of her disgust as lynching became a public spectacle and she started looking into false accusations of rape against black men, frequently used to justify lynching.

But after she stated editorially that some rape cases actually concerned white women who preferred black men, Wells' offices were burned while she was attending an editors convention in New York. Learning her life would be in danger if she returned to Memphis, Wells moved to England to continue her cause but later returned to Chicago where in 1895 she wrote and published *A Red Record.*[37]

By the early 1900s, lynching in Mississippi had taken "a ghoulish turn," as mobs grew larger, often including women and children, and a ritual of torture often prevailed. Despite efforts of Wells and others, the destitute condition of the Delta black was not recognized as a problem.

Great White Chief

In 1903, Mississippians nominated the candidates for all public offices, from the governor down to the local constable, in a popular primary election. The first governor elected under the state's new primary law was James K. Vardaman, a bitter and violent man who came out of the hills of Yalobusha County where he was born in 1861, the son of a Confederate soldier.

Vardaman's political opponents had warned that more black laborers would move out of the state if "The White Chief" was elected, leaving plantations and the lumber districts of South Mississippi without enough workers. This proved true.

Vardaman was a "huge man with shoulder-length hair and a limp right arm that had been mangled years before in a farm-equipment accident." Thousands would come out to see Vardaman, dressed in a white linen suit and a black broad-brimmed hat, often standing on top of a cotton bale, speak for hours at barbecues, fairs and church suppers.

A Vardaman-type rally was far more than a simple political event. Wrote one follower, "It ... brought men together under torches, it filled them with the contagious power of the crowd, it unleashed emotion and set [men] to leaping and dancing."[38]

Tagged the "White Chief" by his supporters, Vardaman campaigned on the slogan, "If necessary, every Negro in the state will be lynched; it will be done to maintain white supremacy." Before and after his election, Mississippi topped the list for lynching well into the 1930s.

During Vardaman's initial 1904 campaign for governor, after a lynch mob in the town of Rocky Ford chained African-American J.P. Ivy to a woodpile and doused him with gasoline prior to roasting him alive, Vardaman was quoted:

"I sometimes think that one could look upon a scene of that kind and suffer no more moral deterioration than he would by looking upon the burning of an Orangutan that had stolen a baby or a viper that had stung an unsuspecting child to death."[39]

When he took office in 1905, Governor Vardaman sent an urgent message to the "law officers" of Mississippi regarding the "vast increase of criminal Negroes." They had become a "peril to the peace of the community and a menace to the safety of the white man's home."

Vardaman urged a hard crackdown by police and prosecutors. His extreme racism eventually clashed with more moderate planters like Leroy Percy of Greenville, who had worked hard to attract and keep black laborers in Mississippi, often in positive ways, but always assuming the wealthy overseer role of noblesse oblige — an assumption that with wealth, power and prestige come responsibilities.

Percy and his cohorts could not afford to allow Vardaman to send more black laborers away from the Delta, even if they had voted for him. These men wanted their workforce for free, and wanted them intimidated — but could not afford to have laborers lynched or so terrified they would leave .

In 1907, the boll weevil answered the labor problem by destroying most of the state's cotton crop, causing thousands more blacks to move north seeking work, if they had not already left the state by the time Vardaman took command.

In same year of Vardaman's election, a notorious lynching took place in Sunflower County involving the family of a future and notorious U.S. Senator.

Eastland Family Lynching

On the Eastland plantation near Doddsville, the uncle and namesake of the future U.S. Senator James O. Eastland was killed. Two black farm hands were blamed for the murder of Eastland's uncle and they were lynched after a massive search.[40]

Lynching was often practiced at the Eastland plantation most Sundays, some county historians and other locals claim.

James O. Eastland was born nine months after the lynching mob that was led by Eastland's father, a pharmacist and planter. Since lynching was often accompanied by celebrations and parties for the white persons attending, it has been theorized the Senator was conceived on this occasion.

Eastland's uncle may have actually been killed by white neighbors during a business argument, and not by the black couple. But formal newspaper reports remained with the status quo.

The February 8 *New York Tribune* reported the lynching was attended by 1,000 people and further details from the *Vicksburg Evening Post* stated:

"When the two Negroes were captured, they were tied to trees and ... forced to suffer the most fiendish tortures. The blacks were forced to hold out their hands while one finger at a time was chopped off. The fingers were distributed as souvenirs. Holbert was beaten severely, his skull was fractured, and one of his eyes, knocked out with a stick, hung by a shred from the socket. The most excruciating form of punishment consisted in the use of a large corkscrew [that] was bored into the flesh of the man and woman ... and then pulled out."

This was neither the first lynching on the Doddsville plantation nor would it be the last. Rumors persist to this day around Sunflower County about other lynching events that regularly took place and perhaps involving the late senator, himself, who was said to be a Klansman.

The lynching of Charley Shepherd in adjacent Bolivar County, reported in the *Jackson Daily News*, might have been close in style to the Eastland event. It was reported that "Over a seven-hour period, the enraged farm and townspeople of the Delta went about their work of torturing."

Before Shepherd was soaked with gasoline, "the mob saw to it that his mouth and nose were partially filled with mud so that the inhalation of the gas fumes would not bring his agony to a premature end."[41]

As Eastland became a prosperous Delta planter and a long-term and powerful senator, he kept himself and other planters wealthy while most of the Delta, including his hometown, was left impoverished. Historians give countless examples of Eastland's ongoing greed that kept money in his family's pockets while poor Delta children literally starved.[42]

Post #5:

The Marcus Garvey Movement Awakened Race Consciousness: The Delta Would Have Changed For Better, Had Garvey Succeeded

"For man to know himself is for him to feel that for him there is no human master. For him Nature is his servant, and whatsoever he wills in Nature, that shall be his reward. If he wills to be a pigmy, a serf or a slave, that shall he be. If he wills to be a real man in possession of the things common to man, then he shall be his own sovereign.

When man fails to grasp his authority he sinks to the level of the lower animals, and whatsoever the real man bids him do, even as if it were of the lower animals, that much shall he do. If he says "go." He goes. If he says, "come," he comes.

By this command he performs the functions of life even as by a similar command the mule, the horse, the cow performs the will of their masters. For the last four hundred years the Negro has been in the position of being commanded even as the lower animals are controlled. Our race has been without a will; without a purpose of its own, for all this length of time."

Marcus Garvey, *Man Know Thyself*

A Professor and a Journalist Arrive, Observe and Report

Two significant white people, a professor of history and a journalist, came into Mississippi at a time when it was once again critical that Mississippi take accountability for its racist acts.

Both men came into the state at this opportune time, between the two world wars, with a fresh perspective. Neither man was influenced by Garvey but clearly both seemed to understand what Garvey maintained, that if a man knows himself, a man can change.

JAMES W. SILVER started his academic career as a history professor at the University of Mississippi in the mid 1930s where he lasted nearly three decades, an especially astonishing feat considering he wrote history books quite liberal for his times, books that would rankle any Confederate-phile.

Born in Rochester, New York, Silver showed great bravery by writing academically about Mississippi's past and present history focusing on the severe mistreatment of African Americans.

Silver would be on campus at the University of Mississippi when U.S. marshals fought to see that James Meredith was enrolled there as the first black student in the fall of 1962. Silver later described himself as "alternately enraged and heartsick" that his fellow Mississippians, particularly the students, felt called upon to engage in a "mad insurrection against their own government."

Silver said, "To me it was and still is nothing less than incredible. Later, when the state of Mississippi was being flooded from within by malignant propaganda about what had happened at Ole Miss that night, I felt a growing compulsion to try to tell the truth, to relate in plain fashion what had taken place and then to put it all in historical perspective."[43]

Silver was also concerned about Mississippi's growing white Citizens Councils, an organization that emerged a year before Emmett Till's murder, following the U.S. Supreme Court's Brown vs. the Topeka, Kansas Board of Education decision. Councils were comprised of angry bankers, physicians, lawyers, ministers, politicians, business people and others who opposed Brown.

About the same time Silver was settling into Oxford, moderately liberal journalist Hodding Carter, Jr. ferried across the Mississippi River from Louisiana to become a powerful newspaper editor in the politically engaged port town of Greenville. For years, Carter had worked as a Louisiana journalist, taking on the notorious and corrupt politician, Huey Long.

A small group of cotton planters, anxious to keep their labor pool in tact, actually recruited Carter to the Delta because they believed Carter could be used to counter some of the highly racist and irrational editorializing in the rest of the state's newspapers.

It was counterproductive for their laborers to be chased out of the state or lynched. Something needed to be done to cool the rhetoric and Carter was brought in for this reason. It would turn out that Carter remained an independent journalist, writing on topics of his choice and keeping his integrity, despite their recruitment.[44]

Both Silver and Carter frequently irritated powerful rulers of the Magnolia state, meeting racism head-on with their perceptions of truth and logic through the written word. Carter would later win a Pulitzer Prize for his editorial writing and Silver would be forced to move his productive career, teaching history, to the University of Notre Dame, after writing a major book with international impact that defined much of Mississippi's moral chaos.

As critical events unfolded in Mississippi, each man took on a significant role. When young Emmett Till was tortured and murdered in the Delta, Silver asked around and did the work of a true historian collecting facts; when James Meredith entered the University of Mississippi, Silver methodically chronicled what he observed; when Cleve McDowell attempted to follow in Meredith's footsteps, Silver spent time with the lonely student, as he had done with Meredith.

Down in Greenville, 140 miles southwest of Ole Miss, Carter stayed busy straining local customs by criticizing the practice of lynching and printing a photograph of black Olympian Jesse Owens. He argued in countless articles and books that Southern whites, not blacks or Northerners, had to change themselves.

Carter eventually died a disheartened man over what he believed to be the extreme direction taken by more radical civil rights leaders after the murder of Martin Luther King, Jr. Silver was finally chased out of Mississippi's premier university in 1964, as his book, *Mississippi: The Closed Society*, was about to be published by Harcourt, Brace & World. He ended his career at Notre Dame where he taught five years before retiring.

Both men made great contributions by describing what they saw during the modern civil rights movement and connecting events to the antecedent history. Their writings remain key to understanding this period and why things happened the way they did.

Years before Carter and Silver came into Mississippi, as World War I ended in 1918, countless white Southerners feared return of black veterans who might spread political ideas acquired in the military, despite there not being any serious challenges to the caste system in Mississippi in the first half of the twentieth century.

Governor Theodore Bilbo "welcomed home" veterans by literally spelling out a warning to returning black soldiers, worded in true Vardaman style:

"We have all the room in the world for what we know as N-i-g-g-e-r-s, but none whatsoever for 'colored ladies and gentlemen.'[45]"

A Democrat, Bilbo served two terms as governor of Mississippi and later became a U.S. Senator in 1935. Described as a master of scathing filibuster and a "rough and tumble" fighter in debate, his fiery defense of segregation brought him eventual shame in the Senate, as did his membership in the Ku Klux Klan.

In his work, *Mississippi: The Closed Society*, Silver gave this account of the returning WWI veterans:

"As elsewhere in the South, there was widespread fear in Mississippi that the Negro would come home from World War I expecting to continue the slightly increased enjoyment of rights and prerogatives he found in the army. But the aims of the Negro were not then particularly high. The 'do-gooder' of that day fought for the Negro's right not to be burned alive, for his recognition as a human being, for a greater moral awareness among white people."[46]

Silver saw a general apathy in the closed society he described of this time. He saw "a lethargic federal government, a widespread agricultural distress, an emigration of the most dissatisfied, and the burgeoning power of the modern Ku Klux Klan."

After World War II intervened, Silver believed that Eleanor Roosevelt bore the brunt of the closed-society offensive against federal meddling in Mississippi. During the war, the Fair Employment Practices Committee had no impact on the state.

Silver saw the walkout of the Mississippi delegation from the Democratic National Convention in 1948 as proof that Dixiecrats would have none of what they perceived as Harry Truman's playing politics with the race question.

It appeared to him that during these periods the closed society was safe from any threat of change. The only potential threat to its way of life was from the outside, mostly likely from the federal government itself, and to Silver, this threat seemed insignificant.

With half the twentieth century gone, Mississippi blacks still did not vote or serve on juries. They held no offices in government and attended poor schools. They lived in slum housing, were treated unequally in the courts and sat in the back of the bus.

Blacks were segregated in illness, worship and even in death, except for sitting in the same electric chair at the state penitentiary. "Good" blacks were least likely to be mistreated because they had learned militancy against the Jim Crow code could be fatal. Resistance was not tolerated.

Silver often bolstered his writing with stories showing murder used as a means of social control, incidents he had personally collected to make his point.

With pride, a "kindly old gentleman" from Tallahatchie County once told the history professor how a crewmember at his Charleston mill was hanged for "talking back to the boss." In fact, the gentleman lost his entire crew of African-American workers over the lynching incident when they all walked off the job. "From the record, one may wonder which race has been living nearer to the law of the jungle," Silver wrote.

DESPITE BILBO and others like him, by the end of the First World War, times were still changing, just very slowly.

The Delta Planting Company, later the Delta and Pine Land Company, with ownership of 45,000 acres of cotton lands in Bolivar County, began using scientific management techniques to mill and market its own lumber, putting 1,000 tenant families to work in better than typical conditions.[47]

The company, unlike most others, did not force the families to shop for all food and necessities in company stores, with high prices and low quality, as did most other plantations.

Recognizing the importance of keeping the labor pool strong, and perhaps sensing Northern migration in the air if violence continued, a few Delta planters tried modeling Delta Planting's modern management — using money for luring workers back to the cotton fields, while other planters continued to rely on brutality and violence against blacks to force them into the fields.[48]

The Elaine Massacre

Over in the small farming community of Elaine, Arkansas, south of Clarksdale and across the Mississippi River, violence remained the choice of planters in 1919. Even with a high market price for cotton, white buyers and landlords were cheating the black growers.

Coming home from a war that had raised hopes for a better life, some veteran black farmers reacted by taking a new tactical direction, joining the Progressive Farmers and Householders Union of America or PFHUA.

Propertied whites opposed the union and clashed with blacks attending a union meeting in a black church at Hoop Spur in Phillips County, Arkansas. The whites later claimed that blacks first opened fire, but blacks stated they had only returned the shooting started by White Raiders, a Klan offshoot from Mississippi.

The first mêlée ended with one white man reported dead and another wounded, after more armed whites entered the county from Arkansas, Mississippi, and Tennessee, disarming and arresting blacks, and confining hundreds in a stockade, keeping them from communicating with relatives or legal counsel. Some blacks hid in canebrakes and were hunted down by white vigilantes.

Up to a thousand planters, sheriffs and other whites from the Yazoo Delta crossed the Mississippi River into Elaine as reinforcements. One journalist described scenes of black men, women and children being shot in cold blood and reported the deaths of "856 Negroes and a wounded list probably five times greater."

Even today, the story goes that at least an equal number of whites were killed and that hundreds of other blacks had been taken to a school house where they were tortured and interrogated for days, some beaten to death. The total death list will never be known, since other estimates were much higher. One teacher who safely hid himself from the gunfire estimated 1,000 dead.

In 1920 the cotton market collapsed once again and, over the following years, black people kept moving to the North. Those who stayed behind became more defiant — while the planters became more oppressive. Attempting to destroy the "New Negro," some planters encouraged a revival of the Ku Klux Klan, resulting in countless acts of violence and terrorism as had occurred in Elaine.

New chapters of the NAACP were being organized around Mississippi, mostly in the Delta. Members helped raise funds to support a congressional anti-lynching bill.

Black gun owners had always posed a great threat to planters, especially around disputes over crop contracts and merchant bills.

While many rural black people carried guns for hunting and self protection, historian Nan Elizabeth Woodruff, author of *American Congo*, asserts the frequency of armed confrontations between planters and croppers may have increased in the decade following World War I, giving countless examples like these:

—In 1921, seventeen-year-old John Noey Brewer worked on Mrs. W.C. Brooks' plantation in Winona and was considered a "good Negro." For ten days he had been "moody and subject to fits of anger" when reprimanded. Brooks asked Brewer to pick up the mail in town. He refused and she threw him off the farm. But Brewer returned that night and shot Brooks, threatened her daughter, and then shot himself.

—In Greenwood, Hal Winters and George Blakely were lynched in 1927 for killing Wisley P. Martin, a plantation manager who raped Winters' daughter.

—In tiny Itta Bena of Sunflower County, D.O. Alexander, a large plantation owner, shot and killed Sam Jefferson over a crop dispute. Alexander heard that Jefferson and his father, heavily armed, were looking for him.

—Sixty miles north, in Clarksdale, a mob killed Lindley Coleman after a jury acquitted him of murdering a plantation manager.

For some white men, shooting black workers was a sport, like shooting deer or quail. In 1923, the Louisiana governor asked the governor of neighboring Mississippi to stop his citizens from shooting their squirrel guns at black men who worked on the Louisiana-Mississippi Highway.

Garveyism Grows

Freedom fighter William Pickens of Arkansas visited the Mississippi River Valley in 1921 and described it as the "American Congo." Pickens was referencing similar violence occurring in the African Congo under Belgium's King Leopold II during the 1890s.

A field secretary for the NAACP, Pickens was in the Delta to investigate a brutal lynching and observed how "labor is forced and the laborer is a slave … in a cunningly contrived debt-slavery, to give the appearance of civilization and the sanction of law."

While Pickens blamed the sharecropping system for increased violence following the war, others would later say that Pickens entirely missed the growing postwar militancy of the Delta's people[49] as chapters of Marcus Garvey's Universal Negro Improvement Association or UNIA were growing across the country in response to the continued violence against black citizens. Jamaican-born Garvey spoke of the lynching, burning, and disrespect of Negroes that was "spreading all over the world."

"If we in this present age do not go out and do something to stop lynching, every inch of ground in the world will become unsafe for the Negro in the next twenty years," Garvey said.[50]

Garveyism began in black Harlem in the spring of 1918 and rapidly grew throughout the black world. Within the brief span of seven years, nearly a thousand UNIA divisions were formed, and tens of thousands of members enrolled.

The Garvey movement "awakened a race consciousness that made Harlem felt around the world," wrote Rev. Adam Clayton Powell, Sr. This growing strength of Garvey's movement, one of the fastest growing black movements in history, would be taken as a political threat by the U.S. government and eventually destroyed.

If Garvey's movement had succeeded, perhaps the Delta would have changed more quickly for the better. But this was not to be.

Post #6:

I was in the middle of posting to this blogbook when ...

Today, August 20, 2009, while looking for any new information on Joe Pullen for the next blog post, I received this short, breaking news release from Ron Herd of W.E. AL.L. B.E. News Radio:

For Immediate Release: *Breaking News *Mob Rule In Sumner, Mississippi!!

Lawyer Organizes Lynch Mob & Uses Machine Guns, Dogs and Tanks To Hunt Down A Black Man Where The Lynching Of Emmett Till Took Place...

While moving closer to the Aug. 28 anniversary of Emmett Till murder, a relative of the defense attorney in the Milam/Bryant trial has been up to his own sort of celebration.

—

This short news story, reported by Ronald Herd of W.E. AL.L. B.E. News, is quickly gaining the attention of the national media.

I sure don't know what is going on down in the Delta but I'll e-mail Jerry Mitchell at *The Clarion-Ledger* and see if he knows anything about this breaking story. Promise to post something as soon as I learn more. Susan

Post #7:

Murder of Joe Pullen, "Another Civil Rights Movement Watershed — Like the Elaine Massacre"

MARY KING WAS a young woman living in Drew, Miss., in 1923 when a gun battle took place in her town that quickly gained worldwide attention.

As a 19-year-old, King was among town members not directly involved in the Sunflower County shoot-out, but was left to deal with the bloody aftermath when dozens, perhaps even one hundred or more men and women lie wounded in the streets and alleys of this cotton ginning town.

When the gun fight was over, Joe Pullen, a returning World War I veteran and Mississippi Delta tenant farmer, was found in a ditch at the edge of town where he had been shot to death by machine gun fire while trying to dodge spraying bullets. All because of a fight over money and the right to determine one's destiny.

King wanted to make sure others would hear the factual Joe Pullen story, she told her Cleveland neighbor, many years later after moving to the seat of Bolivar County, just seven miles away from Drew. Becoming friends with Margaret Block, a civil rights movement activist, King told her story to Block, asking her to write it down for posterity.

"Mary was about 99 years old when she told me the story and she died three years later at the age of 102," Block said. "She was an amazing woman and she wanted to make sure others would hear the truth."

King told her that Joe Pullen "got into it" with W.T. Saunders about money he was due — that he had been cheated by Saunders over money he was owed for work he had completed.

"After the two parted, Saunders sent a gang out after Pullen. He tried to run to his mother's house but ended up hiding in a drainage ditch to protect himself from flying bullets. King said, "Pullen shot Saunders and two others in self-defense. They set the ditch on fire and when flames hit the sky, they could see Pullen. They shot and killed him.[51]"

The Joe Pullen incident is historically significant because it gained national press attention, becoming the first such story to be so widely reported out of the Delta. Interestingly, a second event covered by national and international press would take place 32 years later, at the edge of Drew — the beating of Emmett Till.

Like most Delta history, there are typically multiple accounts, both written and spoken, of the story. Here is what is generally told about the Joe Pullen incident:

On December 15, 1923, Pullen was forced to settle a debt to plantation manager W.T. Saunders, even though he felt the amount owed him was unfair. Heated words flew and Pullen decided to run home for protection.

Several dozen posse members may have been killed as bullets flew and possibly hundreds of bystanders were wounded before Pullen was taken down by machine gunners who brought in their equipment from nearby Clarksdale. Like the earlier massacre in Elaine, Arkansas, no one will ever know how many people were wounded or killed.

For years after the gunfight, a good number of people were using walking canes and displaying other signs of injuries received during the gun battle, some older black Drew residents say to this day.

In yet another popular version, nearly 1,000 white men searched the swamps around Drew to find Pullen. Then, depending on the source, Pullen, himself, killed 4, 17 or 19 whites and wounded 8, 38 or 40 before he was machine gunned down. Pullen either died immediately or was dragged through the streets and then killed. Local news accounts of this event were few and typically, if there had been newspaper coverage, the source would need to be questioned for accuracy and bias.

The weekly Indianola newspaper carried one small paragraph on December 20 of that year, reporting that "J.L. Dogget of Clarksdale and Kenneth Blackwood of Drew, posse men wounded Friday by negro, Joe Pullen, are reported as improving rapidly as could be expected."

An Associated Press report indicated that four men lost their lives in a "spectacular gun battle, which raged until 1 o'clock this morning between Joe Pullen, Negro tenant farmer, and a posse of several hundred men in the swamps of the Mississippi Delta near Drew." The story continues that others were wounded and "three probably fatally."

Pullen was finally captured "...when four members of the posse stormed the drainage ditch in which he was entrenched. The Negro died an hour later from bullet wounds. The trouble started when Pullen's employer came to his house to collect a debt," the Associated Press report states.

Even more interesting accounts are gleaned from stories told by others living in Sunflower County at the time. The late Fannie Lou Hamer, well-known civil rights activist from nearby Ruleville, often told how the shoot-out occurred when she was a child and that Pullen's body was "...dragged into town while people cut off body parts to keep as souvenirs." Hamer would also say that "Mississippi was a quiet place for a long time afterwards."

While local newspapers claimed that four white men had died "in defense of law and order," Mrs. Hamer stated in her autobiography that Pullen killed thirteen white men and wounded twenty-six others before dying.

Dr. L.C. Dorsey, a Mississippi sociologist and friend of the late Mrs. Hamer, remembered how, as a young child living on a Sunflower County plantation between Ruleville and Drew, she heard from her father and relatives the story of Pullen. Like so many other sharecroppers, including Pullen, Dorsey's father often did not receive the money due him by the white landowner.

Dorsey believes general telling of the Pullen incident had much to do with people's fear of questioning "the man." Her family's version asserts that Pullen died because he stood up for his right not to be cheated out of his labor. After Pullen did not clear anything at settlement time, he made arrangements to go live with another black farmer.

Dorsey said, "When he returned to announce his plan ... white folks got angry ... and decided he wasn't going to move ... the man wasn't going to let him take anything off the place. Pullen sent his family away and decided to stay with his belongings ... the furnishings, the livestock, the mules that he needed to work with — and what my daddy called a mob crew, which was really what they called the Klan ... They came to the house to take him out and either kill him or beat him up, to put him in his place.

"He was prepared for them. He shot several of them, killed some of them, and escaped to a ditch and got in a culvert and was able to hold them off for a long time. Eventually, some person poured gasoline in the ditch and set it on fire and he had to come out... and they killed him. And if that wasn't enough, they tied him to a car and drug him through the streets of Drew, cut off his ears, I think, or castrated him ... and put it in jars in the city. Every black person knew that legend. Miss Hamer used to tell it. Everybody knew it."[52]

Unusual for these times, Pullen's family actually protested to President Calvin Coolidge who sent an investigative team "because the man had been in the service, and that was what his family talked about, that this man had served his country and this is how he was treated. He had done nothing wrong and had been killed for trying to defend himself against the crew," Dorsey said.

Historian Woodruff writes that Saunders may have offered Pullen $150 to recruit families to work on the plantation, and when Pullen kept the money without providing the service, the fight began. She terms Pullen's gunfight another "watershed event," much like the Elaine Massacre, as blacks challenged the structure of white supremacy throughout the 1920s.[53]

The frequency of armed confrontations between planters and croppers may have increased in the decade following World War I. Still, no black was safe during the cotton harvest, as evidenced by the Pullen incident.

Observed Clarksdale blues performer Will Stark, "They had to work — or fight! When they come after a man to work, he had to go. For instance, Mister Hobson or Mister Clark or Mister King or Anderson or any of these people out of town wanted some hands to chop the cotton or plow, it make no difference who he was, he must go.

"They would go into colored people's house and get the children out who had never been worked none — schoolgirls — and make them go out and pick cotton ... Of course the boss didn't do all this, the officers here in town would take 'um and when they got out on the plantation they had to work — or fight ... They just whipped 'um up. Some of 'um I heard they whipped to death ... One bossman out here about Tutwiler ... made a man work and chained his wife in bed at night to make sure they wouldn't run away."[54]

THE RULING WHITE Delta families kept their immense social, economic and political power through an efficient capitalist economy rooted in black labor manipulation. Schooling and marriage built strong family alliances, and these white coalitions, like Mafioso, expanded into local economies, from ownership and operation of cotton gins, to real estate, and banking.

Planters ran all of Mississippi. They frequently formed land companies to buy Delta properties; they held political, military, church and other bonds that established a "powerful, vertical integration" of local businesses into more powerful national bodies "such as the Standard Oil Company which dominated the American Cotton Oil Trust."[55]

The plantation bloc dominated political office holders — local, county, state, and national officials who enforced plantation regulations. Under these influences, oppression and censorship returned increasingly to levels experienced before emancipation. World War I made little difference, Pullen and other returning veterans would learn.

In the same year as Pullen's revolt, planters were trying to lure laborers home to the Delta following a mass exodus from the South. Some Blacks actually returned when learning of planters' promises of better housing and pay, especially after finding it hard to survive in new surroundings.

But these were only promises with little true fulfillment, and more and more blacks left the Delta in response to the increased violence and oppression. In the Vicksburg area, alone, more than ten thousand African Americans moved away over the course of three months during the same year as Pullen's death.

A Cleveland, Miss., newspaper reported, "The through trains passing via this city on the way to Northern communities for more than four months have been crowded with men, women, and children forming part of another exodus to the North which is due to lynchings and a general state of unrest of the people."[56]

Some Delta plantation owners actually tried to stop the outflow by paying in cash, allowing workers to shop wherever they wanted, and stocking commissary shelves with meat, cheese, coffee and candy as opposed to the traditional meal and lard.

Night Riders of the Klan drove sharecroppers from their fields and out of the region, negating these planter's efforts. Sexual battery and rape were not uncommon activities for the Klan.

In Ruleville, Isaac Moore and his brother refused to sell their crop to the landowner's brother, and 17 Klansmen broke into Moore's home, sexually harassed his wife, beat her with a rifle and then stole all of their chickens, crops, mules, corn and hogs.

Greenville planter, Leroy Percy, known for his outward civility (and by some revisionists for his hypocrisy), once told his managers how to treat black tenants that could not make enough wages from cotton to pay for their rent, because of boll weevils.

"Take as much as you can get from the Negroes without process of law where they are willing to remain on the place. If they are going to move anyway, it seems to me, you might as well clean them up."

While Mississippi sent more black soldiers to World War I than whites, black men on their return home still found themselves with no more of a voice, something they had fought with their lives to defend ... as did Joe Pullen of Drew.

Post #8:

Emmett Till's Casket Acquired By Smithsonian and My Reaction, Thursday, August 27, 2009

A story in today's *Washington Post* announced the National Museum of African American History and Culture has acquired the original casket of Emmett Till, "whose brutal murder in 1955 energized the modern civil rights movement."

The official announcement of the donation — made by the Till family to the Smithsonian Institution — is set for tomorrow, the 54th anniversary of his death, during a memorial service in Chicago, according to museum officials. Opening of the museum in The Mall is set for 2015.

In the *Post* story, Lonnie G. Bunch III, the museum's director said he had "much to consider before saying yes to the acquisition."

"The family wanted to preserve it in a respectful way," Bunch said. "But it did raise philosophical, ethical and sensational issues that I wanted to think about. And I wanted to consider them as a museum director, as a historian, and someone who has to raise funds. I wanted to understand all the hurdles."

Now wait a minute... I am stunned at this man's remark. Is Lonnie G. Bunch out of his friggin' head? I have to wonder if he even knows this history? Talk about Northern hypocrisy!

Someone who *HAS* to raise funds?

Is Bunch so concerned that if he takes in (to supposedly honor) the casket of a young, black child who was brutally murdered, that donations to the Smithsonian Museum will decrease? Perhaps Lonnie G. Bunch needs a spokesperson to vet his public statements before he makes any more of them.

So, Mr. Bunch goes on to tell the reporter he had no doubts about the casket's significance. His comment: "The story of Emmett Till is one of the most important of the last half of the 20th century. And an important element was the casket."

So, what was Mr. Bunch's problem in the first place? Since he's letting us know that he had "philosophical, ethical and sensational issues" about the casket's display.

Well, I guess one could say that so did Mrs. Till when she decided to let her son's body be viewed in a pine box in Chicago 54 years ago. However, her integrity apparently hastened her in overcoming the same hurdles facing Mr. Bunch today.

This story stinks. What do you think?

Post #9:

Mississippi Flood of 1927, Continued Violence and Government Failure Disrupt the Delta; Scientists, Theologians, Journalists, Communists Try to Help

> "The average planter and public official is firmly convinced that unless he takes drastic steps, white supremacy, Christianity, the American flag and the sanctity of home and family ties will be overthrown by agents of the Soviet Union."
>
> *New York Times* reporter, F. Raymond Daniel who visited the Delta in 1935.

Four years ago this Saturday on Aug. 29, 2005, Hurricane Katrina hit the city of New Orleans with devastating force. Who can ever forget watching images of the poorest residents fighting for their lives while their iconic city drowned as our leaders failed to act?

President George W. Bush's failures compounded the suffering along the Gulf Coast in those fateful days. But this would not be the first time that government left countless Mississippi African Americans to fend for themselves. Consider a catastrophe of similar magnitude back in 1927.

That spring, the powerful Mississippi River flooded 2.7 million acres across the Delta, leaving untold tragedy behind. Louisiana journalist John M. Barry provided an incredible glimpse into this natural disaster in his 1998 book, *Rising Tide: The Great Mississippi Flood of 1927 and How It Changed America.*.

Barry left a wake of surprised and angered white people in the Delta when he reported facts apparently new to his readers, that a long-respected and wealthy Greenville family had not lived up to their expectations during the worst of times.

Red Cross-donated food was placed under planter control, keeping food away from those in most need. Donated supplies were stockpiled by distributors who later profited from sales of the donated food to blacks.

Barry tells the story that during the flood, hundreds of black convicts were treated brutally and even used as human sandbags to stop levees from breaking, and there was indiscriminate murder. James Gooden worked all night piling heavy sandbags as fast as he could on the levee. When ordered to return the next morning by a Greenville police officer, Gooden was exhausted and refused. A scuffle followed and Gooden was shot and killed by the officer.

To calm the black community, the officer was arrested and held for trial. But county prosecutor Ray Toombs was a reputed Exalted Cyclops of the local Klan, and few blacks believed a fair trial would ever occur.

Will Percy, the son of Leroy Percy, head of Greenville's aristocracy, went before blacks gathered in a local church. Rather than making amends or trying to calm the group, Percy blamed the entire black community for Gooden's death, breaking all bonds that existed between blacks and the Percy family.[57]

As conditions worsened in Greenville, refugees were brought in from outlying sections. Cold weather added to their suffering and the situation was becoming life threatening as the water supply became contaminated and food was nearly gone.

Ten thousand people were stranded on the levee and the city was cut off with no rail connections. Supplying Greenville with relief food and medicine would only be possible if refugees were forced to remain living and working on the levee at risk of life.

President Herbert Hoover, having approved an evacuation plan using government steamboats, visited Greenville only to learn local leaders decided to keep thousands of black people stranded on the levee in refuge camps so laborers could continue working to unload supplies for others stranded throughout the county.

The same day of Hoover's visit, a black refugee died, after not eating for days and then gorging himself on bananas. The official story was the man's body was rowed into the middle of the river and thrown in. "But rumors spread that the National Guard had thrown him into the river alive as punishment for stealing the bananas." Other rumors had the police chief regularly towing black bodies, found floating in the streets, to the levee.

Lennie, an uncle of neighboring Bolivar County civil rights activists Sam and Margaret Block — their father's youngest brother — lived in Cleveland at the time of the flood.

"One of the stories he told us was about the sheriff and the Klansmen going around together throughout the Delta and forcing black men to work on cleaning up the aftermath or they would shoot them," Margaret Block said.

"When several whites came to get Uncle Lennie at his home in Cleveland, he was sitting on his front porch and he refused to go. They said they would shoot him and he said he would shoot them back. So they left him alone, but they killed another man who was a friend of our uncle's, Eddie Porter, also from Cleveland.

"They shot him through the head. They didn't need a reason to kill you, if you were black."

The Red Cross ultimately operated 154 refugee camps in Illinois, Missouri, Kentucky, Tennessee, Arkansas, Mississippi, and Louisiana, but only one location would generate criticism enough to bring intense political pressure on President Hoover — the Greenville camp on the levee.

After the flood, there was less reason than ever to stay in the Delta. Homes had been destroyed, belongings lost, and crops ruined. One Greenville sharecropper said that he had to "get my family out of this cursed South land — down here a Negro man is not as good as a white man's dog."

But it was very difficult to leave. Planters still depended on African-American laborers and would do virtually anything to keep them from leaving.

The following year, Congress passed the Flood Control Act of 1928, recognizing that flooding due to the Mississippi River was a federal responsibility, since 41 percent of the continental United States drains down the Mississippi River to the Gulf of Mexico. This act called for levees and floodwalls, floodways, channel improvement and stabilization, and tributary basin improvements.

Passage of this Act still did not stop the exodus of black laborers from the Delta. This legislation certainly gave them no comfort.

Chicago was the favored destination of those leaving Mississippi, and from 1920-1930, the city's population more than doubled. This Great Migration of people was accompanied by Delta blues musicians who carried their musical tradition to Chicago and put down roots in the Northern city.

One story goes that in the week following the murder of Joe Pullen in Drew, several bluesmen were killed one night for violating a local order to shut down Drew's blues alley bars by 7 p.m. each night.

The next day, remaining bluesmen set out for Chicago where they would eventually blend their version of the Delta blues with Chicago blues, to birth a new variation. I learned of this from a Delta blues historian living in Drew. His story, like so many others, is in the oral tradition and if not collected is subject to the ravages of time.

Fortunately, there is a more just ending to the Katrina disaster than there was to the Great Flood as accountability has been drawn into the picture. The Army Corps of Engineers' failure to properly maintain a shipping channel linking New Orleans, Louisiana, to the

Gulf of Mexico led to catastrophic flooding during Hurricane Katrina, a federal court ruled in November 2009.

EMMETT TILL'S MOTHER and her family left Mississippi before the flood, in 1923. "My daddy, Wiley Nash Carthan, had come up a couple of months ahead of us and found work at Corn Products. Mama and I joined him in January 1924 when I was just a little over two years old. As far as Mama was concerned, we didn't come a moment too soon; all kinds of stories came out of Mississippi with the black people who were running for their lives," Till Mobley wrote.

"There had been talk of a lynching in Greenwood. It was the sort of horrible thing you only heard about in the areas nearby. But it seemed like that was the whole point: to send a signal, to make sure that black people in the area were kept under control. Maybe it was that Mama just knew she could never be controlled, or maybe she just knew that there had to be a better life for us somewhere else. And just about any place else would have been better than Mississippi in the 1920s," she wrote.[58] Ironically, her son Emmett would suffer the fate from which Mamie Till Mobley and her birth family fled.

Powerful legislator and planter Walter Sillers of Bolivar County displayed the Delta's typical state of denial when he opined that such continued northern migration was due to recruitment by "labor agents who wanted cheap labor and servants" and not because of white planter oppression.

Yet, he took some responsibility, in acknowledging, "shame of the habitations we furnish our tenants, yet the man who seeks to better conditions goes in debt, mortgages his property and is finally foreclosed."[59]

Share Croppers Union

Thousands of black and white rural families were again left without jobs, food, or homes in the 1930s when mechanized cotton production began replacing their hand labor. Cotton prices kept dropping, and in 1932, those laborers who remained in the fields were earning less annually than what they made in 1913.

A largely black underground organization of sharecroppers, tenant farmers, and agricultural laborers, the Share Croppers Union or SCU was becoming the largest Communist-led mass organization in the Deep South. Founded in Alabama in the spring of 1931, the SCU not surprisingly soon picked up members in Mississippi.

SCU's immediate goals focused on development of smaller farmer and tenant cooperatives and rural unions, based on preventing evictions. Their agenda included racial and ethnic cooperation and securing of federal funds for land reform.[60]

Other reports of Communist Party activity in the Delta during these years included a farm survey done in 1931. Later, flyers were published, urging blacks not to pick cotton at the going wage. Planters, true to their form, punished union members by denying Red Cross food donations, causing some families to starve and, by some reports, to die.[61]

Mississippi's "Caste and Class" Goes Under the Microscope

In the mid 1930s, anthropologist Hortense Powdermaker and social psychologist John Dollard, both colleagues at the Yale Institute of Human Relations, traveled into the Delta to study Indianola and nearby Sunflower, making the Sunflower County seat historically significant as the site of the first anthropological studies on non-Native people in the United States.[62]

Their classic ethnographies, Powdermaker's "After Freedom: A Cultural Study in the Deep South"[63] and Dollard's "Caste and Class in a Southern Town," contributed to a master narrative of the Yazoo-Mississippi Delta and the South that viewed class largely through the lens of race.

An Episcopal priest from Indianola told me about Powdermaker and said that a friend who worked at Parchman found a copy of the significant study was tucked away in a closet! Intrigued, and knowing that I would never find the Parchman copy, I discovered the Mississippi Archives keeps a copy in its general book collection.

Powdermaker's field observations about Indianola, the town she called Cottonville, were stunning. In her first few weeks there, blacks told the famous anthropologist of an incident when the black janitor of a white school was lynched after he reported to the principal that some of the white pupils had thrown stones at school windows.

Powdermaker observed how moods shifted within the white community regarding the possibility of a lynching. One day after a separate lynching attempt, the anthropologist journaled her impressions:

"[A] group of shabby men, their eyes burning, tramped up and down the road and through the woods, mingling their oaths with the barking of their dogs. The middle-class white men sitting in their offices or homes remarked that of course they did not approve of lynching, but that undoubtedly these Negroes would be lynched, and 'what can you do when you have to deal with the primitive African type, the killer?' The Negroes in the neighborhood sat at home all day, afraid to go out. Those in a town thirty miles distant said that things must be getting better because a few years ago, if the mob had not found the men they wanted by this time, they would have lynched someone else."

Powdermaker theorized that lynching encouraged blacks to commit violent acts against other blacks "... because the black person can hope for no justice and no defense from our legal institutions" and therefore must settle his own difficulties, "and often he knows only one way."

Dollard's separate work led to development of a theory of "frustration aggression" through life histories he collected from nine middle-class African Americans. In their respective studies, both scientists stressed the importance of voting and of the deep injustice of the forced caste division they observed.[64]

In 1932, FRANKLIN D. Roosevelt was elected president of the United States and began implementing New Deal relief policies that worked better for whites than most blacks, not surprising, since federal agricultural policies favored the richer agriculturalists. Roosevelt replaced Herbert Hoover, who did not have a good record for helping Delta blacks. This new president appeared to favor the poor, but only in his words.

A group called African Americans in Mississippi hired a secret investigator who studied Roosevelt's relief administration around the state, finding that black people were rarely hired by Works Progress Administration (WPA) or the Civil Works Administration (CWA). Those who were hired received lower pay than whites.

No CWA building projects, such as libraries, were awarded to black communities while most CWA teaching positions were handed out to whites. Planters and their relatives administered relief programs, always to their personal benefit. Blacks were often removed from relief rolls by the planter-run social programs and forced to pick cotton at low wages.[65]

Walter White of the NAACP confirmed that Delta blacks were losing their federal relief for refusing to pick cotton at low wages, creating a condition that "savors of peonage." He documented that:

—In Tunica, White discovered a planter's wife supervised the WPA program and thousands of the 20,000 black residents of the county were dropped from the relief rolls for refusing to pick cotton.[66]

—Mrs. Mary Jane Harris, 85, suffered from high blood pressure. After picking cotton for one month, because of health reasons and the need to care for her daughters, she left the fields and lost her monthly WPA relief check.

New Deal agricultural programs helped large-scale planters the most, allowing them to withdraw up to 30 percent of the acreage of their cotton crops from production. This parity program, requested by planters in the early 1920s, raised farm prices.

These payments harmed smaller family farmers and offered very little for farm workers. Delta planters, who benefited, "welcomed the program as it gave them opportunity to move faster toward mechanization by boosting their profits."

Planters obtained a windfall with passage of the Agricultural Adjustment Act that provided a rental payment from the government on retired lands and a second "parity" check. Tenants and sharecroppers were supposed to receive a share of these payments, but in most cases, they did not. Their portion was either stolen by the planter or taken as they were fooled into signing away their shares.[67]

The AAA eventually led planters to retire croplands. Planters could then use the full subsidy payments to hire back sharecroppers as wageworkers at lower costs. The planters' strategy was to support a great number of tenants to place in the relief programs. Thus, the lower their own expenditures would be for "furnish" or what they provided in advance for food and supplies.

Unions and Cooperative Farms

Movement against the strong tide of racism strengthened, as black farmers worked together trying to bring change, again with outside help. The Southern Tenant Farmer's Union or STFU, founded in 1934, was a socialist organization that attracted support from a variety of Southern white liberals. STFU membership included ministers from a radical movement who followed a social gospel "drawing from the New Testament and Karl Marx."

Noted theologian Reinhold Niebuhr, deeply committed to fighting Jim Crow and an investigator for the NAACP, belonged to the STFU and spent countless months in the Delta, often as an investigator for the NAACP.

STFU called for the end of evictions, appointment of farm labor representation on agricultural boards, and enforcement of Agricultural Administration Act or AAA contracts regarding parity payments to sharecroppers. In 1934, STFU collected evidence for a pamphlet funded by the Socialist Party, "The Plight of the Sharecropper," which "shocked even members of the AAA" with exposure of the planters' misappropriation of AAA payments owed to sharecroppers under the New Deal, Woodruff found.

In 1935, the Delta's major planters reduced cotton-picking wages from 60 cents to 40 cents per hundred pounds picked. Most pickers brought in about 200 pounds per day, so this represented a substantial loss. The STFU called a successful strike in Arkansas that met with success and with this victory union memberships grew. Still, landowners began evicting and blacklisting union members throughout the Delta. Soon, thousands of Delta families were thrown off plantations and out of their homes.

Within four years, the STFU could count eighteen locals and five hundred members in Mississippi, most from the Delta. STFU activities were far greater in Arkansas and received the majority of press coverage. Strikes did occur in the Delta and some were just as bloody as those across the river.

While the STFU moved into other parts of the South and California, some members returned to Mississippi in the 1960s to become involved in the Modern Civil Rights Movement. There were no further successful attempts to organize tenants until Fannie Lou Hamer in Sunflower County formed the Mississippi Freedom Labor Union in 1965.

What was the threat of the STFU? What did planters fear? F. Raymmond Daniell, a *New York Times* reporter, visited the Delta in 1935 and wrote: "The average planter and public official is firmly convinced that unless he takes drastic steps, white supremacy, Christianity, the American flag and the sanctity of home and family ties will be overthrown by agents of the Soviet Union."[68]

Evangelist Sherman Eddy of Memphis wanted to try something new to help Delta sharecroppers and, in 1936 and 1937, he started two cooperative farms — first in Bolivar and then Holmes counties. Both farms were projects of a philanthropically supported corporation, headed by Eddy, with a goal to help Southern agricultural laborers out of their economic plight.

Eddy's first cooperative farm was successful in its early months as 19 black families and 12 white families lived and worked together. Vegetation was abundant and a clinic was built to provide the families with medical attention. The Delta farm was sold in 1942 and all farming activities were transferred to the Providence farm.[69]

Like most cooperatives, the farms simply could not provide enough relief for those who were steadily becoming landless. Family farms were declining around the entire nation and small Delta farms, even with federal help, could not compete with large-scale corporate plantations.

A more successful farming project was initiated outside of Drew in 1920 lasting well into the 1970s. Brooks Farm on Freedom Road evolved from a plantation into a community of black landowners through the efforts of Palmer Herbert Brooks and community residents. The black planter's goal was to help farmers achieve their dream of "having a place where colored folk could have a chance to make a decent living without having somebody always taking away your crops and wages and looking over your shoulder."[70]

Brooks came to Drew in the early 1900s from Virginia after earning money in the lumber business in Ohio and West Virginia. Finding the soil, climate and labor supply good for farming, he purchased 7,000 acres in Sunflower, Leflore, and Bolivar counties. The collective plantation occupied 2,000 acres in Leflore and Sunflower counties. Most important to Brooks was that farmers living in the community not remain dependent. "He wanted these black men to become the boss of their own land and men of their own decision," wrote Valerie Grim in a doctoral dissertation through Iowa State University.

Grim analyzed interviews given by some of the Brooks Farm members, learning that when it became clear Brooks wanted to help blacks, "everybody tried to move out here, but at times there wasn't enough room, so people waited until a house was built or came open."

Brooks Farm workers appreciated the fair treatment offered in the community. Steve Hearon, a former plantation manager for Brooks, told interviewers that, "God sent Mr. Brooks to help us poor color people, 'cause he knowed some of us wasn't being treated right."

Brooks Farm was in place for over fifty years, mostly because of its community members' determination to rise above peonage. Brooks saw to it that farmers acquired knowledge and skills that were not only useful in agriculture, but which also gave residents the choice to make a home for themselves in Brooks Farm.

Both Sarah Walters and Carrie Gordon became licensed midwives and, as community members, they often were called to deliver babies. The community school emphasized a practical education that focused on manual skills, considering the rural character of the community and the limits imposed by segregation.

You can still drive to the site of this important collective farm and see its old storefront, some farming equipment and feel the spirit of its past. I found several abandoned homes, street signs and the skeleton of a cooperative store on the grounds. During the modern civil rights movement, some of the visiting volunteers lived on the grounds of the old Brooks Farm.

Post #10

U.S. Rep. Benjamin Thompson Seeks Attorney General's Probe in Sumner

Here we go again. This short announcement appeared in today's Jackson *Clarion Ledger*.

August 27, 2009: U.S. Rep. Bennie Thompson has officially requested that the U.S. Attorney General investigate an incident in which residents of Sumner conducted a search for a burglary suspect.

—

Don't we wonder what's really going on out in Tallahatchie County? It's fascinating that this story comes out just one day before the 54th anniversary of the lynching of Emmett Till. Remember that the trial of Milam and Bryant took place in Sumner, the second county seat in Tallahatchie County.

If you really cannot imagine that such an incident would take place in Tallahatchie County — the chase of a black man by a prosecutor driving a homemade tank — I would like to share a quick impression of Sumner:

One day I took my son, Barry — who was visiting us after graduating from law school and waiting to take the bar exam — for a drive around the Delta. We drove over to Sumner where he could see the courthouse where the Till trial took place. It was quiet on the courthouse square, almost eerie. Across the street was a small drugstore with a fountain that serves ice cream cones and that sounded good on a hot day.

When we walked up to the fountain, Barry noticed a "no mixing" sign taped to the cash register. Mixing is an old Southern term that refers to the mixing of races and is still used today by white supremacists. You can see the term used on websites like *stormfront.org*. Here's an example of a recent post:

"Races were not meant to be mixed and that is why God made us different. That is why God put them in Africa and Whites in Europe far from each other because we were never supposed to mix."

It was interesting to watch Barry's eyes when he saw the no mixing sign on the register. After a couple of seconds, he quietly asked the store clerk what the sign meant and got this response: "Oh, we just don't want people to mix ice cream flavors. You can have all chocolate or all white."

As I watched my son's stunned expression, I knew that was the day that he fully understood why he had worked so hard to complete his legal education.

Post #11

"Emmett, Down In My Heart" — the 1955 Lynching of 14-year-old Emmett Till in the Mississippi Delta

This announcement appeared Sept. 5, 2009 on the Hamptons.com website:

Kathleen Chalfant, Danny Glover and Linda Powell will star in the reading of Clare Coss's "Emmett, Down in My Heart," directed by James Lawson, for the benefit of the Bridgehampton Child Care and Recreational Center at the John Drew Theater at Guild Hall on Saturday, Sept. 5, at 8 p.m.

"Emmett, Down in My Heart" was written by playwright and psychotherapist, Clare Coss, and was inspired by the 1955 lynching of 14-year-old Emmett Till in the Mississippi Delta.

—

Wish that I could attend. I remember reading once that Rod Serling, the award-winning writer-creator of The Twilight Zone, had already started his career in television when the lynching of Emmett Till took place. Moved by the story, he dramatized the acquittal of Till's killers in a stage script titled "Noon on Doomsday," but it was twice censored by network television.

In both attempts to get "Noon on Doomsday" aired, Serling met with sponsor censorship and network interference that severely (Serling's word) diluted his final work. The script turned into something called "A Town of Dust," and "Emmett Till became a romantic Mexican, who loved the sheriff's wife, but only with his eyes," Serling wrote.

The location went to the Southwest and, according to Sterling, the production "got so far removed from reality it became soup."

Andrew Polak, president of the Rod Serling Memorial Foundation in Great Britain, is quoted in a story posted by Eurweb:

"Serling seemed to struggle with network and sponsor censorship all his career but I believe his trying to tell the story of the Emmett Till case was the pinnacle of this battle."

When word initially got out that Serling was writing about the Till case, Polak says that thousands of protests poured in, mostly from members of the White Citizens Councils. I would guess the postmarks were from Mississippi.

Post #12

Remembering and Honoring Memories of Emmett Till and Dr. Martin Luther King, Jr.

On this day in history, August 28:

In 1955, Emmett Till, an African-American teen from Chicago, was abducted from his uncle's home in Money, Miss., by white men after he had supposedly whistled at a white woman. His body was found three days later in the Tallahatchie River.

In 1963, Martin Luther King, Jr. delivered his famous "I have a Dream" speech in front of the Lincoln Memorial in Washington D.C.

—

Comments From *Vicksburgnews* Saturday, August 29, 2009 9:51:00 AM: I read every word of all your blogs. I had no idea there was a video of this story.

Thanks for the comment. There is a wonderful video by filmmaker Keith Beauchamp, *The Untold Story of Emmett Louis Till,* that articulates the madness of racism in the South of the 1950s.

Beauchamp combined archival photos and footage with emotional interviews and his documentary tells the harrowing story. Keith's work is a compelling documentary that has been shown to large audiences worldwide.

Post #13:

Mississippi Mau Mau; Veterans Return Home From World War II

While researching about teaching civil rights in the classroom, I learned about a professor who tried to help Mississippi better understand its civil rights history. The *Boston Globe*, on December 12, 1995, published a story about history professor James Loewen, who taught at Jackson, Mississippi's Tougaloo College about 35 years ago.

Dr. Loewen asked his students what he thought to be a simple question: What is Reconstruction? All but one student agreed it was a period after the Civil War when blacks governed Southern states but were so recently out of slavery they "messed up" and whites had to take back control.

The professor recalled that his heart sank when he heard his students' response. Loewen explained to the *Globe* reporter there were three misstatements.

First, blacks never took over governments. Southern states always had white governors and almost all had white legislatures. Second, governments during Reconstruction didn't screw up. That was a myth and, in fact, Mississippi had one of its best governments ever, according to Loewen. Third, whites did take control, "but it was because a coalition of white planters and racist Democrats acted against the interracial coalition that had been governing Mississippi."

This experience prompted Loewen to take a hard look into high school history texts, "and sure enough," his students had learned their lessons. "It was the history books that were wrong."

Loewen went to work to correct the misinformation contained in state history books. In 1975, after he co-wrote the first revisionist state-history textbook in America, winning the Lillian Smith Award for "best nonfiction about the South," Loewen had to sue the state to make *Mississippi: Conflict and Change* available to public schools.

The textbook rating committee — with a white majority — decided the book "contained too much black history, featured a photograph of a lynching, and gave too much attention to the recent past."

In April 1980, Loewen won a sweeping court victory based on the First and Fourteenth Amendments. The book found its way into school classrooms and the experience made Loewen aware of history used as a weapon. "My students had been battered by history. Not just the fact of history ... but battered by history books [and] by what we say about the past," Loewen told the *Boston Globe*.

In the summer of 2009, Mississippi announced a new program to teach state civil rights history in its high school classrooms. After learning about Dr. Loewen, I wonder if his book will be part of the new curriculum?

I heard about Mississippi's new attempt at cleaning up its history classes because I got a call from a *Christian Science Monitor* reporter who wanted to know my reaction about Mississippi's new history program.

So, I gave her my reaction: "Depends on who writes the curriculum."

My interview never made it into publication. Her editor apparently thought my remark was out of line for some reason. Even the reporter was not happy about the cleaned up version that made the *Monitor* and apologized.

I had given the reporter Dr. L.C. Dorsey's name and phone number and suggested this award-winning Mississippi professor be interviewed, too. Dr. Dorsey later told me she had the same response and that her remarks never made it into the story, either.

Neither of us was negative about the possibilities and we both suggested that Mississippi could lead the world in the teaching of racial understanding if the curriculum was prepared correctly and if teachers were supported. One of my other concerns was for the white students at private academies. Were they going to learn this history, too?

I thought we gave pretty good, independent interviews. And so did the reporter. The editor was apparently on a slice and dice mission. So — we got sliced. Nevertheless, the history remains, even if school children don't read it from their books ...

NEW IDEAS AND high expectations followed many of Mississippi's returning black World War II soldiers. Some would challenge the state's culture and authority more than ever.

Those returning soldiers who became leaders in the modern civil rights movement — most notably Amzie Moore of Cleveland, Aaron Henry of Clarksdale, and Medgar Evers of southeastern Mississippi — should be long-remembered for their renewed challenges to the racist bullying by Mississippi white leaders.

These three men — Moore, Henry and Evers — were part of nearly one million African Americans who fought in Europe and Asia. Their plan was to capture the freedom for which they had fought, and helped to win, as soldiers. Most returning Southern white veterans did not agree. They had fought this war and expected to keep things the same, and did not expect any changes that would introduce integration.

This book does not extend into the stories of U.S. soldiers who were not allowed to return home but were instead hanged to death by the military, under the orders of Gen. Dwight D. Eisenhower, rather than being shipped home for various criminal charges.

Louis Till, Emmett's father, was one such soldier. He was killed and buried in the Oise-aisne American Cemetery and Memorial in an unmarked grave. The cemetery is located in Fère en Tardenois,

France, said J. Marie Green, an independent researcher who has focused on Louis Till's death for many years.

As the role of black soldiers is documented in the history of World War II, Green is trying to learn about one more distinction of those fighting men: the fact that almost four times as many black soldiers as whites were executed in Europe after military court martial, even though blacks made up less than 10 percent of the troops.

"I am researching this and want to see it made right," Green said. She is using recently declassified military records obtained through the U.S. National Archives. Green, who holds a master's degree in library science from the University of Michigan, is not alone in her investigations.

Professor J. Robert Lilly spoke years earlier with *New York Times* reporter Francis X. Clines about hangings carried out for the American army near Somerset, England, where black and white American soldiers were executed at the prison for charges of murder and rape of English civilians. Lilly accidentally stumbled onto records about the executions while doing research in England on prison punishment in the early 1990s.

With help from a senior research associate at the Congressional Research Service, Lilly uncovered a 1946 summary of court-martial discipline dispensed in the war's European theater, finding "enough racial data to bolster what he had picked up anecdotally in England ... that Black soldiers paid for capital crimes disproportionately at the gallows in the segregated military of that time."

Green recently learned that Louis Till was a cellmate with American avant-garde poet Ezra Pound who later wrote about his experiences being incarcerated with black soldiers. Pound had ended up jailed in France because of his radical views, Green said.

How many black soldiers were executed overseas? Green believes the number of soldiers executed and buried in France, alone, is 80. "We know there are at least two more sites. One is in India; another is possibly in the Philippines."

Lilly, the Regents Professor of Sociology/Criminology at Northern Kentucky University, wrote that the executions of black soldiers supported his suspicions of a Jim Crow sort of racism in American military justice in World War II, a topic covered in his book, *Taken By Force,* published in 2007 by Palgrave MacMillan.

Green hopes that her research will be ready for publication by 2010. She also dreams of one day going to France and arranging for shipment of Louis Till's body back to the United States where he can be buried alongside his son, Emmett. Green said, "It's important for people to know that Emmett Till's father also suffered brutality from racism."

Louis Till's son, Emmett, was not the first fourteen-year-old young black man to be murdered in Mississippi. So many brutal events occurred in this region over the years; some stories have been documented formally but so many others pass orally through the generations:

Two fourteen-year-olds Charlie Lang and Ernest Green were hanged in Clarke County from the Shubuta Bridge over the Chickasawhay River on October 10, 1942. Lang and Green were playmates with a young white girl and when a passing motorist saw them chasing the girl, they were jailed on charges of attempted assault. A mob stormed the Quitman jail, taking the boys, and their bodies were found hanging from the river's bridges.[71]

The killing continued when one week later, Howard Wash was lynched in Laurel. A jury had convicted Wash of killing his dairyman employer but had not recommended death. "The U.S. attorney general ordered the FBI to investigate three lynchings, promising that if the investigation developed a case, "relentless prosecution would follow." No one was ever convicted.[72]

Rev. Isaac Simmons, 66, was abducted by six white men in Amite County on March 2, 1944 and killed with three shots into the back. His relatives discovered that Simmons' tongue had been cut out. Simmons had not been charged with murder or with the "unmentionable crime." Simmons was lynched because he was a successful black man intent on keeping his property —250 acres of debt-free land, historian John Dittmer wrote.

Returning Black Delta Soldiers Efforts Opposed

Two returning racist, white soldiers, Robert 'Tut' Patterson of Clarksdale and Byron de la Beckwith of Greenwood, would take significant actions against the growing civil rights movement, fervidly opposing any changes in the status of blacks, regardless of their military contributions.

During the ten years following the war's end, Mississippians saw black activism slowly rise and expand through what some, including the FBI, loosely termed a *Mau Mau* or "uprising" that began with an accelerated fight for voter registration and voting rights, and escalated to attacks on the state's segregated school systems and public places. There would be blood shed as these factions clashed.

The term *mau mau* comes from an "uprising" from 1952 to 1960 by Kenyan peasants against British Colonialist rule. Members of the Kikuyu ethnic group provided the core of the resistance aided by smaller groups. The uprising hastened Kenyan independence and motivated Africans in other countries to fight against colonial rule, even though it failed militarily. The uprising also set the stage for Kenyan independence in 1963 and is sometimes called the Mau Mau Rebellion or the Kenya Emergency.

Some help came from the NAACP's Legal Defense fund and other groups, but the fight for voting rights began as a mostly homegrown movement that saw Mississippi and Delta blacks become uniquely powerful leaders.

DURING WORLD WAR II, black soldiers rarely were allowed to rise in military rank. They were often assigned the most menial, degrading and physically demanding jobs. The worst tragedy on record, stemming from such mistreatment, involved Mississippi Congressman John Rankin and occurred at Port Chicago, a naval ammunition base northeast of San Francisco, the first pier in U.S. history built for loading and shipping explosives and munitions.

At this port, 71 white officers oversaw 1,400 black sailors, who loaded the ammunition in three round-the-clock seven-hour shifts. White officers had no experience in handling ammunition and ignored all of the grievances reported by the black enlistees.

A tragic explosion of ammunition took place on the morning of July 17, 1944, wherein 320 men were killed instantly, including 202 black enlisted men. Two hundred, thirty-three black enlisted men were among the 390 injured, making this disaster account for 15 percent of all black naval casualties during World War II.

The Navy found the cause to be "incompetence" on the part of the black seamen, letting the racist chain of command completely off the hook. Congress introduced a bill to grant the families of the dead soldiers $5,000 compensation but Mississippi's Rankin objected. Congress blinked and reduced the amount to $3,000.[73]

Amzie Moore, even before leaving Mississippi for World War II, was involved in race relations and once organized a successful rally of some 10,000 blacks in the Delta town of Cleveland on the campus of Delta State Teachers College, now Delta State University.

Born September 23, 1911, on the Wilkin plantation near the Grenada and Carroll County lines, Moore served over three and a half years in the Army before returning to his job at the U.S. Post Office in Cleveland of Bolivar County, where he had worked since 1935. As a soldier, Moore worked with an intelligence unit in Burma and was once ordered to tell African-American soldiers that conditions in the United States would be better when they returned home. Moore knew better, having joined the NAACP while still in the service.[74]

Returning home, Moore learned that one black person was being killed every week in Mississippi. The NAACP attributed many of these deaths to a newly organized "home guard," patterned after a fanatic white-terrorism group from the Delta that operated during and following the Civil War.

When Leon McTatie's body was found in a Sunflower County bayou in June of 1946, Moore, investigating for the NAACP, found the man was whipped to death for "stealing a saddle," a crime that black witnesses said McTatie did not commit. McTatie's wife saw her husband killed. Three defendants confessed to the beating, but it took a grand jury less than ten minutes to release the accused slayers. McTatie's violent killing was just one example of the Mississippi justice that Moore and other veterans returned to witness.[75]

Moore and other black veterans were surprised to find German Prisoner of War camps spread throughout Mississippi, many in the Delta, as Mississippi had served as "home" to all captured German officers.

The POWs were often treated better than the returning black veterans. There were complaints that white prisoners were served in restaurants that would not cater to black veterans, for example. One POW camp was located in Merigold, to the north of Cleveland, while another camp was in downtown Drew, at the later site of the A.W. James building.

Frances Kimbriel Showers, the daughter of an early Drew physician, wrote about the camp in a family history published in 1999 for the Drew Centennial:

"Most of the prisoners were German. Many … were allowed to paint houses for local homeowners. The only cost was [for] the paint. I have been told that for recreation there were dances for the prisoners. Some of the local girls took sandwiches and cookies and danced with the inmates. One of the organizers for those parties was Miss Elvie Netterville. I remember hearing the prisoners singing late in the afternoon on Sundays. They sounded very beautiful. Some of the songs were happy, but most were sad."[76]

Upon his return to Cleveland, Moore opened a gas station with a beauty shop and grocery store on Highway 61 that also served as headquarters for the area's civil rights efforts. His gas station was well known for offering the only restrooms for black drivers between Memphis and Vicksburg.

Moore's house has been described as a "revolving dormitory" and "safe house" for activists during the movement's voter-registration drives in the 1960s, with frequent visits by Rev. Martin Luther King, Jr., Andrew Young, and John Lewis. Thurgood

Marshall, Jesse Jackson and Medgar Evers were also some of Moore's more famous houseguests.

Proud of his family roots, Moore liked to tell about his grandfather, a slave who lived to be 104. "He couldn't read or write, yet he accumulated more than a section of land and had about … twenty thousand dollars … saved when he died."

Left on his own at fourteen, after his mother died in 1925, Moore completed high school but could not realize his dream of a college education. Throughout the rest of his life, he succeeded in becoming a self-educated person and one of Mississippi's most respected civil rights leaders.[77]

Civil rights activist Charles Cobb, who later came into Mississippi for Freedom Summer and was responsible for writing the prospectus for the successful Freedom schools, saw Moore as a "remarkably strong" person who liked to tell stories. Moore was a "classic organizer" as well. In an oral history interview, Cobb said:

"Amzie Moore had us move in and out of dangerous places, successfully and quietly. And he had these stories and you were never sure whether he was talking about now or whether he was talking about twenty or thirty years ago. You'd be passing by some place and he'd launch off into some involved story, some horrible event, some lynching, or something like that. And you'd sort of not be sure if he was talking about something that, you know, happened last weekend or in years past — and he did it quite deliberately."[78]

Aaron Henry used the GI bill at Tulane University to become a pharmacist before returning to settle in Clarksdale, just one county away from Moore. Born on the Flowers brothers' plantation in 1922, about 20 miles east of Clarksdale in Coahoma County, Henry worked all day in the fields starting at a young age. In his autobiography, completed after his death by Constance Curry, Henry wrote about what life was like as a young man.

"It was work or starve or get run of the place, and the work was simpler than the uncertainty of the outside. Nobody ever asked how we felt. They would hear us singing about the heat and the work and the life, and they would turn and tell each other how happy we all were," Henry told Curry.[79]

Tuskegee Institute was promoting trades of the hands at the time and Henry's father learned cobbling through the institute's course by mail. Eventually the Henry family moved to nearby Webb, where his father opened up a small shoe-repair shop. His mother took a Tuskegee course in beauty culture and began to dress hair at home.

In Webb, there was a school for white children, but Henry had to attend the school for black children on a nearby plantation, held in a Baptist church with only two teachers responsible for all grades.

Henry and his schoolmates were taught from well-worn state approved textbooks "that mentioned Negroes only as criminals, just enough to justify the Ku Klux Klan's activity." A new school principal, "soon in Dutch with the county board of education," ensured that black history and literature were included.

For the first time, Henry and his schoolmates were learning in biology that people of color were not inferior. A liberal arts education supplemented the technical and agricultural work. Henry remembered the contrasts in schools, and later gave much of his time to school improvement issues.

Drafted in 1943, Henry and his friend, Charles Hill, quickly learned the "only things not segregated at Mississippi's Camp Shelby were the men in charge — they were always white, and 'in charge' was the operative term."

Military service for most black soldiers in Mississippi meant daily doses of abuse and humiliation. In camp, white soldiers often beat black soldiers.[80] Henry, throughout his entire period of service, searched out nearby NAACP chapters and became involved in civil rights activities.

Once discharged, Henry left for Tulane University in New Orleans where he was involved with an active chapter of the NAACP and also joined the National Students Association, eventually to become Students for a Democratic Society or SDS.

In 1950, when Henry returned home, he was "plagued by problems of police brutality, of rapes of black women by whites, and murders of blacks by whites, with no national organization to come to the rescue."

R.L. Drew, H.Y. Hackett, Leola Guest, Henry and several others decided to form an NAACP chapter.

Ruby Hurley and Rev. Amos Holmes, the state's NAACP president, came to Clarksdale in 1952 and helped organize the Clarksdale branch. Seven years later, Henry became the NAACP state president, heading the organization for over thirty years.[81]

Like Moore's service station business, Henry's pharmacy became a civil rights headquarters for the northern Delta. Henry led boycotts, demonstrations, and other civil rights activities, resulting in the bombing of his home and his drugstore, personal injury and over thirty arrests.

Medgar Evers was sixteen and a sophomore when World War II broke out. Within a year, he quit school and joined his brother, Charles Evers, in the U.S. Army. Medgar Evers was attached to a segregated battalion that served in England and, after the Normandy invasion, in France.

The experience of travel opened up the world to him; the opportunity to leave the South provided an adventure he could not forget. In France, he found "a whole people — all of them white — who apparently saw no difference in a man simply because of his skin color, and this was perhaps the greatest revelation of all," he told his wife, Myrlie.[82]

While Evers grew up in Decatur, Miss., outside of the Delta, he would spend his first several years out of college in Mound Bayou of Bolivar County, working with Amzie Moore, organizing NAACP chapters and investigating murders, and working also selling insurance.

Evers quickly came to know Aaron Henry and the three men began lifelong journeys to change Mississippi. All returning black veterans — Moore, Henry, and Evers — faced the Delta's familiar extremes, both old and new.

Politics had shifted further right. Powerful behind-the-scenes players were building their own blocs such as the Delta Council, a forerunner of what would become the Citizens' Councils, a racist organization evolving to fight integration and change.

A massive farming revolution would further marginalize Mississippi blacks because fewer would be needed to pick the cotton. Usual conflicts between moneyed Delta whites and their poor counterparts in the nearby hill country had eased over the war years, fusing a new race-based voting bloc.

Both groups, fearing federal intervention over race issues, had combined their votes, sending two outspoken, ultra-conservative racists back to the United States Senate — Eastland and Bilbo.

The practice of segregating primary elections, known as White Primaries, ended before the war was over; hence the black vote actually doubled in the 1947 election, but still represented only 10 percent of the African Americans eligible to vote.[83]

Some attempted to hurdle the racial barriers that kept blacks from voting and exercising other citizens' rights. Few succeeded, since the segregationist culture was so strong.

Chancery Judge Harvey Ross, born and raised in the New Africa district outside of Clarksdale, grew up in times when segregation was absolute. He recalled:

"The black school system was almost nonexistent ... there were scattered one-room schools around the county and these schools were always closed when it was time to chop cotton and when it was time to pick cotton....On the Eliza Clark School ground, where all of the swings and sliding boards and sand piles and wading pools were, black children were simply not allowed to set foot on that school ground. If a black child was walking to town from there, rather than walk across the school ground, he had to walk all the way around; and this was religiously adhered to."[84]

At the war's end and the return of black soldiers to their communities, Ross and a small group of whites and African Americans tried to bring change through weekly meetings in Clarksdale. The first meeting in the black county agent's office "was secretly set up because none of us had ever been to such a meeting where we were going to discuss race relations and what needed to be done to improve them. We were nervous about anybody knowing we participated in such a thing."

In the first meeting, Aaron Henry told Joe Ellis, the local newspaper editor, he was bothered that blacks were never referred to as Mr. or Mrs., always just by their first names without courtesy titles.

Ellis agreed, and said things would change. But few changes actually occurred from any of these meetings, Ross admitted.

Patrick Buchanan — Shades of Eastland?

I nearly fell out of my chair last night while listening to pundit Pat Buchanan on television. He was having a chat with news commentator Rachel Maddow when he actually blurted out that black soldiers had never made any contribution to this country — in any war.

After I thought about it for a while, I remembered that Sen. James Eastland said the same of black soldiers at the end of WWII. Near the end of World War Two, Eastland stood in front of Congress and declared that black soldiers were an "embarrassment" to the country and "an utter and abysmal failure." More than 85,000 black soldiers served in the armed forces during the Second World War, and nearly all experienced overt discrimination

But Eastland, despite positive reports from the U.S. military, said that black soldiers were "lazy, irresponsible, and of very low intelligence" and had "deserted their posts at crucial times" and "refused to fight."

Black soldiers, Eastland asserted, "raped white women" while in Europe and "disgraced the flag of their country." At the time, he didn't talk of the executions of black soldiers taking place in Europe and in the United States, after being charged with rape and various crimes. That would come later, just before the trial of Milam and Bryant — in hopes of influencing the jury through the story of Emmett Till's father, Louis.

One year before his soliloquy, Eastland and U.S. Rep. John Rankin, a noted Mississippi racist and also considered to be pro-Nazi, (Rankin once called columnist Walter Winchell "the little kike" on the floor of the House of Representatives) rallied together against black soldiers, acting to halt adoption of a federal ballot for soldiers in the field and thus suppressing the black soldier vote.

When the senior senator blasted black soldiers at the end of the war, Hodding Carter responded editorially that Eastland had done a "disservice both to the tinderbox of race relations and to historical truth." Later Carter won the Pulitzer Prize for editorial writing "on the subject of racial, religious, and economic intolerance."

Now, I suspect Buchanan probably knew damned well what Eastland had openly stated back then. Buchanan's words sounded like Eastland — *Déjà vu once again*.

Perhaps Buchanan has heard of soldiers such as Amzie Moore, Aaron Henry and Medgar Evers. But has he bothered to read Civil War history written by someone other than Shelby Foote? The Civil War expert who once claimed black soldiers in the Civil War could not run forward without falling down? Known to be a drinker, you've got to wonder if Foote, himself, could have run more than a few feet without falling flat on his face

So old Patrick Buchanan is right in there with the worst of them. Too bad Hodding Carter, Jr. isn't around these days to put Buchanan's remarks into context. Carter might not have been a liberal, but he knew his history.

Draper and the Pioneer Fund

What Greenville journalist Hodding Carter and most other Deltans, including Moore, Henry and Evers, did not recognize was Sen. Theodore Bilbo's close relationship to a Northern group with direct Nazi ties.

This liaison began only two years after Bilbo first arrived in Washington, D. C. in 1934, but would impact all of Mississippi for years to come. Throughout his time as a senator, Bilbo constantly caused controversy in the Senate due to his outspoken support of segregation and white supremacy.

Hundreds of thousands of dollars flowed from this outside group, involving Bilbo, into Mississippi to advocate racism, fight against civil rights, establish private, segregated schools, and oppose the Civil Rights Act of 1964. Clear records of these transactions appear in the Sovereignty Commission files.[85]

If it were not for the work of a curious psychology professor at Rutgers University, Dr. William Tucker, and Douglas Blackmon, a *New York Times* reporter, this story would have probably stayed packed away in cartons of old letters, reports and academic papers, never to see the light of day. But here is the gist of what they found and wrote about from related research on the sources of funding for some specific academic research projects:[86]

Earnest Sevier Cox, a white supremacist propagandist, secretly worked for Wycliffe Draper, a wealthy New York City recluse with Nazi ties and a record of paying for research that tried to "prove" that whites were superior to blacks. Draper had old Kentucky blood on one side of the family and old Puritan stock on the other. Born in Massachusetts in 1891, he inherited a multimillion-dollar textile fortune in the early 1920s and never worked at a job, other than military service in World Wars I and II.

Draper's inheritance that his father accumulated and managed was left to the stewardship of Guaranty Trust, which later became Morgan Guaranty — important to remember when tracking down the movement of Draper money, used to fight civil rights and promote racism, that was funneled into Mississippi and laundered by the state.[87]

Tucker found that Draper was a fanatic Howard Hughes-type recluse for his day. Living in a lavish Upper Manhattan apartment, Draper stuffed his walls with big-game trophies he shot on trips to exotic parts of the world. But Draper had other interests as well. In the mid-1920s, he started supporting the cause of eugenics, a pseudo-science focused on "racial purity." Upon his death in 1972, Draper's money had become a critical funding source for scientists who still believed that white racial purity was essential for social progress.

In 1935, Draper attended the Nazi's International Congress for the Scientific Investigation of Population Problems in Berlin chaired by Wilhelm Frick, a prominent Nazi official, serving as Minister of the Interior of the Third Reich who was later convicted during the Nuremberg war-crimes tribunal and hanged in 1946, Tucker wrote.

Draper's conference companion, Dr. Clarence C. Campbell, a former president of the Eugenics Research Association, gave a speech declaring, "The difference between the Jew and the Aryan is as unsurmountable [sic] as that between black and white," and closed by hand saluting, "That great leader, Adolph Hitler!"

Eugenics, Draper's life-long interest, began as a breeding science for horses in the late 19th century. Then, in the early 1900s, two Southern states, North Carolina and Virginia, used it to control the population of humans deemed inferior through mental illness, retardation and handicap. Hitler's Nazi Germany expanded its use to control the population of those determined unfit or unnecessary including gypsies, indigents, gays, slaves, and Jews.

Draper and his friends, eugenicists Harry Laughlin and Frederick Osborn, founded the Pioneer Fund in 1937 to carry forth the eugenics message. A proposed Pioneer budget for the first year mentioned "two German films referred to by Colonel Draper" one of which, The Hereditary Defective, was shown at 28 U.S. high schools, including schools in Mississippi, through Laughlin's efforts.

Draper continued seeking ways to use his money to further science that focused on racial themes, including the funding of a special printing of Earnest Sevier Cox's racist tract, "White America," used by the Army War College in training officers for positions of high command. This pamphlet was sent to every member of Congress, as well as all state legislators in Mississippi and North Carolina, with this message:

"Pigmentation affects the skin only; white civilized culture is the product of the mind's mastery over things material and spiritual. It so happens that white skin accompanies the culturally capable, while black skin accompanies the culturally deficient."

Professor Tucker put Draper and his work under the academic microscope — including his underwriting of the racist tract, "White America," a statement of Draper's support for sending black Americans back to Africa, promotion of a eugenics movement, and radical racial politics, including his influence in Mississippi.

From his findings, Dr. Tucker suggested Draper was "undoubtedly horrified at the prospect of social and political equality for blacks [and] opened wide his purse strings between the late 1950s until his death in 1972, pouring huge amounts of money into various anti-integration projects conducted by some of the most ardent racists."

Bilbo was attracted to Cox's ideas and three years after they first met, the senator introduced his Greater Liberia bill to Congress in 1939. In support, Mississippi's state legislature went on record promoting federal aid "for Negroes who desire to live in a Negro nation," and advising negotiations with France and Great Britain for large areas of land adjacent to Liberia to widen the borders of that country.

Payment for these lands was to be "credited upon debts owed by France and Great Britain to the United States." But Bilbo's legislation was not assigned to a committee and when Bilbo announced plans to run for a third Senate term, Hodding Carter, from his Greenville newspaper, editorialized that Bilbo "sought public office with sickening regularity."

A second Mississippi, Eastland, also had a relationship with Draper, according to Tucker. "Bilbo's understudy [Eastland] and successor in the Senate as Mississippi's chief defender of separatism" served on a committee that distributed Draper's money to scientific recipients.

While hailed by many of his white followers, the Delta senior senator was seen by one of his Mississippi cohorts as a "vituperative racist." Rep. Frank Ellis Smith, a white six-term U.S. representative from the Delta and known as the public official who favored James Meredith's admittance to the University of Mississippi, once wrote that Eastland "stirred up the racism" whenever possible.

"He used it from the time that I went to Congress, even before then. That was what he wanted to symbolize, the resistance to any change in the racial picture in the Delta."

Post #14

Tallahatchie County: Long Known For Civil Rights Violence and Frequent Klan Encounters

Put simply, Tallahatchie County has a BAD reputation. Legions of black people have been murdered there and even today, some unimaginable stories are emerging about African Americans being chased by an armed district attorney in a homemade tank, followed by a pack of dogs. The U.S. Dept. of Justice has been investigating these stories, as well as the FBI and the NAACP, according to news reports.

The place has always been frightening, says Margaret Block of Cleveland, who remembers at the age of 17 "right out of high school" going door to door in Charleston, one of Tallahatchie County's two seats, to hand out voting rights pamphlets.

"People would see me coming and close their doors. They were really afraid. It was much worse than Greenwood," Block said, referring to a town in the neighboring county where her civil rights activist brother, Sam, coordinated voting rights efforts among disenfranchised blacks.

"We were always competitive. When Sam said he was going to Greenwood, I decided I'd do him one better by going to Charleston, since it had a worse reputation. Now when I think about it, that was not a very good idea."

Block means it. To this day, she stays away from Charleston. As a young SNCC worker, she had worked for only several months when a Klansman tried to kill her in front of the county courthouse with a knife.

"I was pulled away by a Justice Department agent just in time. They usually didn't protect us — they weren't supposed to. But he did this time, and I remain grateful."

Soon after Block's close call, a tiny Charleston woman saved her life when Klansmen were reportedly "on their way into town" looking for Block. This time protection quickly came from Birdia Keglar, Tallahatchie County's first black person to vote since the days of the state's second Reconstruction (a short period of freedom for Mississippi's African Americans following the Civil War).

Block said, "I was handing out voting pamphlets downtown and a man came running up to me and said I needed to go to Birdia's office right away. She managed a funeral home and when I got there, Birdia sneaked me away in the back of a hearse. Someone had called Birdia and warned her that the Klan was on the way to get me."

Keglar and her fellow activist friend, Adlena Hamlett, were killed when their car was forced off the road on their way home from a Jackson civil rights meeting. Their deaths occurred the same day in January 1966 that NAACP leader, Vernon Dahmer, was killed in the early morning hours in Hattiesburg. Hamlett and Keglar were killed in the early evening hours, that same day.

Both incidents occurred as Mississippi Ku Klux Klan hearings opened in Washington, D.C. before the House of Representatives' Committee on Un-American Activities. The Klan had orchestrated cross burnings and murders as each state's hearing opened.[88]

More attention was paid to the Dahmer incident that occurred outside of the Delta. No autopsies were ever performed on Keglar or Hamlett. There are no written records of any police investigations, and stories still circulate about what caused their deaths. The state of Mississippi later admitted that some of the highway patrolmen in that part of the Delta were doing double duty as Klansmen at the time.

Block's friend, Birdia Keglar, first appeared on the Sovereignty Commission's radar after investigator Tom Scarbrough visited Charleston on November 17, 1961, and then filed a report about "problems" brought on by Keglar, Grafton Gray, and S.N. Drake, all voting rights activists. Sent back to Charleston to gather details, the former FBI agent met with Sheriff Dogan, Circuit Clerk Tom Harris, and Judge George Payne Cossar who reported they had been summoned by the Federal Civil Rights "Department" to appear in Oxford, Mississippi's Federal Court on December 13, a month away, over voting irregularities in Tallahatchie County.

"All three Negroes [Keglar, Gray and Drake] proffered charges against the two officials alleging they had refused to sell them a poll tax [stamp] and to register them to vote," Scarbrough reported.[89]

Keglar had tried to pay the required poll tax for ten years, but said she was refused each time by the Sheriff's department; no one would accept her money.

"Since [Dogan] has been sheriff, no Negro ever requested to pay his poll tax to him. Therefore ... no Tallahatchie black had ever been allowed to register and vote [since Reconstruction]," countered Scarbrough.

At the trial in Oxford, Miss., on December 14, 1961, Birdia Keglar and John Doar of the U.S. Justice Department were surprised to learn that she was "already listed" on the Tallahatchie County voters list, according to the county's witnesses.

"Shands" surprised Keglar during cross-examination in the federal suit, which charged that county officials discriminated against Negroes who wanted to vote by refusing to let them pay poll taxes. State attorneys on December 13 received a list from the federal government of prospective witnesses, including Mrs. Keglar. Doar told the court that he was "sure Mrs. Keglar would pay her poll tax" because "she's been trying for ten years."[90]

It was not until three and one-half years later, on June 23, 1964, when Victoria Gray, a Mississippi Freedom Democratic Party (MFDP) member, sued to abolish the certificate of nonpayment of poll tax in order to vote in Mississippi and on October 20, 1964, the District Court granted a permanent injunction. Fifteen months later, Keglar, and her friend Adlena Hamlett were dead.[91]

Post #15

"A Child Shouldn't Have To Be Scared"

> "The delta region had the highest number of lynchings [in Mississippi] during the period of 1880 to1930 and therefore, the highest in the nation. Ominously, Tallahatchie and Leflore County were at the top of the list. It was into this volatile land, poisoned by decades of racism and paranoia, that a black Chicago teenager was placed for his summer vacation."
>
> Mark Gado, criminal writer[92]

Just several months after the violent murder of Rev. George Lee, a popular Belzoni minister and voting rights advocate, a Boy Scout campfire was burning down to its last embers over in Tallahatchie County on the outskirts of Charleston, Miss.

It was August 28, 1955, in the early morning hours when Robert Keglar and his scouts were seated around the fire as they heard a story they would never forget. Finding his way into their campsite in the early morning hours, a "very shaken man" told Keglar and his campers of hearing screams of torture several hours earlier. The man said the sounds came from a machine shed on the

Sheridan plantation outside of Drew, about 40 miles southwest of where they were camped.

The visitor reported seeing "several men" taking a body from the barn and hauling it off, afterwards. More than two men were in the lynching party he told Keglar and others as the fire smoldered and died. The tired and bewildered campers finally bedded down. When they awoke for breakfast, the visitor was gone.

Sometime after midnight on that same date, the parents of a white seventeen-year-old Ruleville girl let early-morning visitors stay in their home for the night. J.W. Milam and Roy Bryant, the latter her mother's relative by marriage, were loud and nervous, she would recall nearly 50 years later.[93]

Here is how I heard this woman's story:

She had been down to visit Walter Scurlock, the owner of a small Drew restaurant. After she left, Scurlock called me on the phone and said a woman from town, someone he barely knew, had come into his restaurant crying.

Scurlock said she'd been listening to the news about Emmett Till and the cold case investigation being reopened by the FBI. She surprised him by looking him in the eyes and saying she was sorry.

Scurlock said he was confused, but she kept talking and crying. He listened, and then she said something about her parents knowing the killers of Emmett Till. Scurlock said he didn't really have time to listen to her story since he was busy preparing lunch.

"So I asked her for her telephone number and I told her I know someone she should talk to. I gave her your phone number. Was that okay?" he said. Ten minutes later we were talking over coffee in her living room and she started telling me her story.

Visitors had come to their Ruleville home in the early morning of Aug. 28 in 1955; the day Emmett Till was murdered. "My parents didn't tell me what was going on at the time. J.W. had a full brother, Bud [Milam], and I am very sure he was with them, too. I was in bed, but I could hear their voices," the woman said.

She stopped and asked me, "Please don't use my name." I agreed.

When she awoke at sunrise, all three men had vanished. Her father told her about the visit and said that Milam and Bryant confessed to him what they had done to the young Chicago visitor, stating Till's name.

"They knew the law was looking for them. They also said that Carolyn Bryant was with them when they killed Emmett Till. I don't know when Bud joined them. I think they caught up with him later. He was a nicer person than his brother and I don't think he would have killed someone — I hope not," she told me.

She never knew what happened to the men after they left her home. "I think they knew the law was going to catch up with them. But I also think they felt safe, since most of the police officers were covering for them, anyway. I don't know if they turned themselves in, let themselves be found, or if they were picked up by the sheriff and charged.

"I still can't believe they put our family in such danger; there was so much turmoil after Emmett Till was killed. People in Drew —black and white — were threatening to kill each other's entire families. Some were threatening to kill as many as ten members of another person's family as payback. It got very bad for a long time in our town," the woman continued.

"I know that my parents would have never covered for them. The men came to our house and sat there all night. Later, my parents told me what was going on. But I would never want anyone to think that our family helped them out."

"Most white people in Drew and Ruleville felt the same way. After the trial, the only support Milam and Bryant got came from the Klan, because they were members. Most people didn't want to have anything to do with them; they had killed a 14-year-old child, after all. Maybe they didn't mean to do it, but they did kill him," she finished.

As I started to leave her home, the woman told me she knew very little about Emmett Till and asked if I could loan her a book. Drew is so small there is no library and of course no book store, so I went out to my car and brought her a copy of Christopher

Metress's book, *The Lynching of Emmett Till*. She took it and thanked me.

Several weeks later, I stopped by the woman's home and asked if she was done reading the book. At first a little embarrassed, she said she had read it, found it fascinating, and loaned it to a friend. The book was apparently making the rounds in Drew making me feel like I had helped to change their town forever.

I never again asked for the return of the book, and she never offered to give it back. Somehow I knew it was being read over and over and over. White Drew was finally learning the story of Emmett Till.

Black Drew already knew the Emmett Till story. But I doubted that many African Americans living there knew much about the secretive Sovereignty Commission and white Citizens Councils, since so very few people — black or white — could help me with this history.

The last week we were living at Parchman, I drove over to Drew to take a copy of my book, *Where Rebels Roost*, written about the region's civil rights history, to a black woman who owned a small sewing shop downtown. I had been updating her all along on my progress and asking her questions, as well, since she had taken an early interest in seeing words put to print. I wanted to make sure I'd given Kate a copy before leaving town.

She set the 700-page book under her front counter and I wondered if she would someday take a look. When I came by the next day to pick up some sewing, there were two older black women sitting at the front of her store. One woman was sitting in a rocking chair and rocking back and forth slowly as she read aloud to the others.

I could see Kate listening and working at the sewing machine. She motioned me over and said, "I'm letting my friends read the book. They can't take it home. They have to read it here."

Closing my eyes, I see Kate's kind face, smiling as she kept sewing and listening to the book reading going on in her store. I had a feeling there would be more readings for quite some time to come.

Back in August of 1955, the two half-brothers, after disposing of Emmett Till's body and after visiting the Ruleville home, would be seen by others later that morning outside of a Glendora home, washing the blood off their bodies and clothing, and cleaning out the truck, Robert Keglar later heard.

He also heard that the same man who had visited the campsite, a potential witness, was locked up in the Tallahatchie County Jail during the Milam/Bryant trial. The trial occurred three months later, after both men were accused of kidnapping and murdering Emmett Louis "Bobo" Till.

There are many versions of what happened to Emmett Till — how and where he was killed, and why — and this makes sense. Robert Keglar and the woman from Drew exemplify the oral history of the Emmett Till murder. We tell stories from our factual and emotional perspectives, and we tell stories to help heal our souls. While living in the Delta, I actually heard several "true" accounts of what happened to Emmett.

People seemed interested in what I was writing about and began sharing stories they've lived with — stories they've not been able to escape. Each story, from what happened to Emmett Till to other stories of anguish and horror, seemed to have a special place in the Delta's thick ether. Each story was important to history and the telling of the story, hopefully, represented healing for the storyteller.

One woman sent me three e-mail messages with her account of the Emmett Till story. Filled with spelling errors, typos and broken sentences, it was hard to read. But it was her story and she worked so hard to share what she had been told:

"I'm so glad to se your writing on these murders I cannot wait to se your book by it and put it in my fathers hand. I'm from Drew Mississippi [and] I want to tel my fathers story of emit till. He had a freind thats dead now that told the story. His story was diffrent and he said that one of the Milan ladies had been riding emmit around spending time with emit because he was retarded and she liked the boy and the man was mad at his wife and they told thre men to get emmit and teach him a lesson and instead of these men teaching him a lesson they took him to a barn outside of Drew and beat him.

"The men supposidly did this for just a jug of whiskey. The lady after seeing emit al mutlated suposedly shot emit and put him out of his misery that is when emit was taken to money and dumped.

"This is the story I was told as a child. I do not no what happen to emmit I'l just be glad when the truth comes out my dad is old and always beleived Emmit was killed in Drew and he mentioned the death of Joe Pullen and Joe eartha. Cleve Mcdowel was my fathers lawyer and it hurt dad when he heard how he died your book wil make him feel better."

I e-mailed her back quickly, asking if her father would be willing to talk to me. But she said "no" and explained why:

"I promised my family I would leave this alone so I can't meet you or dig in this anymore This wil be my last letter to you and thanks again for not using my name. My family they were conserned about there name being mention on something that may or may not be true.They are al up in age and stil believe in people getting hurt about such information like this. Just do me a favore don't stop writing about these deaths your on a good start and there's re a lot more to be discovered."

After hearing several such stories, I wondered what it would be like to raise children with such violence going on all around. One evening, while sitting at Walter Scurlock's restaurant, my husband and I found ourselves having coffee with Nettie Davis, one of the first black people from Drew who would talk to me about Emmett Till and other murders. She introduced us to her friend, a man from her church. Both were long time residents of this former cotton ginning town.

It didn't take long for Davis to get to the essence of why people had been, and continue to be, so affected by Emmett's murder. "He was just a kid, that's why this murder was so different than all of the rest."

Nettie Davis made her point for a second time during this conversation. It was important to Nettie that I understand Jim Crow rules are rarely written down and vary by community.

Davis and her friend were patient in offering their wisdom on this cool, fall evening forty-nine years later. And their memories brought fresh reality to the Emmett Till story that night.

"You need to understand. There had been other murders. Joe Pullen, George Lee, so many horrible murders. But Emmett was a young boy, just 14, and he didn't know the rules," Davis said. "Emmett's mother said she tried to tell him, but he couldn't have really understood how much different things were in the Delta than they were in Chicago."

How could black parents ever protect their children in those days, I wanted to know, as I thought of my own rambunctious son when I asked the question. Would I have let him go to the movies alone? Walk to the store or post office? Drive a car?

What if your child accidentally said the wrong thing? Made the wrong gesture, or broke any of the unwritten Jim Crow laws? What if your child was simply misunderstood? How would you keep an active child quiet? Or safe? "Well, you didn't take your children out very much," Davis's friend offered.

"You tried to protect them by keeping them away from places where they could get into trouble, or be hurt, or something bad. But you didn't talk a lot about these things, because a child shouldn't have to be scared," Nettie Davis said.

Her friend had remained on the periphery of this conversation, but then pulled his chair closer and began speaking of his own experiences regarding his sister and Emmett Till's lynching.

She was 14 at the time, the same age as young Till, and a student at the Drew Colored School, only a few miles away from where he was taken into the Drew countryside and, most likely, killed.

The town's children knew about the murder, some knew within hours.

The sister of Davis's friend had been so traumatized and angry at the time, "…she has never spoken to a white person since," he said.

Maybe it would be good for his sister if she would speak to someone now about her feelings, I suggested.

"Maybe she would talk to you," he offered.

Davis's friend pulled out his cell phone and called his sister in Jackson, trying to set up an interview with me. "Could she talk to me when I go there the following week?" I asked.

After a few back and forth phone calls with her brother, the sister agreed to meet me and talk. But the appointment fell through when she backed out the next morning.

"She's still afraid," he told me.

Of course, Nettie Davis is right. Children shouldn't have to live in fear.

Post #16:

Tallahatchie Manhunt, Booze, Guns, Dogs and More

> "There seems to be a pecking order in place. But the trouble is, the ones pecking on top seem to be pecking in the wrong space."
>
> From "Pecking Order," a poem by Margaret Block, civil rights activist and poet

I just read that federal authorities were asked to investigate the reported incident of armed white citizens, using a "military vehicle," while searching for an unarmed black burglary suspect in the Delta.

Remember this incident that took place outside Sumner, in Tallahatchie County? The weekend of August 28 — just 51 years to the date of Emmett Till's lynching?

The article in today's *Jackson Free Press* says that U.S. Representative Bennie Thompson, of Mississippi's Second Congressional District, confirmed the FBI and the U.S. Department of Justice are currently investigating the story.

"Anytime one takes the law in their own hands — if it's in this situation or others — it's absolutely illegal. While people have the right to protect themselves, they don't have the right to put other people at risk at any time," Thompson told Jackson reporters.

The *Free Press* also quotes Mississippi's NAACP President, Derrick Johnson, who says this incident should be investigated as a "racial hate crime."

Well ... at least something is happening down there in the "free state of Tallahatchie County," as some locals call their domain. Yet, I truly wonder why the story is being totally avoided by the mainstream media.

Editors won't touch it, I am told by a friendly journalist, some because of the reporter who was held hostage in Iran several years ago. Jill Carroll, a freelance reporter for *The Christian Science Monitor*, was kidnapped by Sunni Muslim insurgents in Baghdad on Jan. 7, 2006, and held captive for 62 days.

I think that's a pretty lame excuse for not writing about what is going on in Mississippi. But it does remind me of a story about a Jackson attorney, the late Bill Higgs, who was arrested in Coahoma County for driving an integrated vehicle. While in his cell, Higgs ran into an "overlooked" black Freedom Rider from California who was languishing in the Clarksdale jail.

Law student Dewey Peterson had been arrested during the summer of 1961 as he tried to integrate the city's bus depot. He was held incommunicado in Clarksdale for nearly a year before Higgs found him, by chance. The black Mississippi attorney was able to get Peterson bailed out.

Post #17

Brown I, Brown II and Three Mississippi Murders

"There is going to be hell to pay in Mississippi."

Dr. T.R.M. Howard, Mississippi physician, civil
rights leader and entrepreneur

David T. Beito, a professor of history at the University of Alabama, and Linda Royster Beito, a professor of social sciences at Stillman College, are asking why an entrepreneurial businessman and surgeon from Mound Bayou is so often overlooked in civil rights history. The authors of *Black Maverick* have worked diligently to correct this historical oversight.

T.R.M. Howard, a flamboyant and wealthy black planter and surgeon, was pivotal in both investigating and publicizing the Emmett Till case. Howard's importance in American history went far beyond Emmett Till, however. Without Howard, the world might never have heard of Rosa Parks, Fannie Lou Hamer, Medgar Evers, or even Operation PUSH, the Beitos say.

Howard was an unlikely civil rights hero, a prosperous and entrepreneurial businessman who spared no expense in his wardrobe, sped down the highway in expensive Cadillacs, gambled regularly on horses, ran a successful hospital that provided affordable health care, hunted big game on African safaris, owned a 1,000-acre cotton plantation, and preached a gospel of entrepreneurship and self-help.

In whatever role he chose, Theodore Roosevelt Mason Howard, born in 1908, was no stranger to controversy. As a civil rights activist, Howard successfully organized a grassroots boycott against Jim Crow in the 1950s. After earning his medical degree, Howard became one of the wealthiest blacks in Mississippi. The tireless activist found time to mentor civil rights activist Medgar Evers. He became a nemesis of J. Edgar Hoover and not surprisingly, Howard was a target of the Ku Klux Klan.

It was Wednesday, August 31, 1955, and Howard, a man of great influence, was leaving Chicago. Howard had been doing organizing work for the Regional Council of Negro Leadership, a society he founded to promote a program of civil rights, self-help and business ownership.

At Chicago's Midway Airport, Dr. Howard spoke to reporters from the area's media, including the *Chicago Defender*, about Emmett Till's disappearance and of other murders also concerning him — murders of two black men that had taken place shortly before Till's disappearance: the Rev. George Lee and Lamar Smith.[94]

The Rev. George Lee, while driving his car along Belzoni, Mississippi's, Church Street on May 7, 1955, was killed as two gun blasts shattered the night stillness. His Buick sedan ran over the curb and rammed into a frame house as Rev. Lee was returning home from a meeting on organizing blacks to register to vote.

The lower, left side of his face gone, Rev. Lee actually staggered from the wreckage, but he did not survive. The popular minister had lost control of his car and died when his dental fillings blew up, the county sheriff, Ike Shelton, first explained.[95]

It was a mysterious death, Shelton told the NAACP's state coordinator, Medgar Evers. Shelton would later conclude that Rev. Lee's fillings had not exploded after all, but that he was murdered by another black in an argument over a woman. No arrest was ever made.

Three weeks after Rev. Lee's "mysterious death," the U.S. Supreme Court handed down Brown II on May 31, 1955, ordering the South to proceed with integration "with all deliberate speed." The wording seemed harsh to many segregationists, as Brown II spoke plainly in reaffirming the first decision, Brown v. the Topeka Board of Education.

Then, two and a half months after the Brown II "All Deliberate Speed" Decision, on Aug. 13, a second Mississippi man was murdered. Lamar Smith, a 63-year-old black farmer and World War I veteran and organizer of black voter registration, was shot to death in broad daylight at close range on the lawn of the Lincoln County courthouse in Brookhaven, Miss.[96]

Some contemporary reports say there were many white witnesses, including the local sheriff, who saw a white man covered with blood leaving the scene. However, at the time, no witnesses would come forward. The three men originally arrested for Smith's murder were set free.

YOUNG EMMETT LOUIS "BOBO" TILL arrived in Grenada, Miss. from his Chicago home by train on Saturday, August 20, 1955, to visit relatives in Money, Miss., a tiny cotton hamlet on the eastern edge of the Delta. This was to be a summer vacation with his mother's relatives in the Delta countryside.

Emmett was "big for his age," his cousin Simeon Wright first noticed as Emmett, Wheeler Parker, Jr. (Simeon's nephew), and Rev. Mose Wright (Simeon's father) stepped off the train. Mose Wright had gone to Chicago earlier for the funeral of an old parishioner and brought Emmett and Wheeler back to Mississippi for a visit with his cousins.

"He [Emmett] must have weighed about 140 pounds and was a little over five foot six. I weighed about ninety pounds and was just five feet tall," Simeon Wright later recalled.[97]

The Wrights headed out for Money, actually to East Money, for the family's four-bedroom home located down "a lonely, ominous byway that we called Dark Fear Road," Simeon Wright states in his account, *Simeon's Story*:

"If you ventured down that road at night, you would see why – it was one of the darkest places in the world, filled with menacing woods and snake-infested lakes. But old-timers say it got its name from the many lynchings that took place in the area."[98]

Emmett's mother, Mamie Elizabeth Carthan, the daughter of John and Alma Carthan, was born in Hazlehurst, not far from where her son was headed with his uncle and cousins. At the age of two, her family moved to Illinois where she grew up and eventually married Louis Till.

Emmett had brought along his father's ring for the special trip. He would never know his father, who was shipped out to Europe as an Army private. Mamie and Louis Till separated in 1942 and his father's silver ring was later given to him as a remembrance. Louis purchased the silver ring in Casablanca and had it engraved with his own initials and a date, May 25, 1943.

The ring was always too large for Emmett, but as he packed for his upcoming visit with his Mississippi relatives, he tried it on and found that it fit his middle finger perfectly. His mother permitted his to wear the ring on his trip to show his cousins and his friends.[99]

Before his summer trip to Mississippi, Emmett's mother also cautioned him to mind his manners with white people. "If you have to get on your knees and bow when a white person goes past, do it willingly," she told her only son.

But something happened when Emmett later visited the small Money grocery store owned by Roy and Carolyn Bryant. There are so many versions of what happened inside the grocery store. Mrs. Bryant, described by the New York Times as a "pretty brunette," had her own account, of course.

In a Mississippi courtroom, with her husband and J.W. Milam on trial for the murder of Till, the store owner's wife would assert that Till grabbed her at the waist and asked her for a date. She said that he used "unprintable" words.

While it would have helped her husband's case, Mrs. Bryant was not allowed to testify in front of the jury. Aware that a Mississippi jury could well find cause for murder if a Southern woman was harassed by a black male, the judge ordered the jury removed during her testimony. Prosecutors wanted her entire testimony excluded and Judge Swango reserved decision on the matter.[100]

When his cousin, Simeon Wright, took him outside the Bryant grocery store, Emmett allegedly said, "Bye, baby." Till had a slight stutter that Bryant might have misinterpreted. Some have speculated that he might have been mildly retarded and any unexpected behavior on his part might easily be misconstrued.

Wright recalls visiting the store after a hard day of work in the cotton fields, to satisfy his restless cousin. After milling around in front of the store Wheeler entered to buy some pop or candy and Emmett went in after him. Wheeler left, and Till remained inside, alone.

Wright entered the store immediately, concerned about his cousin being left alone. Till had gotten into earlier trouble in town after setting off firecrackers inside the city limits. Nothing happened in the store, according to Wright, but as they left Mrs. Bryant came out behind them and Emmett whistled at her.[101]

Wright waited until 2010 to formally give his account of what took place when he wrote his book, leaving others to fill in the blanks. One version — Till stuttered and may have accidentally made a whistling sound as he tried to correct what he said, something which he was known to do from time to time.

The official FBI report backs Wright, stating that "On August 24, 1955, Emmett Louis Till, age 14, entered the Bryant Grocery & Meat Market in the town of Money, Mississippi. Till exited the store, and shortly thereafter the store owner's wife, Carolyn Bryant, a white woman, exited as well. Upon her exit, Till whistled. The relatives accompanying Emmett knew this whistle from a black male could cause trouble, and they left with Till in haste."[102]

By the time Roy Bryant, 29, returned home from a road trip three days after his wife's encounter with Emmett, it seemed nearly everyone in Tallahatchie County knew about the incident, and every conceivable version.

Bryant, angered about the stories of his wife's encounter with Till that were flying around the county, decided that he and his half-brother, J.W. Milam, 40, would meet Sunday to "teach the boy a lesson."

At around 2:30 a.m. on August 28, Bryant went to Mose Wright's home, Till's great-uncle who resided in a small home on the outskirts of Money, and demanded to talk with young Till. As the story goes, both Bryant and Milam forced their way into the back bedroom where Till was sleeping, woke him up and made him go outside to their car. That was the last time any of Emmett Till's relatives saw him alive.

A story appearing September 3, 1955, in the *Jackson Advocate* suggested that three white men were involved in the kidnapping, marking "the first suggestion that more individuals were involved in the abduction than either Milam or Bryant let on."

The Mound Bayou physician, Dr. Howard, contributed his own version of the kidnapping and murder that appeared in a small booklet in February 1956, *Time Bomb: Mississippi Exposed and the Full Story of Emmett Till*.

The author was Olive Arnold Adams, the wife of Julius J. Adams, publisher of the *New York Age*, but Howard was her main source and he wrote the foreword. In addition to *Time Bomb*, a series of articles appeared in the *California Eagle*, a black newspaper in Los Angeles.

A mysterious white Southern reporter who wrote under the pseudonym of Amos Dixon offered a more detailed description of the possible roles of three additional men, Loggins, Hubbard, and Collins. Dixon also alleged that still another brother of Milam and Bryant, Leslie Milam, took part in the crime.

Post #18

Update: Manhunt Rumors Haunt Mississippi Town With Troubled Past

This morning, with a cup of coffee in hand, I am reading an article by Holbrook Mohr of the *Associated Press*. This is good — perhaps the media is beginning to wake up to the story unfolding in Sumner. He writes:

"SUMNER, Miss. September 7, 2009 (AP) — In the Mississippi Delta, nothing spreads faster than a rumor that an armed white mob chased black thieves through a cotton field. Throw in an armored personnel carrier and a racially charged past, and it's no surprise federal investigators are checking it out.

"Suspicion is especially deep in Sumner, population about 400, the town where two white men were tried and acquitted in the notorious 1955 slaying of Emmett Till, a black Chicago teenager lynched for whistling at a white woman."

Well, halleluiah! Just maybe a real reporter has arrived on the scene! At least we are beginning to hear some details.

A real journalist, the late and great David Halberstam, was no stranger to Tallahatchie County. Halberstam not only covered the Bryant and Milam trial, but he stayed on for the trial of a white man who shot a black service-station attendant, Clinton Melton, less than a month after the two men who killed Till were set free.

The father of four children was shot in cold blood by a friend of Milam's, in a Glendora gas station located only four miles from where Emmett Till's body was dumped into the Tallahatchie River.

Clinton Melton's young wife, Beulah [Melton] was killed under suspicious circumstances shortly before the murder trial opened. She had been trying to gather information to help convict the man who killed her husband when her car "accidentally" veered into a bayou and she was drowned.

The sheriff said Beulah Melton was a bad driver, her daughter, Delores Gresham said. Gresham survived the crash and remembers water coming into the car. She describes her mother as an active, curious person who would have naturally tried to uncover information about her husband's death and believes this is what got her mother killed. But the death of Beulah Melton has never made it to an FBI cold case list.

The trial of the man accused of killing Clinton Melton ended in an acquittal. Halberstam, knowing what was about to take place in the courtroom, offered his assessment even before the trial began:

"A friend of mine divides the white population of Mississippi into two categories. The first and largest contains the good people of Mississippi, as they are affectionately called by editorial writers, politicians, and themselves. The other group is a smaller but in many ways more conspicuous faction called the peckerwoods.

"The good people will generally agree that the peckerwoods are troublemakers, and indeed several good people have told me they joined the Citizens Councils because otherwise the peckerwoods would take over the situation entirely. It is the good people who will tell you that their town has enjoyed racial harmony for many years, while it is the peckerwoods who may confide that they know how to keep the niggers in their place; it is the good people who say and mean, 'We love our nigras,' and it is the peckerwoods who say and mean, 'If any big buck gets in my way it'll be too damn bad.'

"But while the good people would not act with the rashness of and are not governed by the hatred of the peckerwood, they are reluctant to apply society's normal remedies to the peckerwood. Thus it is the peckerwoods who kill Negroes and the good people who acquit the peckerwoods..."[103]

I would imagine if he was alive today, Halberstam would already be camping out in Sumner with his notebook and cell phone running hot.

Post #19

"Negroes Up North Have No Respect For People" — "It's a Shame Emmett Till Had To Die So Soon"

> "We grew up with the hurt of what happened to Emmett Till. My brothers were always afraid that someone would take them away and kill them, too, just like Emmett Till."
>
> "X" of the Delta.[104]

Late August in the Mississippi Delta is cruel. It's commonly in the mid 90s that time of the year and while that might not sound too hot, typically it is so humid that if you've been sitting a while and stand up, your backside sticks to your clothes, even if they're made of cotton. Horseflies buzz your body with voracity and there's rarely any shade, even under the most voluminous pecan trees.

One terribly hot and humid Saturday morning Fred and I thought it would be refreshing to walk down to the sand bars of the Mississippi River over near Rosedale, about 35 miles west of Parchman. "Don't go down there after 9:30 in the mornin' or it'll be too hot to walk back," a Mississippi friend warned.

We waited until 10:30 a.m. to head out for the river channel and an hour later it came to me that I was not going to make it back from the river's edge, and my husband had to convince me it would be the best thing to just keep walking and that he was NOT going to call 911.

WHEN COTTON WAS KING, and it still held that powerful role in the mid 1950s, black Delta families worked the cotton fields despite unbearable heat. Everyone, even the youngest child, was expected to show up for work. An absent cotton picker could be beaten by a plantation owner.

This directive included Emmett Louis "Bobo" Till. It was late August of 1955 when Bo arrived, the beginning of the picking season, and the young man complied, going into the fields the first day of the season.

"The Wright boys showed Bo how to pull the cotton out of the boll. There's a certain way you have to catch it, get right into the boll and pull it clean out so that you don't get all the debris mixed in with it. Nobody wanted dirty cotton. But you also had to take care that you didn't stick your hand on the ends of the bud. And if you didn't get it just right, it would stick you," Mamie Till Mobley wrote.[105]

Bo's uncle, Papa Mose, quickly saw that Emmett couldn't work the cotton and decided to give Bobo a break. The sun was too hot for him to pick much cotton, even when wearing a hat. So during the day, while his cousins were out working the fields, Emmett helped his aunt Lizzie around the house and in the family garden.

Workdays were shorter at the beginning of the cotton picking season, so day's end often came by 4 p.m. in time for the boys to have some fun. Emmett would entertain, telling stories.

Emmett liked to tease his Mississippi cousins and kept them entertained by singing Bo Diddley tunes or showing off his treasured Frankenstein comic book, his mother wrote, but his cousins had their own activities to share with the big-city cousin, including swimming in the Tallahatchie River with its moccasin snakes. They had to drive the snakes out first by making commotion in the water.

There was fishing for bass, bream and catfish using bait placed in a glass jar and left in the water. Mornings, the boys found jars bobbing with fish that couldn't back out, requiring them to "catch" the jars holding their fish.

They could listen to popular shows on the family radio or drive Papa Mose's car around the neighborhood and through the fields and over to the plantation store. But the small plantation-run establishment didn't have the treats like gum and soda pop, the stuff carried by Bryant's Grocery and Meat Market over in Money, three miles away, with its ongoing checker game on the front porch. This much we know is true:

On August 24, seven boys and one girl headed out for Bryant's Grocery and Meat Market for refreshments to cool off after a long day of picking cotton in the hot sun. At some point, Emmett went into the store to buy bubble gum. Some of the kids outside the store later said they heard Emmett whistle at Carolyn Bryant.

At about 2:30 a.m. on August 28, Roy Bryant, Carolyn's husband, and his half brother, J.W. Milam, kidnapped Emmett Till from Moses Wright's home. Others may have been involved.

Within one day of the disappearance of Emmett Till from his uncle's home, officers from Tallahatchie County and nearby Leflore County arrested Roy Bryant and J.W. Milam in Leflore County and charged them with kidnapping Emmett Till. This surely set a Mississippi speed record for an arrest involving a white on black crime.

Both men were jailed in Greenwood and held without bond after admitting they had taken Till from his great-uncle's home. But they also claimed they had turned him loose the same night.

In Chicago, the FBI had been quickly informed about the kidnapping, but didn't get involved. An initial report dated August 29, 1955, from the Chicago, Illinois bureau issued by "Mr. Price" to "Mr. Rosen" shows Price was told that three white men, armed with revolvers, forcibly removed Till from Mose Wright's home in Money, Miss.

The contact person, whose name is redacted throughout the FBI report, stated his information came from Till's mother, who said she learned this from Mississippi relatives.

Price's report stated no apparent violation of the federal kidnapping statute had occurred. Price reported that he instructed the contact to call the bureau office back if he received anything new indicating interstate transportation of the victim.

Stories of the missing teenager were soaring about the Delta. Some thought Emmett's relatives were hiding him out of fear for his safety. Others believed Till was sent back to Chicago for safekeeping.

As the search progressed, black leaders Medgar Evers and Amzie Moore disguised themselves as cotton pickers and went into the cotton fields searching for any clues that would help find the young Delta visitor.

After collecting stories first hand from the field laborers, with no luck finding any news about Till, Moore estimated that *more than 2,000 families* had been murdered and lynched over the years, with their bodies thrown into the region's swamps, rivers and bayous.[106]

Three days following his abduction, on August 31, Emmett Till's decomposed and disfigured and swollen body was pulled from the Tallahatchie River. Moses Wright identified his nephew's body from a ring with the initials L.T. Journalist Hodding Carter, Jr. reported in a UP wire story that 17-year-old fisherman Robert Hodges found Till's decomposed body barb wired to a 75-pound cotton gin fan. It was floating in the Tallahatchie River 12 miles north of Money.

Emmett Till had been stripped naked, pistol-whipped and shot through the head with a .45-caliber Colt automatic before he was thrown into the muddy river, his body weighted down by a gin fan, the sheriff's report concluded.

Young Till's body was first taken to Greenwood, the seat of Leflore County, even though it was found in Tallahatchie County. Then quickly, the body was transported to an undertaker in nearby Tutwiler to be embalmed and then shipped by rail to Chicago, the latter demanded by Mrs. Till, who feared her son's body would be buried in the Delta.

On Friday, September 2, Mrs. Till arrived at the Illinois Central Terminal to receive her son's casket, surrounded by family and photographers who snapped her photo collapsing in grief.

In an editorial appearing that same day in his Greenville newspaper, Carter asserted that "people who are guilty of this savage crime should be prosecuted to the fullest extent of the law." It was an extremely brave suggestion for any Mississippi newspaper editor to state and remain out of harm's way, even Hodding Carter, Jr.

In the small town of Tutwiler, Woodrow Jackson was assigned to embalm Emmett Till's body. As the black assistant to his town's white undertaker, Jackson drove 42 miles from Tutwiler to Greenwood to pick up young Till's corpse and transport it back, he told me from his home.[107]

I met with Jackson several days following a state ceremony to dedicate the same route Jackson drove back in 1955 as the Emmett Till Memorial Highway — a 30-mile stretch of US Highway 49 East from Greenwood to Tutwiler.

"There was a patrol car in front and one in back. Billy Ray Cole, a state highway patrolman from Tutwiler told me not to stop for anything, and I didn't," Jackson recalled.

Jackson remembered arriving back in Tutwiler at approximately 4 p.m. with Till's body and working throughout the night until 8 the next morning, trying to make the body look better.

"It was terrible and that's why it took a long time. I remember thinking his body must have been in the water for three or four days and maybe longer. It was clear to me that he died from blows to the right side of his head," he told me.

When Jackson finished his work, he put Emmett Till's body in a shipping case and sent it back home to Chicago by train. "I never met his mother, but I always hoped I helped her in some way."

Despite Jackson's efforts to make Till's body less horrifying, in Chicago gruesome pictures of the young man's corpse appeared in *Jet* magazine, drawing national attention. Some reports indicate that over 100,000 people walked by his open casket before the funeral took place, while hundreds of thousands read about his murder.

Till's mother, after meeting with NAACP officials, insisted the world must see what was done to her son. The casket would not be closed.

In the film documentary, *The Untold Story of Emmett Louis Till*, conceived and directed by Keith Beauchamp, Till's mother tells the Chicago funeral director, "If you can't open the box, I can. I want to see what's in that box."

What she found, according to movie critic Roger Ebert, was the already decomposing body of her son that had spent three days in a bayou of the Tallahatchie River, a heavy cotton gin fan tied to his neck with barbed wire. The mother was purposeful as she described what she saw:

"She always thought her son's teeth were 'the prettiest thing I ever saw.' All but two were knocked out. One eyeball was hanging on his chin. An ear was missing. She saw daylight through the bullet hole in his head. His skull had been chopped almost in two, the face separated from the back of the head." [108]

Emmett Till's mother made history as thousands of the city's residents filed past her son's remains. On September 6, Emmett was buried at Burr Oak Cemetery.

"A photograph in *Jet* magazine made such an impression on journalist Ed Bradley that, 50 years later, as a 60 Minutes reporter Bradley told Beauchamp, the photograph caused him to become obsessed with the case."

It took Beauchamp nine years to investigate the Till lynching and his work is considered primarily responsible for the Justice Department reopening the case in 2007.

Down in Mississippi, while Hodding Carter's editorials called for punishing Till's murderers, the journalist also didn't like the scenes from Chicago and asserted the "macabre exhibitionism, the wild statements, and the hysterical overtones" had been planned to inflame hatred and would result in a reverse reaction in Mississippi, where there had been a reaction of "honest indignation."[109]

Rumors kept moving around the Delta about Till's death, especially in Drew, only a few miles from the Sheridan plantation's machine shed where Till was taken, tortured and most likely murdered. On the night of Till's abduction, there had been whispers that a woman's voice was heard in the dark when Till was taken from his uncle's home.

Simeon Wright, Mose Wright's son, who later became a Chicago minister, often tells of hearing his father recount to him and others, how "They took Emmett out to the truck to ask, 'Is this the one?' And a female voice confirmed it was.[110]

"There were so many rumors. We all knew, right away, that Emmett was killed in Sunflower County and not over in Tallahatchie County," Woodrow Jackson told me.

"There were others involved besides Milam and Bryant. And we knew that some of the witnesses were held in Charleston's jail during the trial."

At the 50-year anniversary of Till's murder, while living in Parchman, I was concerned for the people living in the home adjacent to the shed where Till was killed. I'd met this young, professional white family who lived there and knew they were not the same family that had lived on the property back in 1955. In fact, the original home had been demolished and replaced with a new home. The machine shed, which had been partly restored, was located about a minute's walk to their front door.

As I spoke with them, about to mention the 50th anniversary of Till's death and to see if I could tour the shed, I realized they had no inkling of the significance of this shed or Till's murder there. I wondered if they even knew the story, at all.

So, I spoke to a professor at nearby Delta State who was helping to coordinate the region's civil rights history, telling him I feared that visitors might show up one day at their front door, asking to see where Emmett Till died. In my mind's eye, I could envision someone knocking on their front door intent on touring this civil right's shrine. This young family's ignorance could result in a most unfortunate encounter. The professor agreed this could be a problem and promised to pay a visit to the couple before the Aug. 28 anniversary.

"... get the FBI on the case ..." August 30, 1955"

To:Mr. Gloster B. Current, Director, Branches NAACP, New York, New York

From:Medgar W. Evers, Field Secretary, Mississippi

On Sunday, August 28 at 2 A.M., a fourteen year old Negro boy, Emmett Till of Chicago, was forced from his home at Money, Leflore County, Mississippi, by three white men and a white woman who alleged that Till had made remarks that were displeasing to a white grocery owner's wife.

One man has been apprehended by the Sheriff of Leflore County, the other man is being sought. If it is possible to get the FBI on the case, maybe we can get some results.[111]

MISSISSIPPI WRITER Ann Moody tells the story in her book, *Coming of Age in Mississippi*, how she was walking to her after-school job the evening she heard the news about Till.

A group of girls and boys were walking home from school. The boys were walking and talking quietly among themselves. But all of a sudden they began shouting at each other and Moody heard a boy say:

"That boy wasn't but fourteen years old and they killed him. Now what kin a fourteen-year-old boy do with a white woman?"

Moody asked who had been killed and was told Emmett Till was killed "by some white men."

When she reached the home where she worked as a housekeeper, the woman of the house entered the kitchen and asked Moody if she had heard of Till. She was eating her dinner and said she had not heard anything, but choked down the food as she responded.

Till was killed, the woman stated, "because he got out of his place with a white woman. A boy from Mississippi would have known better than that. This boy was from Chicago.

"Negroes up north have no respect for people. They think they can get away with anything. He just came to Mississippi and put a whole lot of notions in the boys' heads here and stirred up a lot of trouble."

Asking Moody her age, the woman continued, "See, that boy was just fourteen, too. It's a shame he had to die so soon."[112]

Post #20

Sumner, Miss., Milam/Bryant Murder Trial; 'First Great Media Event of the Civil Rights Movement'

Fred and I met Ada Guest of Sumner one Sunday afternoon while driving around her small Tallahatchie County town. In fact, the silver-haired woman had been following us, not very subtly, in her fancy white Cadillac for a good half-hour. After letting her chase us around the neighborhoods for a while, we finally got curious and stopped our car, pulled over to the side of the road across from the town's small drugstore, and she pulled over, too.

With a little friendly back and forth chit-chat through car windows, we assured her that we — Yankee strangers — were simply driving around her pretty town because of its history. She relaxed and gave us a tour of the bridge crossing the Cassidy Bayou, the Tallahatchie County courthouse, the town's old churches and then shared some personal memories about the day she attended Sumner's biggest event ever, back in the fall of 1955.

In her mid-eighties and still living independently in the town where she grew up, Ada Guest told us about attending *The Trial*, or as she said, "the biggest week ever in Sumner." She went to the trial for one day, as guest of her boss, a Sumner attorney, who arranged for her to stand at the back of the hot and humid courtroom.

"He told me this was something I should not miss. I remember the courtroom was crowded and it was so hot. Mostly I remember that Emmett Till's mother came to the trial every day, very well dressed. Her car door was opened courteously by the black courthouse janitor each morning when she arrived at the courthouse."

I could tell quickly the image of a man opening a door for a black woman was a concept that surprised Ada Guest to this day. Guest remembered seeing the black reporters working at a table separated from white reporters. "The black congressman was sitting by the black reporters at their table," she said. By now, we had parked our cars in front of the courthouse.

Wives of the defendants sat with their husbands throughout the trial and their children stayed close by, she told us. Ada remembered how "the children played sometimes, and they slept and got cranky, too."

Could I come over to Sumner and talk some more with her about the trial? Ada Guest gave me a telephone number and I never saw her again.

Mamie Till Mobley

Emmett Till's mother, Mamie Till Mobley, and her family left Mississippi and its inherent meanness when she was just a baby. Like many black Mississippians, they moved to Argo, a small community on the outskirts of Chicago, to escape the misery of the Delta.

Throughout her life, Emmett Till's mother carried a frightening story close to her heart — a story she often replayed in her mind. Back in Mississippi, a little black girl — brought to work by her mother out of necessity — had become a playmate of the white family's daughter. One day the white child complained to her father about something the black child had done. The father became so angry that he slammed the black woman's child into a tree. The black mother was forced to complete her housework before caring for her child; her daughter ultimately died from the injuries.

For black people, every generation has a cautionary tale much like this — a story based on real or imaginary events and that teaches something important, Mrs. Till Mobley wrote.

Before Emmett left for the Delta, she wanted Emmett to be aware he would be leaving the world of Chicago, the only world he knew, for a place that could be extraordinarily mean to black folk, even to black children like the cleaning lady's daughter.

She coached her son to be aware of the unwritten Jim Crow rules: Don't start up conversations with white people, only talk if you're spoken to, respond with "yes, sir" and "no, ma'am." Step off the street for white women and lower your head. Don't look white women in the eye and when passing on the sidewalk, keep going and don't look back. If you must, get onto your knees and apologize.[113]

Raised mostly in Chicago, how could she know these rules so well, the basis of reality for Mississippi blacks? As a 12-year-old child, Mrs. Till Mobley once returned to Mississippi to visit grandparents, and her grandfather let her wander alone downtown while he was conducting business. She had left his side and walked into a drugstore, alone, where she unknowingly disobeyed the rules of Jim Crow, going into a white-only store to buy toilet paper — and being brazen about it.

Because her grandfather was well known and respected (as much as any black man in the Delta could be), he was able to remove his granddaughter safely from the store and take her home without incident. But upon return to her grandparents' home, she was scolded and warned never again to cross over to the white side of town. "He told me about the great danger that I had just faced, how I simply could have disappeared."

After her grandfather explained the impact on her parents — should something ever happen to her while in Mississippi — the fear of "every black person in the state of Mississippi, had been pounded in to me." This was a lesson that Emmett Till's mother would never forget.

Till's mother had struggled emotionally with the decision to allow her son to visit Mississippi, based on this experience. Would he be safe?

At the time,, it was not uncommon for children to visit their Delta relatives. A number of years had passed, after all, since her own frightening experience in Webb, and with assurances from her relatives, combined with Bo's intense desire to see his roots, Mobley gave in, deciding the trip would be a good experience for her son.

The trip was going well, as Emmett wrote in a letter to his mother:[114]

> Dear Mom
> How is everybody? I hope you and Jean is fine. I hope you'll have a nice trip. I am having a fine time will be home next week. Please have my motorbike fixed for me (pay you back). If I get any mail put it up for me. I am going to see Uncle Crosby Saturday. Everybody here is fine and having a good time. Tell Aunt Alma hello. (out of money)
> Your son, Bobo

The first telephone call to Mrs. Till came early Sunday morning, August 28, from Emmett's aunt, Willie Mae. The message was short and simple: Emmett was kidnapped in the middle of the night.

What would be done? Would any officials care that a black child was missing in the Delta? Here is where the Emmett Till story takes an historical upturn. Unlike most black families, Emmett Till's family had some limited connections and clout, and quickly put them to work.

First, Mrs. Till's hastily called press conference gave reporters the initial facts. Emmett was abducted from her Uncle Moses Wright's home in Money in the middle of the night by white men.

Papa Spearman, her mother's husband, told Till Mobley to contact his nephew, Rayfield Mooty, a union official and head of the Steelworkers Local who had good contacts with the steelworkers, autoworkers and sleeping car porter unions.

Mooty knew important politicians and civil rights people and, as a man of action, he quickly got to work. By the next morning, Mooty had arranged for Mrs. Till to meet with the Chicago branch of the NAACP where they spoke with William Henry Huff, the Chicago NAACP counsel, who promised to put their resources to work.

With the power of the unions behind him, Mooty stirred the pot and the Emmett Till kidnapping story, appearing in Chicago newspapers, took on its own life.

Local and state officials, including Chicago Mayor Richard J. Daley, Illinois Governor William Stratton, and William Dawson, the city's powerful Southside congressman, quickly got involved. A plane from a relative's company, Inland Steel Container Company, was put into the air, flying over the area in Mississippi where Emmett had been kidnapped.[115]

The second call came to Emmett's mother from a news reporter on Wednesday, August 31. Emmett's body had been removed from the Tallahatchie River.

"In a way, life had been too easy for me. Always someone there to look out for me, to take care of the hard things. Even Bo. I could see that things were about to get very hard, more difficult than they had ever been. Impossible, really. And the only one I could count on would be myself," Mrs. Till would later write.[116]

While she had been surrounded by strength, it would be Mrs. Till who insisted on an open casket funeral for her young son. She took the next brave step by going to Mississippi for the trial of her son's murderers. This was the impossible part.

Mooty did not abandon the Till case, once he started the ball rolling. He traveled to Mississippi in September with Mamie and her father, Nash "John" Carthan, for the murder trial.

Later Mooty would write and speak about the incident, noting that two things made the Till case different: "...the ugly brutality of it all," and the "public outrage at this gruesome act" that "marked the beginning of the modern civil rights movement." He also signed a petition urging President Eisenhower to call a special session of Congress in order to recommend passage of anti-lynching and anti-poll-tax laws.[117]

—

"X," a black Delta businessperson, grew up in Minter City and was ten when Emmett Till was killed. "My mother was so worried about us. I had brothers and sisters, and she told the girls and then the boys about what happened. Sometimes we traveled to Drew and my mother was afraid for our safety."

"She said Emmett whistled at a dog that was sitting on a chair, and Carolyn Bryant thought Emmett was whistling at her."

X learned from her mother about the rumors that Emmett Till was castrated before he was killed. "We grew up with the hurt of what happened to Emmett Till. My brothers were always afraid that someone would take them away and kill them, too — just like Emmett Till," she told me.

Post #21

Sumner 'a Good Place to Raise a Boy': The Emmett Till Murder Trial

> Found dead people in the forests, Tallahatchie River and lakes. Whole world is wondering, what's wrong with the United States?
>
> From "Freedom Highway," recorded by the Staple Singers, a popular gospel and blues group that originated in Drew, Miss.

On September 15, *Jet* magazine, a nationwide black publication, introduced photographs of Till's corpse. The *Chicago Defender* published similar photos two days later.

Shortly after, on September 19, the kidnapping and murder trial of J.W. Milam and Roy Bryant opened in Sumner, Miss., the county seat of Tallahatchie County. Jury selection began and, with blacks and white women banned from serving, an all-white, 12-man jury made up of nine farmers, two carpenters and one insurance agent was selected. Mrs. Till left from Chicago on that same day to attend the trial.

Tallahatchie County is one of ten counties in Mississippi with two county seats, Charleston and Sumner. These counties are geographically larger than the others and the dual system was done for the public's convenience. The word Tallahatchie comes from the Choctaw language and means "rock of waters."

Sumner's standing courthouse, built in 1909, like most other county courthouses in Mississippi, features a somber monument to the memory of Southern Civil War soldiers. It was here in historic Sumner — a mile and a half from the birthplace of Emmett Till's mother — where the Milam/Bryant trial unfolded in the fall of 1955.

Journalists and others were stunned to be welcomed to this Delta town by its slogan emblazoned on a prominent sign: "Sumner — a good place to raise a boy."

Scores of national reporters and photographers — white and black — would come face to face with Sheriff H.C. Strider each day of the trial, " ...a big, fat, plain-talking, obscene-talking sheriff you would expect to find in the South," wrote John Herbers, representing United Press.

A number of trial accountings focus on the sheriff. Not used to caring for an international pool of journalists and photographers, Strider made sure black reporters were "provided" a Jim Crow card table to the side.

When Detroit's black Congressman Charles Diggs came to Sumner to observe the proceedings, Strider wouldn't allow him into the courtroom until the presiding judge made the sheriff do so. Then, Strider escorted Diggs to the Jim Crow table to sit alongside the black reporters. Strider, who died in 2009, was memorialized by state legislators when they named a portion of a highway after him.

Opening Monday and ending that Friday, this trial was named the "first great media event of the civil rights movement," by journalist David Halberstam, then a young correspondent covering Mississippi.

Along with Halberstam, more than seventy reporters and thirty photographers attended, including Booker Simeon for *Jet* magazine; John Chancellor for NBC news; John Gunter for the *Memphis*

Commercial Appeal, Robert F. Hall for the *Daily Worker* and Halberstam for the *West Point Daily Times Leader*.

An all-white grand jury had surprised most people in the first place by quickly ordering Bryant and Milam to stand trial. It was unusual in Mississippi for any action to be taken against whites that committed violence against blacks. It was not the first time a Mississippi court would hear a case of white men accused of murdering a black, but it would become one of the state's most famous examples.

The entire jury was composed of white men from the defendants' home county. At trial, lawyers asserted that the body recovered from the river was not Till's body. Instead, they claimed Milam and Bryant had taken Till but had let him go. They alleged that the NAACP and Mamie Till had dug up a body and claimed that it was Till. Now Till was hiding out in Chicago, they said.

It would be dangerous for any black person to testify against a white person in Mississippi and so it was difficult to find witnesses for the prosecution. Those who knew something were afraid to come forward.

A group of black journalists had tried to help the prosecution team of District Attorney Gerald Chatham and Robert Smith, a former FBI agent appointed to assist by Gov. Hugh White (because "the people of Mississippi are anxious that justice be done").[118]

Prosecutors based much of their case on Willie Reed, a black eighteen-year-old high school student, who testified on the stand in barely a whisper that he had seen Bryant, Milam, and another man with Till. Reed said the truck pulled into an equipment shed near the town of Drew and he heard "licks and hollers" that sounded like a beating.

When Mose Wright took the stand, he testified that Milam and Bryant took his nephew at gunpoint from his home. After Reed and Wright testified, they were quickly escorted out of Mississippi by the NAACP.

Wright had decided from the beginning that he would testify, thus forever changing courtroom testimony of blacks about whites in the state of Mississippi, according to crime reporter Mark Gado:

Gado's story goes that Moses had put his wife, Elizabeth, on a train to Chicago, for her safety. She had begged him not to testify and most local whites didn't think he would show up. But once the trial opened, Moses defied all odds and spoke before the jury. Gado writes:

"Moses Wright was called to the stand. He was a very thin, wiry man with taut black leathery skin and gray hair. Wright wore a white shirt with a blue tie and suspenders. He came to the witness chair with an air of dignity and determination. Wright said he was awakened by a banging on his door on the night of August 28. When he opened the door, he found Mr. Bryant and Mr. Milam standing there and demanding to see the boy from Chicago who did the talking.

"He said Milam had a gun and walked into his house to get Emmett Till. Wright described the next anxious minutes as Till was awakened from sleep and forced to get dressed while Bryant and Milam stood over him. He said his wife Elizabeth [Wright] offered to pay the defendants for any damage Emmett may have caused, if they would just let him be. District Attorney Chatam asked if he could point out the man with the gun in the courtroom.

"Yes, sir! Wright said without hesitation. He stood up slowly and with an act of courage and defiance that would reverberate across the state of Mississippi and signal the beginning of the end of white supremacy in the South, an old, black sharecropper pointed a gnarled finger at white J.W. Milam and announced in a loud, clear voice, Thar he!"[19]

Gado got a little carried away. In fact, Papa Mose said, "There he is," according to others present in the courtroom, including Emmett's mother.

Her first official appearance in the courtroom was Tuesday, September 20. With the humidity and heat, "...it felt like we had walked into hell," Emmett Till's mother later wrote.

Mamie Till Mobley testified that the body she buried was her son, Emmett Till. A key piece of evidence in the trial was a silver ring that Emmett wore. The ring was engraved with the letters L.T., the initials of his father Louis Till. Emmett's father had left him the ring when he died. According to Mrs. Till Mobley "Emmett was definitely wearing it when he left Chicago."

Mobley had a bad feeling from the start, about how the trial would end. She could tell "a lot" by faces of the black spectators in the back of the court. "Some were staying in their places, but others were getting out of there, and those were the ones I studied."[120]

Were others involved in the kidnapping? At the time of the trial, and over the years, there has been speculation that others were involved in Till's kidnapping and murder — that several potential witnesses had been locked up in the Charleston jail, for instance. Historical researchers David T. Beito and Linda Royster Beito believe this is entirely plausible, *just not provable.*

"It is entirely possible that others, besides Milam and Bryant, took part in Till's kidnapping and killing. Proving this is another matter entirely. Key witnesses, including, of course, Bryant and Milam are dead. Memories have become hazy and unreliable. Taken together, we believe that the evidence is too thin, too circumstantial, and too contradictory, for definitive answers," they state in "Why It's Unlikely the Emmett Till Murder Mystery Will Ever Be Solved."

Neither Milam nor Bryant testified during the trial that lasted five days. In the defense's closing argument, Milam and Bryant's attorney forewarned the jury, "Your ancestors will turn over in their grave, and I'm sure every last Anglo-Saxon one of you has the courage to free these men."[121]

After the jury deliberated for only 67 minutes (lasting that long only because they stopped to drink soda, the story goes), the jury found Milam and Bryant not guilty, concluding that the prosecution had failed to prove the body recovered from the river was Emmett Till. Some in the press corps wept when the jury acquitted Emmett Till's murderers, several reports state.

Journalist Hodding Carter, Jr. asserted the tension from the murder and trial was the worst he had ever seen. The Greenville publisher believed that matters were going to get "more violent down this way before things take a turn for the better," and told others he had never felt quite as discouraged about racial relations and attitudes, his biographer Ann Waldron wrote.

Reactions around the Delta to the entire Emmett Till saga were nearly as swift and mean as were most of the earlier reactions to Brown vs. the Topeka Board of Education and then Brown II. Wrote the *Yazoo Herald* editor, "Through the furor over the Emmett Till case we hope someone gets this over to the nine ninnies who comprise the present U.S. Supreme Court. Some of the young Negro's blood is on their hands also."

On January 24, 1956, just four months after the trial ended and Milam and Bryant were set free, *Look* magazine published their confessions. The two agreed to tell their story to black journalist William Bradford Huie for $4,000.

They admitted they beat Till with a .45 in Milam's barn and then took him to the Tallahatchie River where they said they made him undress and then shot him in the head. A gin fan was tied around his neck with wire in order to weigh the body down in the river. Till's shoes and clothes were burned, they said.

Despite the confession, Milam and Bryant could not be legally prosecuted because of the constitutional prohibition against double jeopardy. Yet in their home community of Ruleville, Milam and Bryant were ostracized for "disgracing" their community for what they had done.

Black residents and some whites started boycotting the Bryants' store soon after the trial, which forced the Bryants out of business. Both men remained in Mississippi until their deaths; Milam died of cancer in 1980 and Bryant died of cancer in 1994.

In 1996, filmmaker Keith Beauchamp initiated background research for a feature film he later produced about Till's murder, asserting that as many as 14 individuals may have been involved. Beauchamp spent the next nine years creating *The Untold Story of Emmett Louis Till* and his film led to calls by the NAACP and others for the Emmett Till case to be reopened.

"I promised Emmett's mother that I would find out who killed her son and that I would find out what happened to all of the other black people who were killed," Beauchamp said in a 2009 interview.

In 2001, the Beito research team tracked down and interviewed on tape two key principals in the case, Henry Lee Loggins and

Willie Reed, while doing research for their biography of Dr. T.R.M. Howard. Like Beauchamp, they believed it was entirely possible that others, besides Milam and Bryant took part in Till's kidnapping and killing, but they did not believe the number was as high as 14.

When interviewed by the Beitos, Loggins denied any knowledge of the crime or that he was one of the black men on the truck outside of the equipment shed near Drew. Reed repeated his trial testimony, that he had seen three black men and four white men (including J.W. Milam) on the truck but did not name Loggins as one of them.

"Any black man who helped in the crime was probably not a free agent in any meaningful sense. For all these reasons, we are dubious that reopening the case will produce a satisfactory conclusion," the Beitos reported.

Mamie Till Mobley died in 2003 at the age of 81. On May 10 of the following year, the United States Department of Justice announced reopening of the Emmett Till case to determine whether anyone other than Milam and Bryant was involved. Although the statute of limitations prevented charges being pursued under federal law, they could be pursued before the state court, and the Federal Bureau of Investigation and officials in Mississippi worked jointly on the investigation.

Emmett Till's murder was finally afforded the dignity of a professional forensics investigation. His body was exhumed by the Cook County coroner on May 31, 2005, from the suburban Chicago cemetery where it was buried. The body was reburied by relatives on June 4 after it was positively identified as that of Emmett Till.

In 2007, the FBI and a Leflore County Grand Jury empanelled by Joyce Chiles, a black prosecutor, found no credible basis for Keith Beauchamp's claim that fourteen individuals took part in Till's abduction and murder or that any remained alive.

The Grand Jury decided not to prefer charges against Carolyn Bryant Donham, Roy Bryant's ex-wife. Neither the FBI nor the Grand Jury found any credible evidence that Henry Lee Logginsliving in an Ohio nursing home, had any role in the crime.

Award-winning reporter Jerry Mitchell of the Jackson, Miss. *Clarion-Ledger* labeled as legend a rumor that Till had endured castration at the hands of his murderers. The recent autopsy, as reported by Mitchell, confirmed Till Mobley's original account that her son was not castrated and showed no evidence of castration.

In March of 2007, the FBI released its 464-page report stating that Till died of a gunshot wound to the head and that he had suffered fractures to his wrist bones and skull and legs.

But the story of Emmett Till didn't simply fade into history. On July 9, 2009, a manager and three gravediggers at Burr Oak Cemetery near Alsip, Ill. were charged with digging up bodies, dumping them in a remote area, and reselling the plots. Till's grave was not disturbed, but investigators found his original glass-topped casket rusting in a dilapidated storage shed.

The casket was taken to the Rayner and Sons mortuary to be restored for display in the future National Museum of African American History and Culture in Washington, D.C. Rayner and Sons had also prepared Emmett Till's body for burial in 1955.

As of 2009, Carolyn Donham still resides in the Delta town of Greenwood, refusing to talk to the occasional news reporter asking to hear her side of the story.

—

Still Another Story Still Floating Around the Delta

Thirty-seven-year-old Michael Rosa of tiny Itta Bena, Miss. lost a research paper he wrote as an undergraduate student. "I wish I had been a more serious student, back then. And I wish I had realized what I'd written and the importance," he told me on the telephone, during a call a couple of months before this book was published.[122]

Stories like Rosa's have a way of appearing when I'm almost done with a book. And it's a wonderful thing — a gift — that I have come to look forward to. The day we left Parchman Penitentiary, Nina Zachary Black called me from Minneapolis because she had forgotten to tell me something very important about her grandmother, Adlena Hamlett, a teacher and civil rights advocate. Hamlett was killed, under questionable circumstances, with a friend while coming home from a civil rights meeting.

Nina said she once went to the courthouse in Charleston with her grandmother. "She got a ballot and someone took it away and tore it up. She told me not to worry, because some day this would change and I would be able to vote. I think of my grandmother Adlena and sometimes I still want to cry."

It was a stunning story and I was glad that she called me — even though I was rushing around, packing for our move.

This time, Rosa had a terrific story to share, too. He was trying to figure out how to find the paper he wrote in 1994 on Emmett Till — a paper that included a personal interview with one of Till's murderers, Roy Bryant. Rosa wanted the information for a new paper he was writing 15 years later — for a graduate class.

Bryant? I had never interviewed anyone who got close enough to this man to have a conversation. I'd tried talking to a relative of Bryants, once, but had no luck, and I've been told that Bryant, himself, always wanted a lot of money to talk about Till's murder, so I was especially interested in what Rosa learned.

"Back then, we didn't have computers, printers and copy machines. But I wish I could get the original paper back. That would certainly help with this assignment," he said. Besides, the lost paper surely represents the most historically significant paper he will ever write.

Rosa was studying black history at Valley State University, the small, historically black college near his hometown in the heart of the Mississippi Delta when a black history professor issued the first assignment.

He wanted to write about Till back then because the murder happened near his hometown. Further, Rosa's grandfather, "probably a Klansman," had bonded out Till's murderers from jail in nearby Greenwood.

"My grandfather, Landy Walker, lived in the same small town of Phillips near Money. It was a small community and everyone helped each other, so that's probably why my grandfather did this," Rosa said.

"Wait — why would he do that? Why did he help Bryant," I asked Rosa.

And then I realized that Rosa, with his slow Delta accent was white. I had just been assuming he was black until he got to the part of the story about his grandfather. Rosa has a good sense of humor and quickly reminded me he talks "Deltan" and is white.

Rosa said his cousin, Pete Walker, offered to help him with his research paper by providing a first-hand opportunity to meet Roy Bryant face to face.

Rosa thought the interview would help his paper, so the two traveled over to Ruleville, about 30 miles northwest of Itta Bena, where Rosa remembered meeting Bryant at his vegetable and fruit stand on the corner of the highway heading west to Cleveland.

"He was cordial when I told him about my paper. Then he started talking in great detail. He was giving his personal view about what happened that night — he really didn't mention J.W. Milam or anyone else, but I could tell he hadn't changed one bit since that night.

"He used the *N word* over and over — maybe 100 times — when he was telling me about what happened. He said at first, after his wife told him what Till had done — that he was just going to whoop the boy. But he said Emmett made some remarks that pushed him overboard. So they killed him."

Bryant told Rosa he was very drunk that night and said they killed Till and tied the gin fan around his neck while they were still in Drew. "It sounded like Till was either dead or unconscious when they did that to him," Rosa told me.

Talking to Bryant was "... like talking to a stone cold killer. He showed absolutely no remorse. It was like he was able to vividly recall what happened that night."

Bryant said his wife, Carolyn, was with the men, Rosa remembered. "He said he came home to the store and she said a 'nigger came on to her.' He said she went with him and Milam to the uncle's house to kidnap Tilland that she identified him, that she pointed him out."

Bryant told Rosa they killed Emmett Till because "...'he didn't understand where the hell he was — that he was in the South,' and that he wasn't scared at all, 'like he should have been.' "

Bryant, Rosa said, appeared a bitter man who was angry at the white community for refusing to do business at his "watermelon stand." Bryant claimed that Milam "got all the money," referring to the news magazine interviews about the Till crime. Roy Bryant died two weeks after the interview.

After Rosa told me this story, we got to talking about his own life. A racist grandfather can easily poison his family's beliefs for generations to come. But the circle was broken for Rosa. His mother worked hard; his care, from the age of 6, was left to his maternal grandmother who was a kind soul, he said.

The family was poor, he told me, and lived at the edge of the black side of town where Rosa "saw racism while I was growing up, on a daily basis." Other white kids went to the town's all-white private academy. But Rosa lived 100 feet from the public school and decided to go there — from elementary through high school. "Some of the white families got together and offered to pay for my tuition to the white school. They didn't want to see me go to the public school with black kids. I was the only white student."

A neighbor woman once offered to pay for his schooling through college, if he would change to the private academy. "I told her 'no' and she said, '...well, at least don't associate with any of them.' "

Rosa's own family was split on the race issue and he knew as a young child he didn't want to "be this way." While his mother's mother raised him not to be racist, Rosa says his father's side "comes from a land owner's background and is definitely racist." His father died when he was 13, Rosa said.

Recently, as a mentor at the public school, Rosa was asked by the administrator if he had any ideas about how to reach out to white children and get them to come to the public school. "I told him it's tough. When I was growing up, one side of town was all white. Now there are only three white families left. Everyone else has moved out into the country and they home school or send their kids to the Pillow Academy over in Greenwood."

Rosa plans to sit quietly and try to remember as much as he can about the interview he had with Roy Bryant so many years ago. "I really do remember most of what he said very vividly."

Surely it's a story Rosa may someday want to erase from his memory. He was so nice to call me — a complete stranger — and share a fascinating piece of Mississippi history. Like Black-Zachary, who surely "grew up with the hurt" of this dark Mississippi history, taking the time to remember creates an opportunity to heal their hearts, and the souls of others.

BLOG Comments

Michael Rosa said: After reviewing this blog I find that it is very interesting. Though over the years there has also been revised information since the time that it happened.

Susan Klopfer responded: This is the stuff of history! There will always be modifications and more modifications — layers and layers — put down. And that's what makes collecting history so much fun and so intriguing. Stories, recollections, real events and imagined all come together in a tapestry.

Some tribal members believe it is better not to write down stories but to allow them to unfold over generations through storytelling. Communication, after all, is the practice of replicating memories! (I learned that definition once in a communication class, and I knew it would come handy some day!)

Alan said: This is an amazing story. It brings up a few questions: Is this the first time that Roy Bryant directly implicates his wife in the kidnapping? How did Bryant survive working at a watermelon stand if people know who and where he was, and while he talked so openly and bitterly about Till and his cohorts?

Susan Klopfer responded: You can still see remaining boards and other bits and pieces of the small produce stand that Bryant operated in Ruleville. Margaret Block told me she knew about the stand and that few people in town, black or white, would make purchases. Others have told me the same story. Margaret said that Bryant also tried to open up a junk store in Cleveland and it also failed. Once, I wrote a story about a reporter, Cloyte Larsson, who covered the first trial and went back to visit the *Land of Till*. About midway through she visits Cleve McDowell and they go to the store.

Also, I heard about Carolyn Bryant when I interviewed a white woman in Drew Bryant and Milam came to their home, after killing Till, and told her parents the story. She said her father was told by both men that Bryant's wife was with them when they picked up Emmett.

Post #22

Cemetery Where Emmett Till Buried; Handed Back to Owners

An AP Wire News report is stating today that some people with relatives buried at Burr Oak — the resting place of many prominent African-Americans, including lynching victim Emmett Till — have expressed dismay over news the cemetery is to be handed back to its owners.

"Why would they give control back to the people who created the mess? It doesn't make sense," said Gregory Mannie, who has several relatives buried at Burr Oak, including his father, grandfather and grandmother.

"The more I think about it, the more upset I get."

Post #23

Still Another Unsolved Mississippi Murder? Cleve McDowell Investigated Delta Murder Victims, Including Emmett Till

I became fascinated in a person named Cleve McDowell right after we moved to the Delta. It was his story that peaked my interest in Emmett Till and in all of the other Mississippi ghosts whose souls roam the Delta's rich soil.

One day, I was a passenger in the car of a woman from Drew. She was a member of the town's culture club and I was listening to her talk about her club's programs while wondering at the same time how one would ever come up with a year's worth of programs for a "culture" club in this funny, little town.

Yet, I admired what she was doing and also realized I would never be asked to be a member because of my "damn Yankee" status. And that was okay.

My Drew acquaintance was driving me home from some event and, over on the left side of the road, I saw for the first time a rusted, white metal fence with two closed gates. There were weeds growing around the fence and you could see a couple of poles sticking straight up in the air on each side of the lot, like someone had abandoned a building project years earlier.

"What's that?" I asked. "Oh, it's really nothing. A lawyer was building a house there and he was murdered. So he couldn't finish it. He wasn't a nice man."

"Who was he?" "Cleve McDowell. That's really about all that I know."

I knew that I was being dismissed. So I tucked away the information. But I did want to know more and looked up McDowell that night in Sovereignty Commission files. He was the first black law student at the University of Mississippi. He'd been kicked out quickly for carrying a gun (for self protection, he'd said) and ended up going to school in Texas. McDowell came back, bucked the state's licensing board and became a licensed attorney. He even worked for a while with Dr. Martin Luther King, Jr.'s Southern Christian Leadership Conference, SCLC, group in Chicago.

The more that I could find out about McDowell, and the more that I was learning about Emmett Till I realized their two lives came together and yet never really touched.

I had come to the Delta knowing nothing about Emmett Till and now I was learning about two different people, born two weeks apart, who were murdered years apart but in close proximity. Both had a place in the modern civil rights movement.

After several months of catfish lunches in downtown Drew — my questions tucked between bites — Walter Scurlock, the owner of a small restaurant was trusting me and took some time to fill me in about Cleve McDowell, the man who was murdered on the same day he'd put up pilings for his new home on that large lot at the edge of Drew.

And boy, did Walter have some stories to tell!

After sharing everything he could think of about McDowell, Scurlock said I should go down the block and introduce myself to Nettie Davis, Cleve McDowell's former office manager.

I found her home that afternoon and knocked on the door. And it was like she had been waiting to talk to me for quite some time.

Cleve McDowell

Hearing that his close friend, Harry S. Mims, had committed suicide, Cleve McDowell's mojo kicked in and the Delta lawyer drove to Montgomery, Alabama, speeding the 380 miles to do the obvious.

It was easy enough to maneuver himself around the funeral home and find Mims's body in order to check out the story.

From nearly three decades of practicing civil rights and public defense law, assessing what happened to his friend would not — and did not — take more than a few moments alone with the corpse.

Back home in Drew, McDowell told his friend and minister, Rev. Jesse Gresham, he'd found Mims body with bruises and broken fingers. "There were signs of torture," he said. Mims was found hanging from the garage ceiling with a ladder under his body, the widow told McDowell, but from her description, McDowell knew the ladder wasn't far enough from the floor to make sense.[123]

"Cleve wanted to talk when he got back to Drew," Gresham said. Their conversation took a new direction when McDowell asked the minister to promise he would conduct his — McDowell's — funeral when the time arrived.

"…And he meant it," Gresham said. "I thought he was kidding at first, and I told him I would be dying before him since I'm quite a bit older. But he was serious and he looked scared." Gresham tried to better understand his friend's request, and directly asked McDowell if he knew what happened to Mims.

McDowell had been blunt. Mims didn't kill himself; the story had to be a cover, he had told Gresham.

"I asked Cleve if he knew who did it. He said 'yes,' and then looked down and said nothing else."

To Gresham's sorrow, he had to honor his friend's request five years later. The former blues musician played for McDowell's funeral, after the lawyer was murdered in his own home.

The morning of March 17, 1997, Cleveland McDowell's body was discovered by his younger sister and his long-time office manager, and the following day the *Associated Press* reported:

DREW, Miss. (AP) - A civil rights attorney who was the second black to attend the University of Mississippi was found shot to death at his home, and a judge immediately slapped a gag order on investigators.

Cleve McDowell, 56, was found dead in an upstairs bathroom early Thursday after relatives called police to say the door to his apartment was open and his car missing. Police continued to look for McDowell's Cadillac on Friday.

McDowell had been a public defender in Sunflower County for three decades. He was part of a group of black leaders organizing to pressure district attorneys and revive interest in many never-prosecuted cases in which blacks were killed for doing civil rights work.

During the 1980s, McDowell was the executive field director of the Mississippi chapter of the National Association for the Advancement of Colored People.

—

That McDowell was "part of a group of black leaders organizing to pressure district attorneys" in civil rights actions, would never make it to obituaries published in Mississippi.

McDowell was well known around the state. He was appointed to the state's Penitentiary Board in 1971 and named as state Head Start director in 1972, the first Mississippi African American to receive a governor's appointments.

In later years, the Delta lawyer revived the state's NAACP, first opened in 1954 by his mentor Medgar Evers, Mississippi's first NAACP field secretary. McDowell also served as a Sunflower

County judge from 1978 to 1982 and ran unsuccessfully for the state legislature twice, in 1978 and 1987.[124]

For a short time, he was a legislative aide to conservative U.S. Senator Trent Lott, leading some friends and political observers to question his motives. But friends say McDowell was a thoughtful and somewhat conservative civil rights advocate who was simply trying to better understand the motives of politicians like Lott.

It seemed that only his office manager, Nettie Davis and a few close friends knew of McDowell's longtime relationship with Mamie Till Mobley, who, at 75, was still alive when McDowell died.

For years, McDowell studied the Till lynching, Davis said, most likely because Till was killed a few miles outside of Drew when both young men were 14, and the murder had been particularly traumatic for Drew children. The event helped direct McDowell into the study of law.

McDowell updated Emmett's mother with occasional telephone calls and visits to Chicago about his efforts, while filling law office corners with stacked cardboard boxes holding papers and records he'd collected on Till and other unsolved murder victims, Davis said.

Some of the records were kept locked in his office safe, along with a dozen or more guns that McDowell always kept on hand for self-protection. But six months after he was murdered, all of McDowell's investigative papers disappeared when his unoccupied law office caught fire, according to Davis.

The fire occurred the same week the State of Mississippi finally opened half of its secret Sovereignty Commission investigation files, kept under lock since 1972 — a long 25 years after losing a court battle with the ACLU to make records public.

A share of Mississippi's thousands of missing and potentially embarrassing Sovereignty Commission records could have landed in McDowell's office for analysis and safe-keeping before disappearing again during the fire, it has been suggested.

Juarez Webb, one of McDowell's public defender clients, who initially hoped McDowell could make his recent burglary charges go away, was tracked down and arrested within three days of his lawyer's murder.

Jet magazine reported March 31, 1997, that the 19-year-old was caught in Indianola, seat of Sunflower County, charged with capital murder and held without bond.

Webb was seen with McDowell late in the day of the murder, District Attorney Frank Carlton told Jet. A police officer found McDowell's body early the next morning in an upstairs bedroom when responding to reports from the victim's family that the front door to his home was open and his car, a brown 1995 Cadillac, was missing, Police Capt. Albert Robinson said.

McDowell, who lived alone in Drew, in a house he built using sections from his family's sharecropper home, was shot twice, Robinson said. Authorities soon found his car in Indianola. Webb was not in the car, but faced grand larceny charges for its theft.

Carlton told the *Journal Constitution* that there were "indications that Webb had driven McDowell's car from Drew back to Indianola," about 40 minutes away.

Following McDowell's murder, Sunflower County law enforcement and court officers insisted on enforcing the initial gag order on all related police and court records for 12 consecutive years.

Davis questioned why such an order would remain — not an unfair query, considering a gag order's intention. The order to keep such papers out of the public reach was first placed on the investigation to halt a local police chief from further damaging the crime scene and spreading inflammatory rumors, she said.

CLEVELAND MCDOWELL HAD distinguished himself early on, from the time he was a student at Drew High School where he won awards as a speech and debate competitor going on to study at Jackson State University.

In the summer of 1963, as the second black student after James Meredith to be admitted to the University of Mississippi, McDowell followed suit, becoming the first African American ever to study law at what was then the James O. Eastland School of Law, named after Sunflower County's well-known U.S. Senator and avowed racist.

Shortly after the murder of his friend and mentor, NAACP Field Secretary Medgar Evers, McDowell learned that both he and Meredith were next in line for assassination, a fact he told oral historian Owen Brooks, which was confirmed years later by a retired Parchman Penitentiary guard who told me he was asked to kill McDowell by a Delta planter.

McDowell brought a gun to the University of Mississippi campus after being chased home several times and receiving other verbal and physical threats. "Most everybody else had one," McDowell told Brooks, "but when mine was discovered, I was expelled." McDowell used data to prove students commonly carried guns at the University of Mississippi, in an attempt to be reinstated, but to no avail. Later praised in a letter of support by Mississippi's law school dean, McDowell finished his education at the Thurgood Marshall School of Law, Texas Southern University, a "better and safer" place to be."

The University of Mississippi law school dean refused in 2003 to acknowledge existence of the letter of support in McDowell's files, turning away a Freedom of Information request. A call made to his office in 2009 was referred to law school archives where an archivist said the letter was definitely not in the school's possession. Several weeks later, the head archivist provided a copy of the letter that praised McDowell while he was a student in Mississippi. It had been found in a department file on the University of Mississippi campus. In fact, Texas Southern proved a better place for McDowell to finish his law degree, because the Texas law school was emphasizing civil rights law while the University of Mississippi was far behind, McDowell told Brooks. McDowell excelled there as a leader, becoming president of the student body.

Juarez Webb

On August 21, 1997, Juarez Webb was indicted by Sunflower County grand jurors on charges of capital murder and robbery of McDowell. And for several months, the charges stuck.

It would be hard to make a case against Webb because there was tampering at the crime scene and there were no witnesses to the shooting. The city's police chief was called to McDowell's home once the body was discovered, Nettie Davis said. "He told us all to leave the house, all of us including the police officer, and he stayed in the house for a long time, literally tearing up the floors and walls — like he was looking for something.

"He walked out with a small sack, but I don't know what he had. It was obvious that he messed up the crime scene before the state investigators could get there."

"About 20 minutes" after the police chief's departure, Sunflower County Circuit Judge Gray Evans filed orders to seal the premises and to make discussions of any findings or evidence from the crime scene illegal for any officers and personnel working the crime scene.

The gag order remains in effect as of 2009, even though the investigation was closed years ago, asserts the county's assistant district attorney who, in the fall of 2003, refused access to any of the police investigation or court records stored in the courthouse basement in Indianola, even though the gag order never covered court officers.

"The police chief was saying awful things about Cleve when he came out of the house that morning. I know that Judge Gray [Evans] was just trying to tone things down before the gossip got out of hand," Davis said. "But I wouldn't think he meant for the gag order to never be lifted." McDowell's family would have to approve lifting the gag order, a county judge said in 2003 after receiving an Indianola attorney's informal request for McDowell's records.

But Webb's case files, kept in the Sunflower County courthouse basement, were accessible. They included a copy of McDowell's autopsy report — performed in Jackson the night of McDowell's murder — by Steven T. Hayne, M.D., the state's controversial deputy coroner. It was a good find, since the state of Mississippi claims to no longer have the original autopsy report or a copy on file.

How did I discover a copy of McDowell's autopsy report when the state of Mississippi claimed to have no such records? When it became apparent that the county assistant prosecutor was not going to hand over any records on McDowell, I decided to take another approach. I would quietly go back to "the girls" who worked the desk in the judges' office of the courthouse and ask for Webb's case files.

One of the clerks made a second trip down to the basement and found a box of papers that included the McDowell autopsy report. She lugged it back up the steps to their office where I could make copies. And I was in!

Post #24

The Autopsy of Cleveland McDowell

Dr. Hayne's report states there were "negative" signs of any drug abuse. Cause of death was listed as a "gunshot wound of the left neck, distant and perforating." The death was listed as a homicide.

Three gunshot wounds fired in "close temporal proximity" but not at close range, perhaps up to a distance of 15 feet," were described by the coroner:

...a "nonlethal" wound consisting of a "nonlethal distant and perforating gunshot wound of the left back;" a "nonlethal distant and perforating gunshot wound of the left shoulder with re-entry penetrating gunshot wound of the left temple;" and a "lethal distant and perforating gunshot wound of the left neck."

These descriptions could not be put into sequential order, the report stated. Perhaps what is *not* included in the autopsy report leaves more questions than what was stated.

This officially stamped copy of McDowell's autopsy report does not give information regarding the range from which the gun was fired. In 2004, I asked a physician practicing forensic medicine to read the report and give his opinion. He was not given McDowell's name or any further information about the crime.

The physician told me it appeared the shots could have been fired from fifteen feet away. The physician also speculated there could have been more than one shooter, given the angles of the three shots. Further, it surprised him that usual and expected information about the condition of bullets causing these wounds was not included in the report.

The forensics physician, looking over McDowell's autopsy, would not be alone in stating his doubts about the work done by Mississippi's deputy coroner and medical examiner. Hayne has been formally accused on various occasions of "causing innocent people ['there may be some on death row'] doing time at Parchman Penitentiary due to his testimony," said J.D. Sanders, a former Columbus, Miss., police chief who now works as an assistant police chief in Franklin, Tenn.

Interviewed by Radley Balko of ReasonOnline, Sanders cited an instance in 2007 when the Mississippi Supreme Court, by an 8-to-1 vote, tossed out Hayne's expert testimony in a case of a 13-year-old boy accused of killing his sister's husband.

Leroy Riddick, a state medical examiner in Alabama who has testified in opposition to Hayne, told Balko, "All of the prosecutors in Mississippi know that if you want to be sure you get the autopsy results you want, you take the body to Dr. Hayne."

Sanders and Riddick state that according to standards set by the National Association of Medical Examiners (NAME), the field's pre-eminent professional organization, a single medical examiner should perform no more than 250 autopsies per year.

At 325 autopsies performed per year, the group considers a doctor to have a "Phase II deficiency." At that point, it will not accredit a practice, regardless of any other criteria.

"Hayne has repeatedly testified under oath that he performs more than 1,500 autopsies per year—a staggering number ... That's more than four per day, every day of the year, for the 20 years Hayne has been in Mississippi. In a 2002 deposition, Hayne put the estimate at 1,800," Balko wrote.

SIX MONTHS AFTER McDowell's murder, a fire was set in downtown Drew, devastating the town's largest department store and McDowell's vacant office next door. And all of the records McDowell had collected over the years from his personal research on unsolved race-based murders and lynching, including his records on Emmett Till, were stored in the vacant office. McDowell's records were either taken away or destroyed in the fire.

These records had remained stored in McDowell's office since his murder because the family wanted to make a museum there some day and left all of the records where they would be put on display. That was the story understood by Nettie Davis.

The fire's flames were so high that some Cleveland residents reported seeing the "lighted sky" 17 miles southwest of Drew. Others heard an "explosion" in Drew at the beginning of the fire, newspaper reports state.

Drew police chief Burner Smith, in 2003, refused to release the records of the fire, stating they had been turned over to Sunflower County.

—

"No."

That was Hailey Gail Bridges' immediate response to my request for the Drew fire records, and she was sticking to it. Bridges told me quite firmly that "if they are at the courthouse, the records are not available to the public."

I was beginning to understand why some say that McDowell didn't like her very much. Bridges, who earlier refused to turn over any records the county had on McDowell's murder, was never a friend to the late public defender. As a graduate of the University of Mississippi, she had never gotten along with McDowell, several former colleagues said, including Davis.

"He would beat her nearly every time in court. And then he would make fun of her. She really hated him," Davis said. Specifically, McDowell was known for waggling his tongue at Bridges whenever she lost a case to him, Davis told me.

Bridges was no help to the FBI in solving the Emmett Till cold case, either. During the summer of 2006, Bridges was given the task of overseeing the Emmett Till cold case project initiated by the FBI. To date, no court action has been taken. Some civil rights movement veterans, including Margaret Block, assert Bridges "will never do anything to resolve the 1955 murder."

On Feb. 17, 2007, *Clarion Ledger* reporter, Jerry Mitchell, reported that the Leflore grand jury indicted no one in the 1955 killing of Emmett Till, bringing an apparent end to the resurrection of one of the nation's most notorious hate crimes.

"Assistant District Attorney Hailey Gail Bridges said she could not comment because it is a grand jury matter," Mitchell wrote. "Such reports typically become public days or weeks after a grand jury finishes. The grand jury considered possible charges against Carolyn Bryant, now 73 and living in Greenville. She has told relatives and the FBI she is innocent."

The Case Against Webb

From records coming into the sunlight from years stored in the Sunflower County courthouse basement, it was apparent the case against Juarez Webb took odd twists and turns — at one point acting more like events surrounding James Earl Ray, convicted of killing Rev. Martin Luther King, Jr. back in 1969.

On the advice of attorney Percy Foreman, Ray had pleaded guilty to avoid the death penalty. He was sentenced to a 99-year-prison term and then recanted just three days later, saying he had been framed.

Webb's court records show that he filed a Petition to Enter a Guilty Plea, reducing his plea from capital murder to manslaughter on January 26, 1998. In his request, Webb said he "shot and killed Cleve McDowell, without malice, in the heat of passion" and "not in necessary self-defense."

But like Ray, Webb also asserted that he was "coerced" into pleading guilty to manslaughter by his attorneys:

"They told me I wasn't going to be able — I wasn't going to be able to get nowhere in this case, that I might as well go ahead and take a plea; otherwise, it would be over with me.... I guess they were talking about my life," Webb's records state.

On July 22, 1998, court files show that Webb reversed himself and filed a "jailhouse" petition to withdraw his guilty plea, citing "a series of interrogations, threats and promises [made to him] by various law enforcement officials" and "a series of statements of an incriminating nature [that were] obtained from Petitioner in taped, written and oral form against the Petitioner's will and conscent [sic]."

Interrogations, Webb claimed, were "unsolicited" and "initiated by ... the instance [sic] of arresting officers and other varies [sic] courthouse officials." Webb said he did not waive his rights to silence or counsel or self-incrimination, but that he was forced unwillingly, and without counsel present, to answer questions.

Webb said he was "repeatedly interrogated and threatened as well as coerced to admit to the crime in an involuntary nature, thus rendering my guilty plea involuntary as the result of being threatened by the officials to receive the death penalty."

Records stated that Webb was taken for a psychological examination to determine if he was potentially suicidal.

Appointed counsel, Webb went to trial January 27, 1998, and "maintained his innocence," his petition states. His family was "repeatedly harassed by law enforcement officials" and was told by his attorneys that he would "get the death penalty" if he did not "take a plea for a lesser charge of manslaughter."

Webb asserted the charge of capital murder was dropped to manslaughter "due to the pressure and threats and unlawful statements obtained as well as other evidence and unlawful arrest against my will."

Webb admitted giving "false statements in court to end the truma [sic] and nightmare" and to protect his family from "further threats and harassments." The guilty plea, he stated, was "made unwillingly, involuntarily" and he was "coerced" to give his plea to "avoid a big trial and publicity" on his family.

What Webb wanted was permission to withdraw his plea of guilty and to prove his innocence "so that the real suspect can be caught."

At the time of his slaying, McDowell was Webb's court-appointed attorney on earlier burglary charges. "The police thought Webb killed Cleve to steal his Cadillac, money and jewelry. It was all missing from his home when his body was found. They said Webb confessed to the killing when he was arrested," Davis said.

At Webb's preliminary hearing, according to a *Clarion-Ledger* news report, Drew Police Chief Burner Smith testified that Webb, 18, told police, "McDowell had thrown him on the floor and tried to pull his pants down to sexually assault him."

That charge never resurfaced.

District Attorney Carlton said accepting Webb's plea was the best decision, since the case was "not iron-clad" and that McDowell "needed to be remembered for what he did as a leader in the Civil Rights Movement at a time when that wasn't too popular."

On July 9, 1999, Circuit Judge Gray Evans denied and dismissed Webb's motion. Evans wrote that it had "probably" been a "wise" recommendation by Webb's attorney to urge Webb to plead guilty to manslaughter rather than face the possibility of a death sentence from a conviction of capital murder. At the end of 2009, Webb remained incarcerated in a Greenwood facility, according to the Mississippi Department of Corrections. One of his friends said that Webb was seeking an early release.

BACK IN 1956, during the legislative session following the murder of Emmett Till, and in the wake of national and international condemnation, Mississippi legislators installed a quiet and effective spy agency known as the Mississippi Sovereignty Commission. Its purpose was to quell all integration efforts while also cranking up efforts for better Mississippi public relations.

Like so many other blacks (and pro-integration whites), McDowell had been a target of the Sovereignty Commission and a moderate number of records remain available to the public concerning McDowell. Only a fraction of Sovereignty Commission files have ever seen the light of day, since thousands of records were reportedly destroyed or removed before they were made available to the public when the state was ordered to open its secretive vaults.

Some former Commission employees have stated they purposely removed important records and they or their relatives have refused to turn over these records while the state appears to have done nothing to regain them.

Davis said that McDowell received some of his personal Sovereignty Commission reports to look over before they were made public — just one week before his murder — adding he did not appear particularly disturbed over the unsealed records made privy to him.

Shortly after McDowell was killed, "Someone came to the office and took everything off his computer. I don't know who it was. But everything was so strange at the time — Cleve had even spent a few days before he was killed updating his resume — making a big deal out of it," Davis said.

One Sovereignty Commission record named a possible Jackson "homosexual partner" to McDowell. The record also declared McDowell as a young black man "on the rise," as someone who "impressed" the Governor. Davis did not remember if this particular record was made available to her former boss for his review.

As Davis spoke about McDowell's murder, she recalled something else that struck her as unusual: "When Cleve was murdered, the strangest thing to me was how neat his coffee table looked. I went into the house with Cleve's sister and that was the first thing I noticed. "It was always a mess, with papers, files, and books stacked up and even falling off the edges. Everyone who knew him would remember that coffee table. But that morning it looked like it had been cleaned up when we went into the house. Every paper was stacked neatly into a pile.

"There were these neat piles all over the table. My eye caught the coffee table immediately, as soon as I walked in. I had never seen it like this before," Davis said.

Woodrow Jackson had also talked to me about McDowell, earlier, and agreed with Davis over the cleaned up coffee table. The retired funeral home assistant, who had prepared Emmett Till's body before it was shipped back to his mother, was also a friend of McDowell's. Jackson said he found it "more than intriguing" that McDowell's coffee table was straightened the day his body was discovered.

"This says something. His coffee table was always very messy. He would never have straightened it up, himself. I didn't see his body, but from what I could reconstruct from the rumors going around, there might have been two people involved in the shooting."

Jackson talked softly. "I knew Cleve very well. I didn't embalm his body; I believe it was someone from Cleveland who did...Cleve was a good lawyer and we often spoke about Emmett Till because he was interested in finding all who were involved in the murder. "Cleve kept boxes of records in his office. I know, because I saw them. I remember a year or so ago before Cleve was murdered he brought Emmett Till up again and still seemed upset, but he would never give out any details. When his office burned down after he was murdered, a lot of important papers had to have been lost," Jackson said.

Nettie Davis, besides noticing the status of her boss's coffee table, also observed that McDowell's prized guns were missing soon after his murder. "He had guns in many places throughout the house and his office. He was always within reach of a gun. I don't know how he could have been so surprised as to have been shot. I never learned what happened to all of his guns in his house or in his office. He also kept guns in his car."

McDowell and the FBI

The FBI, responding to a Freedom of Information request, first asserted no records on McDowell exist. "Strange," said Davis and several of McDowell's close friends, recalling that FBI agents visited McDowell's office several times in the years before his death.

Later, two records were made available by the FBI regarding a minor incident during McDowell's tenure as a Tunica Judge. Other "tax records" were not available to the public, the FBI stated.

Rev. Jesse Gresham said he always wondered if McDowell's murder could have been related to a "very large" settlement he won for a client who lived near Tunica and "may have involved something to do with a utility company." Davis agreed when told of Gresham's observation.

McDowell had invited Gresham and his wife to dinner several days before he was murdered. "He said he had won 'the big' case he'd been working on and, for once, had lots of money. I didn't know anything about this case, but I did hear that no attorney in Memphis would touch it. Some say there might have been mob involvement," Gresham said.

The Mimms' story holds additional mystery when trying to figure out who killed Cleve McDowell, and why. McDowell's immediate reaction to Mims' sudden death was that it would be "impossible" for Mims to have killed himself; it wasn't in his personality, Rev. Jesse Gresham said.

McDowell had set out immediately to learn what had happened to his friend. When Gresham and several others from Drew decided to drive to Alabama for the funeral, McDowell decided he would "go out first and try to find out what happened" and then call back to give an update before the others left town.

McDowell arrived in Montgomery and went to his friend's home, but Mims' widow refused to let him view her husband's body and McDowell learned she was demanding a closed casket during the funeral.

McDowell would not have taken such news sitting down, but most likely went to the funeral home to examine the body himself, McDowell's own minister, Rev. Gresham, said. "Cleve would have worked to find out what happened to Mims and he would never take 'no' for an answer."

McDowell had sounded "shaken" on the telephone call back to Drew and said he would not stay for the funeral; he also suggested that his friends not drive to Alabama, as planned, Gresham said.

But McDowell's friends drove out to the funeral and were surprised at "all of the California people" who attended. "So many, that most of his Mississippi friends could not get inside of the church."

Mims was a graduate of the City College of Los Angeles, and apparently had maintained contact with the Californians. Still, his Drew friends were surprised at the number of people from the coast who so quickly gathered to honor a man who now lived in Alabama. When McDowell and his minister got together back in Drew after the funeral, McDowell again asserted there was no evidence of a suicide and said that Mims showed definite signs of torture.

Mims' Drew relatives have all refused interviews. One family member said they were afraid to talk, with the common Delta signature: "Don't give my name." Mims' wife, reportedly still living in Montgomery, refuses to return my telephone calls.

I called the county courthouse in Alabama and found a law clerk that agreed to answer some questions about Mims, asking not to be named. In a whisper, she said, "rumors flew around" Montgomery that Mims was murdered. "But no one wanted to talk about it."

McDowell made enormous changes in his life after his friend's death. He had studied to be a Baptist minister and now he began seriously decreasing time spent working in his law office to build his newly formed church.

The Holly Grove church had purchased a small building in downtown Drew and members were working to build their congregation.

"Cleve spent more time picking out the dishes and other special purchases for the church than coming to work," Davis said. "Sometime I'd get worried about Cleve's absence from the office and tell Cleve 'we' might get sued," she laughed, explaining that she found herself doing a good share of the legal work via McDowell's telephone instructions.

"He just really changed after the Alabama trip, and it was so important for him that everything be done exactly right for the new church. That mattered to him more than anything else in the world."

A former Parchman prison guard — like many Deltans with secrets, asking for anonymity — talked about McDowell's murder. "Most of us know that Cleve's death was not just a matter of a young kid shooting him because he thought Cleve was trying to molest him.

"Molestation would be impossible, anyway, because Webb was too old, legally, to be molested. But, there had been FBI hanging around here, and I personally think Cleve had to be one of the reasons why. His family and friends, I think, are still afraid to talk. They know what it is still like in the Delta, and so do I, since I know how some of the richest people work."

In 1962, when James Meredith was attempting to enter the University of Mississippi, a "rich, white planter" had approached this prison guard and "tried to hire me to kill Meredith." Even though the event took place over 40 years ago, the retired guard, who also told me he had cancer, would not give the planter's name.

"He wanted me to 'do something' about Meredith. Of course, I said no. But that is how it has always been around here — rich, white people paying off others, including blacks, to murder black people. They think this keeps us in line. And this has not stopped — it still goes on."[125] The guard later died from this disease, his brother said.

Meredith actually was shot in 1966 while walking from Memphis to Jackson, Miss., in a march to protest racism. Throughout his lifetime, Meredith was known as an outspoken conservative who could easily upset liberals as well as conservatives and this was the first time Meredith had led such a demonstration.

McDowell, mentored by Meredith, never made such a splash on the civil rights scene. In an oral, taped interview, McDowell described himself as "the briefcase guy" during undergraduate days at Jackson State University where he quietly assisted Freedom Riders who were coming into Jackson bus stations.

Unlike Meredith's entry to the University of Mississippi, McDowell's entrance to the law school was quiet and uninterrupted; Mississippi state records show that Sovereignty Commission spies tried to find evidence to block his application — combing through grade school and high school files, interviewing teachers and family friends — but nothing negative was ever found, according to their reports.

Medgar Evers, also Cleve McDowell's early mentor, had persuaded him to apply to law school; and through his years of state and national NAACP involvement, McDowell met Dr. King, who visited him on occasion in Drew.

Rev. Jesse Jackson, John Lewis, Rev. Fred Shuttlesworth and a host of other civil rights heroes also stopped by McDowell's office, when coming into the region, Davis said.

Over the years, as civil rights heroes Evers, then President John F. Kennedy, Rev. Martin Luther King, Jr. and Sen. Robert Kennedy were all slain, McDowell became noticeably more outspoken.

Interviews with national press became more frequent for the Delta lawyer and, by the 1980s, McDowell was stepping outside of Mississippi and giving interviews to the national press about resolution of civil rights murders. His tone was more strident.

In 1988, McDowell told of his sense of devastation following the murder of Evers for a 25th-anniversary story published by the *Jackson Clarion-Ledger* and called for a watchdog organization to locate and identify persons responsible for civil rights murders, "just as Nazi war criminals were prosecuted."

"There ought to be some organization to track them down...Right now some of those people are smiling and grinning in our faces and asking us to vote for them," he said.

McDowell and two other lawyers (".... perhaps Texans who went to school with Cleve," his only nephew, Kwasi McDowell of Chicago suggested) were doing their own investigations, according to his nephew — from the murders of Emmett Till, Medgar Evers and forward, gathering every piece of information they could lay their hands on to solve crimes against black people at the local, state and national level, a close friend confirmed.

Kwasi McDowell, at first interested in talking about his uncle, backed off after two interviews, saying his parents warned him not to talk.

In the fall of 1991, McDowell told National Public Radio reporter Vicki Monks there had been "a meticulous effort to reconstruct many of these murders and many of these people are in fact known, but it's just a question of whether you can get to them legally."

McDowell as referring specifically to the 1966 murder of an NAACP voting rights organizer whose Hattiesburg store and home were bombed by Klansmen. Interviewed with Vernon Damer's son, Dennis, and a former county district attorney, Jim Dukes, McDowell asserted there was "enough new evidence and enough of a change in attitudes that it's now possible to get conviction."

While Dukes disagreed, citing passage of time, evidence, deceased witnesses and "the legal constitutional question of speedy trial," McDowell asserted that convictions were not the point. That it was a matter of making the attempt to address old injustices.

Three years before McDowell was murdered, he spoke to The *Philadelphia Inquirer*'s Washington Bureau reporter Donna St. George, shortly after prosecutors opened their third trial in the Evers case — attempting for the third time to prove that Byron De La Beckwith was the midnight sniper who killed Evers.

Two earlier trials had been a "sham," McDowell told St. George.

THERE WAS a quieter side to McDowell's life. He and several other well-known civil rights veterans were gay, perhaps giving family members and some close friends reason not to give interviews because of embarrassment or denial.

The civil rights period was a time of forced anonymity, since gays were considered immoral, if not communistic. Their lives would have been in peril had they practiced homosexuality in the open, a London researcher explained. Sovereignty Commission files show that agents reported by name any alleged gay behavior of blacks (including a brief mention of McDowell as well as records naming James Meredith and Aaron Henry).

Of course, there is little mention of any white gay behavior, unless the person mentioned was against segregation. One rumor that never made it to Sovereignty Commission files was a strange tale that continues to circulate throughout Mississippi. It was rumored that a white governor (and a Citizens Councils member), was also a closet gay and "slept with at least one well-known black activist."

Professor John Howard of Queens College in London offered an insight to gay activities in the Mississippi Delta during the modern civil rights era in his thesis on "The love that dare not speak its name in the Bible belt."[126]

"Generally speaking, before the 1960s, gay Southerners, black and white, participated in similar practices and networks. But they were doing so in two parallel, segregated worlds. "A deep-rooted and longstanding homosexual homicide mythology associates gay men with dangerous lifestyles and disgraceful deaths," Howard said.

Up until the late 1960s, homosexuality in the South was "largely accommodated with pretence of ignorance, a system of mutual discretion in which much was understood but left unsaid," Howard said.

Howard questioned rumors that occasionally surface painting McDowell a pedophile. "Of course, his enemies would have wanted that sort of idea to circulate. But do you have proof that he had sexual intercourse with children? With pre-pubescent youth? It's worth mentioning that the legal age of consent here in Great Britain is sixteen for both heterosexual and homosexual sex."

The professor questioned if McDowell's partners were ".... incapable of consenting? I mention this because such accusations are a classic form of intimidation by white supremacists."

"Bill Higgs [a well-known, white Mississippi civil rights attorney], as you know, was accused of having sex with a sixteen-year-old. This may have been true. But it also may have involved what I would refer to as a set of consensual acts. You need only look back several decades to find a time when the age of consent in

Southern states was what would now be seen as shockingly low," Howard said.

The statutory age of sexual consent was increased from 14 to 16 in Mississippi as of January 1, 2000.

What information Cleveland McDowell took to the grave and how he will be remembered, if he is remembered at all, perhaps rests on whether or not McDowell's friends and family will ever talk and advocate for him, and if official files will ever be found and released — an absence that is helpful for the state of Mississippi, which wants to avoid most issues of the civil rights era, and for many of McDowell's old friends and family members who appear still embarrassed over sexual aspects of his life.

Meanwhile, Cleveland McDowell's ghost is quickly fading:

—The Mississippi civil rights collection housed at the William Winters Library in Jackson shows no records on file for McDowell, even though he was appointed to several state positions by former Governor William Winters and was the first black to attend the state's premier law school. Library assistants say they had "never heard of him" when asked for assistance in finding any records. It has been impossible to access any papers on McDowell at the library. There do not appear to be any records of his existence, including his contributions to state government.

—Officials from the law school at the University of Mississippi, including the dean, consistently refused to share records about his short attendance at the law school. There is no indication on campus he ever attended the school.

Some old friends and colleagues won't talk about him, or they say very little, when asked for interviews. Those who do speak, typically ask to remain anonymous.

—Charles McLaurin of Indianola, an active civil rights advocate and SNCC member who knew McDowell well, would not comment about his old friend and deferred questions to McDowell's family. Conceding that family members would not talk about McDowell either, McLaurin offered, "They think it's better to let a sleeping dog lie," before quickly ending the phone call.

—One friend of McDowell's confirmed that she often accompanied the attorney to statewide events, serving as his female companion for appearance sake — "so people wouldn't know he was gay." She would only talk to me if — of course — she did not have to give her name.

—A young man from McDowell's hometown at first told me he was "molested" by McDowell "for years" and "wish I'd shot him, myself." But the Drew native, who did not want to give his name for publication, also said that an attempt in later years to "make [McDowell] look like a pedophile" was a "set-up."

Parents of a young child in nearby Cleveland made the accusation, he said, "but no charges were ever filed." He remembered the day McDowell was murdered. FBI personnel were in Drew "by noon" after McDowell's body was discovered. "They had been watching him," he said, but added he did not know why.

—Mississippi attorney Constance Slaughter, who'd known McDowell professionally and personally over the years, told Jackson, Miss., Clarion-Ledger reporter Eric Stringfellow that "Cleve McDowell has a place in history. I thought he was a person who felt that he had paid his dues and one who knew that he made quite a few sacrifices to try to achieve equality for everybody. He stood up when it was crucial." But Slaughter refused to be interviewed for this book.

Kind remarks come from Myrlie Evers-Williams, the widow of slain Mississippi civil rights leader Medgar Evers, who told a *Clarion-Ledger* reporter that she first met McDowell when he studied at Jackson State University and was involved in the NAACP. The long-time friend was described as speechless when told of McDowell's death, Stringfellow reported.

Her strongest memories of McDowell were that "when Cleve applied to Ole Miss and the difficulties and the harassment, and how proud I think the entire community was."

"He was one of the few who would mention Medgar as a role model, and he did it during a time when others wouldn't mention Medgar — either they had forgotten or chose to forget. Whenever

Cleve would speak, he would always mention something about Medgar," she said.

THE FAMILIAR SMELL of pan-fried catfish and steamy greens soaked in lard wafts as an old friend of McDowell's talks about the man he knew for so many years.

Walter Scurlock stops preparing lunch for a moment at his restaurant on the center block of Drew's Main Street, a couple of building's away from McDowell's former law office, and chuckles about his old friend as he recounts several stories of this small town's first black city councilman and a former Masonic leader.

"He would always make sure that everyone's Masonic dues were paid every year. He would pay them himself just to see that no one lost their membership. He was a conscientious leader."

"Yeah, Cleve was a special kind of guy," Scurlock says as he sets out the deep-fried catfish, collard greens, fried okra and sweet tea.

"I sure miss Cleve — we all do."

Post #25

Mississippi Reporter Fought Racism; Jerry Mitchell, Wins MacArthur Award

Jerry Mitchell, an investigative reporter at *The Clarion-Ledger* newspaper in Jackson, Miss., who focuses on cold-case murders from the civil rights era, says he will use money received from the 2009 MacArthur Fellowship to help write a book on the subject.

Mitchell is among the 24 recipients of the $500,000 "genius awards" presented by the John D. and Catherine T. MacArthur Foundation.

"I never in all my life expected this," Mitchell, 50, told the *New York Times* in a Sept. 21, 2009, story reported by Felicia R. Lee.

I have never met Jerry Mitchell in person, but we've shared email and have spoken on the telephone when I've had a question, and it is inspiring to know him in just that small way. I think he's contributed so much, considering he's worked from the *belly of the beast*. To sit there in Jackson and report on civil right atrocities takes guts.

Sometimes I think he's a little too cautious, too conservative, but if he had been radical, he would have never lasted. He might have lost his life. It's wonderful news that he has been so honored. I just wish he would write about Birdia Keglar, Adlena Hamlett,

Sonny Boy Keglar, Cleve McDowell and some of the other less famous people who were killed.

Post #26

Burr Oak, New Overseers; Emmett Till's Grave Unharmed

SOPHIA TAREEN, Associated Press writer from Chicago, reports today (Sept. 22, 2009) the owner of a historic black cemetery in suburban Chicago, where hundreds of graves were dug up as part of an alleged plot-reselling scheme, agreed Tuesday to appoint an independent chief operating officer to oversee daily operations.

The move came after Illinois Attorney General Lisa Madigan filed a motion last week for independent oversight at Burr Oak Cemetery in Alsip, claiming incompetent and dishonest management.

Tareen broke the original story about Burr Oaks the week of July 9, 2009.

Post #27

Sick and Tired of Being Sick and Tired of Racist Remarks By Glenn Beck

Today I've had it.

I am thoroughly disgusted with what I'm seeing, hearing and reading by junk news pundit, Glenn Beck. His tirades against President Barack Obama and health care insurance, particularly the public option suggested legislation, have been going on 24/7 and they are not worth repeating.

So here's my letter to the editor. Have you written yours?

Dear Editor; As someone who has spent years researching, reading and writing about the history of African Americans in this country, I am just "sick and tired of being sick and tired" (thank you Fanny Lou Hamer) of seeing the space given to Glenn Beck and his racist dialogue. What he is doing is bad for democracy regardless of anyone's political party or beliefs.

Beck is stoking racial fear and paranoia and, in doing so, attempts to divide this country. His hateful rhetoric plays on fear and is frequently not based on facts.

Why he is given this free space through constant media efforts, I'll never understand. But what he has to say is not news and does not deserve the attention it is given. When people carry guns to public meetings, it shows what kind of an atmosphere he creates.

In my town of Mount Pleasant, Iowa, a mayor was once shot and killed by an angry person who brought a gun to a public meeting. We do not need any repeat of what took place in our town.

More than 60 major companies don't want to be associated with him, showing that he is far outside of the mainstream.

Distorted facts presented in a contemptuous rhetoric are not helping this country. I ask that people who opposed government officials use their intelligence and decency in giving their side. We owe this to our communities and to our children.

Now, if you do not know the story of Fanny Lou Hamer, the black lady from the Mississippi Delta who was "sick and tired of being sick and tired," may I suggest that you have some catching up to do with civil rights history?

It's worth a trip to the library or some time spent at the bookstore. Hamer was known as a poor sharecrop farmer from the Delta, who learned she actually had the right to vote from young college civil rights volunteers who came to her community in Freedom Summer of 1964.

She put the fear of God into Lyndon Johnson, Hubert Humphrey and the Democratic Party at the 1964 convention in Atlantic City — and Fannie Lou Hame is probably the chief reason that Johnson took a second look at voting patterns.

Please help tell FOX-TV to get rid of Beck. His racism stinks.
Susan Klopfer
Mount Pleasant, Iowa 52641

Post #28

Final Post: The Beginning or the End?

> "There are two lasting bequests we can give our children. One is roots. The other is wings."
>
> William Hodding Carter, Jr., Mississippi journalist and winner of a Pulitzer Prize for civil rights reporting

> "Have you ever sent a loved son on vacation and had him returned to you in a pine box, so horribly battered and water-logged that someone needs to tell you this sickening sight is your son — lynched?"
>
> Mamie Till Mobley, mother of Emmett Till

In midsummer 2009, a 40-second video clip circulated on the Internet of an Iranian girl, a philosophy student named Neda Soltani who was allegedly shot dead by a Basij soldier.

On her way to a music lesson when struck down, Soltani's violent death came as Iran faced demonstrations in the magnitude not seen since the 1979 Iranian Revolution.

Throughout the world, people watched the scene of this 16-year-old girl, with a single bullet wound in her chest, lying on her back as her family tragically unsuccessfully tried to save her. Blood was leaving her chest, and later flowing from her mouth and nose as her face was eventually left covered in red. In a few moments, Neda was pronounced dead.

Another story of a teenage girl, very much like this tragedy, happened across the planet back in 1971 at the end of the school term when Jo Etha Collier was shot to death in the streets of Drew, Mississippi as her friends looked on.

Collier, 18, was celebrating her high school graduation. Drinking soda pop with friends out in front of a small grocery store, her life ended. Like Neda, she had only been an observer of recent protests and clashes going on all around her as the modern civil rights movement progressed — or tried to.

Neda is the Farsi word for voice. Jo in Hebrew translates to He will enlarge and Etha, a variation of the Old English name Ethel, means noble.

In the end, these two martyrs were cut down before they had an opportunity to give voice to their dreams, to enlarge the opportunities open to them and confer nobility to their culture.

Yet in these stories of young and old murder victims, if one listens quietly, it is possible to hear their voices and the songs of others like them from the rivers, bayous and terrain of the Delta as they whisper their freedom songs.

Yes, the river in Minter City sings and so do the bayous and bogues throughout all of Mississippi. To hear the sorrow as it flows through time, just listen.

Simply listen.

BY THE END of the 1960s and into the early 1970s, well over a dozen years after Brown I and Brown II and the murders of Rev. George Lee, Lamar Smith and then Emmett Till and others, violence was once again accelerating in Mississippi. More black people were being killed or turning up "missing" than there had been in recent years.

Attempts increased to destroy individuals and organizations bent on stopping this violence. The Black Panther Party and lesser-known volunteer groups, sometimes church run, worked to help Mississippi's blacks either change their conditions or flee the state.

Both the Panthers and the Box Project, the later aiding sharecroppers to physically escape plantations, were perceived much like Chicago's ACORN in 2009 — their efforts at community organization and related activities often misunderstood or misrepresented.

Fear of events outside of the South such as the Watt's burning in 1965 translated into attempts to halt expansion plans by the Panthers, who in 1969 were quietly trying to organize college students at Delta State University in Cleveland, 17 miles southwest of Drew.

After moving out of the South following Freedom Summer of 1964, some movement veterans were now returning home from the major cities like Detroit, Los Angeles and other boiling pots. Isaac Henderson Shorter of Cleveland returned home from Detroit where he had led demonstrations, hoping as a Delta State student to galvanize students through the Black Panther organization. The Sovereignty Commission was spying on Shorter and others who had, by an agent's report, "returned from Berkeley with a stack of Black Panther newspapers." For an agency two years away from winding down, the returning community organizers breathed new life into the Sovereignty Commission's investigations. State archives show 25 files on Shorter, alone.

In Greenville, as the city's well-known journalist Hodding Carter, Jr. was coming to the end of his career, another murder of a black child took place; a child even younger than Neda Soltani, Jo Etha Collier or Emmett Till — a child who was simply surrounded by violence and could do nothing about it.

Flora Jean Smith

Thirteen year-old Flora Jean Smith was sexually assaulted and murdered on July 19, 1969. Smith was reported missing after she failed to return from a babysitting job and soon after her body found in a nearby lake.

A Sovereignty Commission report dated August 1 stated that "Sidney E. Taylor W/M, 36 years of age, of Greenville, a house painter" was charged with her kidnapping and murder. Ninety persons marched in memory of the young girl and Taylor would serve a short prison sentence before disappearing from Greenville altogether.

Still, few people outside of Mississippi's more rural battle zones knew what was happening in the state's smaller towns when problems occurred, especially in places like Drew, Ruleville, Greenville and Charleston, since news reports were few and sporadic.

Some news of violence and murders made it into the mainstream media while other skirmishes — from mild to death-producing, such as the murder of Flora Smith — simply came and went with little recognition.

Phillip Gibbs, James Earl Green

Even violence in the state capitol, at Jackson State University, sailed through history with little comment. During a two-day student protest starting on May 14, 1970, 20-year-old Phillip Gibbs, a junior, and James Earl Green, a Jackson bystander, were slain and several others wounded when police fired a barrage of gunfire on a dormitory and a dining hall. Upon hearing false rumors that slain leader Medgar Evers' brother, Charles Evers, had been killed along with his wife, students had gathered on Lynch Street and began rioting.

These Jackson killings are often forgotten in the shadow of Kent State, which took place ten days earlier. Local media coverage was limited and racist, as usual. The university newspaper would not report the incident until a special edition was issued one year later. The Grand Jury refused to indict any of the officers involved in the shootings and in 1974, a US Court of Appeals ruled that the officers could not be held liable for the two deaths despite concluding they had overreacted. In 1982, all but two U.S. Supreme Court Justices refused to hear the case.

Young Students Rebel

In some rural communities, high school students were becoming more involved in civil rights clashes, as the movement began to regroup in Mississippi.

On October 20, 1970, over 125 black high school students were arrested in Charleston and taken to the prison at Parchman Penitentiary, some 33 miles southwest of their school. Two were jailed in Sumner.

The students had been marching and picketing "under the direction of the county's NAACP director, Lucy Boyd...also a congressional candidate," Sovereignty Commission director W. B. Burke learned from his investigator, James Mohead.

On Friday, high school students began walking around the school singing freedom songs and chanting. Warned of possible arrest, they kept up the same activities, starting out fresh that Monday morning when they were once again warned they could be arrested. Mohead and Boyce differ on what happened next. "Those under 18 years of age were returned to Charleston after records were made of names, ages, etc. and they were never [taken] beyond the records office." The students were returned to churches in Charleston where they were released to their parents, Mohead told his boss.

Years later, when Boyd finally saw Mohead's report in old Sovereignty Commission files first released in 1997, she said the investigator lied. "The children — all of them — spent the night at

Parchman Penitentiary in cells. The Sovereignty Commission was always twisting their facts around and this is just one example."[127]

Mohead claimed he "took the offense," and contacted Clarksdale civil rights leader Aaron Henry about the incident "after hearing a rumor that Henry had been in Charleston."

Boyd said she had been talking with Henry by telephone throughout the day. The pharmacist who resided and worked in Clarksdale, about 40 miles northwest of Charleston, stayed close to his business phone as Boyd's calls came in, she said. Mohead's report insisted that Henry was the instigator of Charleston's student action, having picked up the idea from "the Coffeeville action."

Coffeeville's African American students were being bussed to their school — the town is about 50 miles to the East of Charleston, outside of the Delta — for part of a day, and then to another school, under court order, and they were trying to get back into court "in an effort to bring a change in the procedure," according to Mohead.

Charleston school children showed great bravery after being locked up all night in Mississippi's most notorious prison, Boyd said. But they had a strategy — and it worked. Their loud screaming resulted in prison officials getting sick and tired of the noise and sending them home, confirmed Robert Keglar, a former Charleston schoolteacher.

Birdia Keglar, Adlena Hamlett and James "Sunny Boy" Keglar: So, Who Makes the Cold Case "Rules?"

Civil rights cold cases are heating up since the FBI announced in November of 2009 that agents were seeking to interview next of kin of people who might have been victims of hate-crime based attacks. But before the FBI will take action on a cold case, a victim's name has to get on the cold case list, and this concerns Nina Zachary-Black, the granddaughter of Adlena Hamlett, a voting rights activist who was killed in the late afternoon hours of Jan. 12, 1966, at the age of 78. Hamlett was a school teacher.[128]

So far, no one from the FBI has knocked on Zachary-Black's door to ask about her grandmother. Responding to the FBI's nation-wide request for next of kin to call the agency with information, Zachary-Black contacted the FBI in December of 2009, but the answer from an agent of the Minneapolis FBI office was stunning:

"Minneapolis has decided not to pass on this information to the FBI in Mississippi. We would need a police report in order to prove that it was civil rights connected," the agent reportedly said.

Zachery-Black wanted to know who made this decision not to investigate or pass on the information to Mississippi and asked for their name, to no avail. "The agent told me that the FBI does not have jurisdiction over murder cases unless they happened on federal land," Zachery-Black said. "And they would not give me the names of the agents who made this decision. They would not let me talk to anyone else."

"I said this is a cold case — what could be colder than this?"

The FBI agent was "particularly irritating" to Hamlett's granddaughter when she questioned why her family "waited so long" to report the death. "I told her we wrote to the Justice Department early on and never got a reply."

Zachary-Black, a Minneapolis school teacher, also wants to know why a police report from Mississippi would be required. "That doesn't make sense," she said. "Some of the police officers back then were known to be Klansmen back they. My relatives would have been killed if they had tried to call the police and ask for help."[129]

So much for the cold cases.

Murder came in waves and hit all ages as the intensity of civil rights activities grew in the mid and late 1960s. Not only were children being killed and bullied, but elder activists like Keglar and Hamlett were harassed, too.

Both women were killed in the early evening hours of Jan. 12, 1966, outside of Greenwood in a suspicious car wreck. Birdia

Beatrice Clark Keglar, 58, a voting rights activist, was involved with forming a local NAACP chapter in Tallahatchie County. Keglar was the first black person to vote in Tallahatchie County since the end of Reconstruction.

Their car was reportedly forced off the road in Sidon, a small town near Greenwood in Leflore County, as they returned from a civil rights meeting in Jackson, said Robert Keglar, who was first told about his mother's death by a close friend who claimed to have witnessed the accident. This was not the first time they had been chased, one of the driver's relatives said. A friend of Robert Keglar confirms earlier car chases, too.

Keglar said the local district attorney visited his Charleston home that night to tell him of the accident. The prosecutor said a drunk driver had hit their car, forcing it from the road and killing both women. The prosecutor also warned Keglar to stay home and not go to the accident scene. But, despite this warning, Keglar immediately went to the site, a small town known quite well for Klan activities.

Keglar said he was interviewed several times in 2009 by the FBI. He said agents told him the case was closed and that his mother died from injuries received in an auto accident. They had no answers to offer regarding the death of his brother, James "Sonny Boy" Keglar, who died three months later.

Interviewed by me on January 4, 2010, Robert Keglar said he doesn't believe the FBI has any further interest in his mother's death. "I am not satisfied with what the FBI told me about my mother's death. I believe that she and my brother were victims of a crime. None of our relatives believe what the FBI told us," Keglar stated.

Three months after his mother died in the wreck, Birdia Keglar's youngest son, James or "Sonny Boy" died in a mysterious fire when his home burned down. Reportedly, he was three months into a personal investigation of his mother's death and, according to Robert Keglar, FBI representatives still claim there are no files on James Keglar.

Relatives of both Keglar and Hamlett believe there was definite evidence of foul play. Both women had been subjected to bullying and harassment because of their civil rights activities. Hamlett was hanged in effigy months earlier, records show

Zachary-Black believes the murder of her grandmother, Adlena Hamlett, could have been prompted by her own father's well-known hatred of the late U.S. Senator James O. Eastland and her father's political activism, as well.

"When he [James Black, a school principal] heard about Adlena's murder, my father wept and said that Eastland had finally gotten to him by murdering Adlena. My father often collided with the senator, who was a noted racist."

"My father tried really hard to get someone to go to the site. By the time my grandfather, Berry Hamlett, got to the scene, everything was cleaned up. It had been washed away. They used hoses and he said there was nothing left to see."

Despite possible motives and details of the actual incident, Hamlett's granddaughter knows what she saw at the funeral home.

Zachary-Black and her brother, James Black, Jr., examined her grandmother Adlena's body at the funeral home and it was apparent that body parts had been severed, indicating possible Ku Klux Klan involvement, she said during interviews in 2005 and again in 2009. Coincidentally, at the time of the accident, according to later FBI reports, some highway patrolmen in that particular region were also known Klan members.

Zachary-Black said that funeral home personnel told her and her brother it would be better for the caskets to stay closed: "My brother said 'no, it would be open,' and so they said they would let my brother see the casket. I came up behind when he was examining the body and I saw that her head was too small for her body. I saw my brother lift her head and it seemed to be that her head was detached from her body. "He said to me, 'We're not going to say anything about this.' "

"I just listened to him. There wasn't anything we could do. My mother, Jimmie Louise, never looked at the body. But her daughter, my aunt who lived in Kansas City, Julia, looked at the body when the funeral home director wheeled it by her and she started screaming and saying, 'That's not my mother.' She knew that something was very wrong with her body."

Lila Hamlett, Adlena's youngest daughter, also saw her mother's body at the funeral home, Zachary-Black said. "She told me there were gloves lying across Adlena's body but there were no hands in the gloves."

Zachary-Black said she wants the FBI to take a better look at the death of her grandmother and Keglar. "I have wanted this to be investigated since she died. I've been recently thinking about it and have hoped something will happen while I'm still living." Zackary-Black turned 75 on Nov. 15, 2009.

But will the FBI listen? Or has this cold case — that was never put on the list in the first place — already been closed, due to a conflicting report by a white passenger in the car?

Richard "Dick" Simpson, a survivor of the crash, gives a different view of what happened, and asserts both women were killed on impact, even though he admits he was sleeping in the back seat at the time of impact. Simpson, after being tracked down for an interview by the FBI in the fall of 2009, said he believed the crash was an accident.[130]

As a 27-year-old civil rights SNCC volunteer from Massachusetts, stationed in Belzoni, he was traveling with the two women and two other black men home from a Jackson meeting.

Simpson, the only white person in the car, said he was fighting to survive as he crawled from the back seat of the car through the back window, that he was sleeping when the crash occurred and did not see what happened. But when he woke up, he said, "They looked dead to me." From that point forward, Simpson was not able to recall further events until he found himself in the hospital.

Simpson, who I also interviewed in the fall of 2009, said he is sympathetic to their deaths but said his memories of the crash are "still vivid," even though the accident took place 43 years ago. I asked him if he was aware that trauma victims sometimes report false memories (often using the term "vivid") and he said 'no.'

Apparently the FBI has chosen not to investigate the accident any further, using Simpson's report, without ever interviewing Zachary-Black or any of her surviving relatives. Even though Simpson admits to being asleep in the back seat when the crash occurred, the FBI counts him as an eye witness to the accident.

Zachary-Black says she is "more than disappointed if this is the case." "I have a friend whose husband is a psychologist. He told me that it is not unusual for people suffering this some type of trauma to believe they can remember an incident vividly. Important details may be wrong or missing and some things that seem vivid may not, in fact, have happened at all.

"I know what I saw at the funeral home and want my grandmother's body exhumed, too, just like Emmett Till's. I want to talk to the FBI. I don't think this case should end with Simpson's questionable memories."

Grafton Gray, Birdia Keglar's cousin who was the driver, was also injured seriously and taken to the Mound Bayou hospital, said Gwen Dailey, Grafton Gray's great-niece. She states she is also displeased with the FBI's lack of interest.

Gray suffered emotionally afterwards and "was never the same," she said. Dailey could tell that her father was suspicious of what happened to his brother and to the others who were injured or killed: "My great-uncle was already a quiet man. He received under-handed threats while in the hospital to keep quiet about what happened, my father learned.

"Employees and visitors would come into his room and tell him to 'be careful,' but not in a caring way. When he came home, the threats continued. "He would go out into the fields by his house and stand, gazing away. He rarely talked. Even my own father became far more cautious with his own children, and he watched Uncle Grafton like a hawk. Mr. Brewer, another passenger, was injured too, and he was never the same. His reaction was the same as my great-uncle."

Margaret Block, an old friend of Birdia Keglar's, said she was told years later by journalist Plater Robinson of New Orleans, who often wrote for the *Times Picyune*, that "the undertaker who picked up the bodies said it was not an accident but a murder. The undertaker was from Greenwood and Plater recorded the interview." Robinson, apparently traveling in 2010, could not be contacted for details in time to meet this book's publication date.

BOTH KEGLAR AND Hamlett were long-time civil rights activists and met with U.S. Senator Robert F. Kennedy sometime during 1965, say family and friends. Both women testified in hearings before the U.S. Commission On Civil Rights taking place in Jackson, Miss. in February of that year, telling of the years of harassment they'd been through for their involvement in voting rights. At one meeting, the senator warned his audience that both women had better return home safely, Robert Keglar said. Family and friends are unsure of the place and date of that meeting, but remember hearing from the two women about RFK's remarks.

John D. Sullivan

Coincidentally, another Mississippian dying that same month in 1966 was a white detective from Vicksburg, John Daniel Sullivan, a former FBI agent and frequent Sovereignty Commission consultant on segregation enforcement cases. The facts surrounding Sullivan's death are also hazy. Sullivan reportedly died from a self-inflicted gunshot wound following a hunting accident — shooting himself in the groin and then bleeding to death, his relatives state.

Sullivan had been working under contract for Guy Banister of New Orleans, a former FBI agent who in 1963 began working for Mafia criminal defense lawyer G. Wray Gill, also a Mississippian, and Gill's client, Carlos Marcello, the New Orleans-based Godfather of the American Mafia Family whose operations were centered in Louisiana, Mississippi, Alabama, and Texas. Sullivan knew Banister from the Chicago FBI office where they once worked together.

Banister's known involvement with Marcello centered on attempts to block Marcello's deportation, ordered by Robert F. Kennedy. Did Sullivan know too much? One family member says that two weeks before Sullivan died, he told one of his sons that he had run into information "so far over his head that he did not know where to go." In 1979, the House assassinations committee concluded that at least two shooters were involved in the John F. Kennedy assassination, and that a list of most likely conspirators included Marcello. Banister has also been implicated in the JFK assassination.

Maybe Sullivan ran into something bigger than the Delta's kudzu could hide.

Jo Etha Collier

Collier, the Drew High School senior murdered at graduation, was officially killed by Wesley Parks, 25, of Drew. It was a murder that "seemed to have no motive," said a sheriff's deputy.

Parks, his brother and their nephew, Allen Wilkerson, 19, of Memphis were in the truck and all three were arrested in nearby Cleveland within three hours of the shooting. A 22-caliber pistol "with one bullet missing" was found in the car along with a 12-gauge Army issue riot gun and a 22-caliber automatic rifle, according to Sovereignty Commission reports. No police department or state agency has been able to produce copies of the autopsy report.

Others in Drew's black community disagreed with the sheriff's assessment at the time, including civil rights leader Fannie Lou Hamer of nearby Ruleville, who at the time said she was "convinced that Collier's death was connected with the current voter registration campaign."

Collier was not active with the campaign going on at the time, but visiting reporters at Collier's funeral were reminded that black political activity in the Delta — where blacks outnumber whites — had "long met with a proportionate increase in white harassment."

FBI agents went to Drew and studied the crime, according to Sovereignty Commission reports. But all FBI records on the death of Collier, requested by this author in April 2004, were reported by the FBI as "destroyed on March 16, 2004." No reason was given.

Police Chief J. D. Fleming of Drew told news reporters the three men involved "were very much under the influence of alcohol." Fleming said he took Collier's two companions to Cleveland to identify the suspect. The three men offered no resistance when arrested in Cleveland, Fleming said.

About 45 minutes before the shooting, the men were seen sitting in their truck at a service station located less than a block away from the grocery store. When a black male asked for a light, "one of the occupants of the vehicle reportedly pointed a revolver at the negro male and told him, 'I'll put all your G.D. lights out,' " the investigator's report stated.

Collier was reportedly killed by a single bullet, which hit her in the neck as she stood in front of a grocery store "in the negro section of town." At her funeral, Rev. Ralph David Abernathy, chair of the Southern Christian Leadership Conference, eulogized Collier before an audience of 2,000.

"The foes of evil have robbed us of one of our most dear and talented sisters…How long will black people be mistreated in Mississippi? How long will black people be shot down in the Delta?" the SCLC leader asked those gathered in the auditorium of Drew High School. Abernathy called for massive change that would come with black voter registrations to put blacks in office "…so that we can see that her living and dying was not in vain."

Drew's Mayor W. O. Williford, seated on the main stage during the rites, told a reporter he was surprised at the large turnout of blacks, and spoke of recent gains by Delta blacks: "If that many Negroes had gathered in one place when I first took office there surely would have been bloodshed."

The atmosphere was peaceful enough that Williford quickly sent away the highway patrolmen who were there in case of an anticipated flare up. Days earlier, the mayor imposed an 8 p.m. until daylight curfew and called in the officers to help enforce it. After the ceremony, Collier, regarded highly by teachers and friends, was buried in the all-black section of Drew's community cemetery.

Another version of the Jo Etha Collier story that still lingers in this small town with a unique history of African American murders, suggests that some students reported a teacher was riding in the car. This person was reportedly harassed so much by students in the years following Collier's murder that he finally left to teach in a private, segregated academy.

Cleve McDowell, practicing law in Jackson, returned to Drew to help keep his hometown calm. Concerned about the community and the safety of its children, he decided to make this move permanent. Meeting with the mayor before Collier's very public funeral, McDowell was required to pledge that no outsiders — "especially Fannie Lou Hamer" — would come into Drew and cause problems during several planned marches. Hamer was well known for her state and national activism and never met a politician that scared her away from stating her demands, President Lyndon B. Johnson and Hubert Humphrey, included.

Collier's family was extremely poor and McDowell paid all funeral costs expenses. Working hard to maintain calm, he requested and was granted a permit for mourners to hold peaceful daily marches in the downtown section of Drew and at the same time, the attorney was careful to praise the "swift police work" in apprehending the three men. "Now there must be vigorous prosecution. Responsible people are angry at this senseless murder," he told a visiting newspaper reporter.

Once back in Drew for good, McDowell ran for city council, becoming Drew's first black assistant mayor. A Sovereignty report filed September 16, 1971, noted, "Chief of Police Fleming…advised that Cleve McDowell, N/M, formerly of Drew, now of Jackson, is spending a lot of time in the Drew, Ruleville area. These visits are believed to be political, in nature."

McDowell eased back into his birthplace and by the following year was named to the state Penitentiary Board in July by Governor Bill Waller and was reappointed for a five-year-term in 1972. He was the first black to hold this position, until then reserved for whites. At the end of his term, McDowell told Ron Harris of the Associated Press he hoped his appointment helped pave the way for other African Americans, and that he had "pushed hard" to get the appointment because he felt blacks needed to become involved at the decision making level.

"Three Killings in a Week"

Prompted by the murders of Collier and others, Aaron Henry telegraphed President Richard Nixon to protest the "wave of senseless killing in Mississippi of black citizens by white citizens." Henry said it was the "third such killing in less than a week."

"There was no provocation and no words were passed. It's doubtful that they knew Miss Collier," Henry told a UPI reporter. "They apparently were out to kill a black, any black."

All three men were initially charged with murder but only Wesley Parks was tried. Charges were dropped against the other two men. Parks was sent to prison for five years, but served less than three years of his sentence and then, like Flora Jean Smith's killer, he dropped out of sight.

This blatant inaction prompted Henry to question George Everett, district attorney for the three-county region. There were potential dangers from Everett's decision to drop charges, Henry warned in a letter to the prosecutor:[131]

"Your statement today...really pulls the rug from under those of us in the NAACP who worked so hard to prevent violent retaliation against whites by determined members of the black community. Particularly you have seriously undercut the good will efforts of Mrs. Fannie Lou Hamer and attorney Cleve McDowell.

"There are not as many of us in the Black Community as there once were who took a forthright position condemning violence, for whatever the cause. Now there are many Blacks anxious to engage in the "eye for an eye," "tooth for a tooth," type of violence. Putting it another way, "white man for black man" retaliation. When announcements come out such as you issued today, they only give reason for those prone toward violence to exercise it.

"Those who once had the confidence of the community, on the sides of non-violence, are losing the confidence of the Black citizens of our communities, especially when we were the ones to caution and advise the masses to have confidence in the law or the legal system.

"You see, if a jury acquits a man who is tried, and in this case a white man for the murder of a Black citizen, then at least there has been some attempt to secure justice. But when the District Attorney pronounces that those charged will not be brought to trial, then we are almost back to where we were in the "Dred Scott" U.S. Supreme Court decision of a hundred years ago, that established that a Black had no rights that whites were bound to respect.

"Of course this also meant the privilege of a white to take the life of a black with no fear of ever coming to trial, just as your announcement today. Once the pent up violence that exists in many members of the Black Community begins to explode, then the cry of the white community is going to be a call for "peace." …You can help us in our position, or render us useless, and those prone toward violence will be in the position of advising our people what steps to take next…. Think it over!"

Henry's quote was taken from a letter signed by Henry and received into state archives in 2003 for "processing." As of August 2009, this letter and all other Tougaloo College records of Aaron Henry, including the telegraph to President Nixon that were presented to the William F. Winters Archives, were "not available" for viewing. The letter was found buried in papers held by the college archives before the school donated Henry's paper to the state institution. It will be interesting to see if the letter ever makes it to the "processed" bin.

One older Drew resident, of course asking to remain anonymous, said that random shootings frequently took place in the community for years, and sometimes still do."This was happening everywhere in the Delta, and no one would do anything about it. Whites rode around on our side of town and shot at black people. There was no reason for it, except they were usually drinking." While traveling around the Delta, I heard the same stories of random shootings from elderly blacks in Belzoni, Goat Hill and Charleston.

Eddie McClinton and Edgar Higginbottom

In neighboring Tallahatchie County, a murder took place two days before Collier was killed, according to Henry's records. On May 23, 1971, military veteran Eddie McClinton was allegedly killed by a white "night marshal" in Sumner in a fight at a pop machine. Sovereignty Commission investigator Mohead learned from county deputy sheriff Downs, doubling as the town marshal, that McClinton was shot three times and killed by a white man outside of Sumner.

Mohead reported that McClinton was observed by Sumner Night Marshal Tom Trannam "kicking and beating on a change machine" at a self-service gas station. When Trannam intervened, McClinton threatened to kill him, Downs told Mohead.

"McClinton started for Trannam, in a threatening manner, Trannam fired one shot to the right of McClinton attempting to stop him. McClinton continued to advance and told Trannam, 'If you don't kill me, you white S.O.B., I'm going to kill you.' At this time, Trannam shot McClinton once in the arm and once in the chest with a 45 cal. pistol," Mohead's report stated. No hearing or coroner's inquest was held, and Downs said he would get back to Mohead after he conferred with Trannam "and the two negro witnesses."

During the week of November 1, 1971 Sovereignty Commission investigator Fulton Tutor reported from Pontotoc, west of Tupelo, where the grand jury reported out "without returning an indictment against Jake Denton, W/M, who shot 'the Negro' a few months ago in Ecru. There is a possibility of some reaction from the black community over this."

Tutor did not name the victim Edger Higginbottom in his report. Also during the week, Tutor "did some checking on white voters to see if all were out to vote." In Holly Springs, Tutor learned from Mayor Coopwood that "for the first time the whites all worked together in this election and this really paid off, as the blacks only won the Justice of the Peace post."

Sid Harrison

As state NAACP president, Henry often received letters like one dated December 21, 1972 from a resident of Jonesboro, Arkansas regarding her missing brother, Sid Harrison of Holcomb in Carroll County.

In late October 1972, Harrison disappeared from his family without a trace of him or his automobile. "Since several of Mr. Harrison's relatives believe that he has been murdered in the manner of the three civil rights workers of 1964 near Philadelphia… along with his relatives appreciate…your immediate cooperation."

Like so many other Mississippi endless stories, this man's disappearance appears to have faded into history. No other related letters or reports about Harrison could be found in Henry's archival papers at Tougaloo.

In April of 1972, Mississippi lost its most famous journalists to natural death after a series of health problems, Hodding Carter Jr., the courageous editor of the Greenville *Delta Democrat-Times*, Mississippi's most liberal newspaper during the Civil Rights era, died at 65 of a heart attack during a workout at an athletic club in Greenville.

"He knew his enemies' virtues and would recite them, and his favorite retort to the righteously angry was, 'Yes, but …'

He told great stories, full of villains and heroes and morals, stories for passing on. We will remember," wrote his son, Philip Carter, in an editorial for his father's newspaper. Hodding Carter II was serving as the newspaper's publisher but the family quickly sold the publication.

Daisy Savage and Grandson

In May of 1973, Mrs. Daisy Savage and her 11-year-old grandson of Hollandale were murdered, probably by Klansmen, believes Charles Sudduth, a Deltan who researches and writes about the Mississippi Klan. Sudduth says that Savage had provided room for the two white civil rights workers assigned to the small town near Belzoni in 1964.

"What I heard was that a city official and a party of 4 to 20 Klansmen stoned them to death. I also heard that at least one black person witnessed her killing and that person is said to still be alive. That was also confirmed to me by a black civil rights attorney who was originally from Hollandale, Jesse Pennington."

The killing may have taken place in south Washington County, near or around the Yazoo Wildlife Refuge. "If it in fact this is true, then Federal authorities have jurisdiction in the matter…On the other hand, I also heard the murders took place right at the county line between Issaquena and Washington County, so this might indicate a still unresolved question of jurisdiction."[132]

Lillie Mae Bumpers

I found this undated, anonymous message appearing on a Clarksdale Internet discussion group, ClarksdaleWebinfo.com:

"I lived in Clarksdale from 1971 to 1989 and am searching to find archived obituaries or newspaper articles on deceased family members. My mother, Dorothy Sykes was murdered on May 5, 1977 and her body was found in a ditch just outside of the Clarksdale area. She had seven bullet wounds to the head. I do recall that there was a typo in the spelling of my mother's last name in the obituary. Her address was 324 Bolivar Street.

"Also, my aunt, Lillie Mae Bumpers, was killed and her body was found in Moon Lake around June to September 1982. Rescue workers were searching for the body of a couple that were suspected to have drowned in a fishing boat and they discovered her body during the search. The funeral home that handled my mother's body was Delta Burial Funeral Home and I think that Smith Funeral Home handled my aunt's body. "I ...would be more than happy to come and pick up any material that you may be able to provide for me. If there is a cost for obtaining this information, please let me know as well. Thank you for your time."

Civil rights leader Aaron Henry never gave up trying to stop the bloodshed. Records show he met with Governor Cliff Finch and his Director of Minority Affairs, R. L. Bolden on September 16, 1976, to "acquaint and remind them of the upsurge in racism that is pervading Mississippi, with its most pronounced manifestation being in the area of police brutality."

James Calhoun

The two most recent worst acts of this kind, according to Aaron Henry were the "apparent lynching" by Klansmen of sixteen-year-old James Calhoun in the Bolivar-Sunflower area[133] and the killing of a young black by a highway patrolman in Sturgis, Mississippi.

The Sovereignty Commission was not above harassing Henry and there would be payback for these and other complaints made to officials outside of the state. According to papers turned over to the Winters Archives by Tougaloo College [but not available for reviewing as of Aug. 2009], the day after meeting with the two Mississippi officials, Henry spent the following day in Oxford and then attended a meeting on the Gulf Coast with Georgia Governor Jimmy Carter.

Saturday was filled with Democratic Party Administrative Committee meetings in Jackson and with leaders of the Mississippi Carter-Mondale campaign, Head Start meetings, and dinner with friends, running until 10 p.m. that evening. Henry returned to his hotel room but was awakened shortly after midnight with a call "informing me that a black youth was being beaten by the police in the park across from Central High School" a few blocks from the hotel. Deciding to observe the action, he dressed and walked around to the park where he saw two young men sitting on a park bench at the park's entry. The NAACP director asked if they had seen a black youth being beaten by the police and both replied they had not. Henry took their names — David Bronstein and Isom Herron — and then saw a man approaching him with handcuffs in one hand and a portable radio in the other.

Henry asked the officer about the beating of a young black man and was told that he was "sticking my nose into too much in police business." Upon the officer's suggestion, they both headed back to the hotel "to talk" but the officer became "suddenly angry" and asserted Henry was interfering with the legal activity of a police officer.

Henry was placed under arrest, while reminding the officer that he had "... been in jails before, larger than the ones in Jackson." Henry was taken to the station and charged with disorderly conduct with a bond set at $500. A court appearance was set for the following Monday. This was a resurgence of racism, Henry later wrote:

"We are in the process now of formulating plans to challenge this resurgence of racism. Some personalities in Mississippi still feel that the repressive tactics of the 1960s will still work. Although the Sovereignty Commission no longer legally exists, its tactics are forever before us. The judgments against the NAACP by two recent Mississippi judges, the attacks upon black and white personalities in this rebirth of vicious Dirty Tricks will live for a while, but in a short time they too will pass away. Although there are some Mississippians unhappy about the progress of the Black and White Community away from racism, the reality of the uniting of the Democratic Party with blacks and whites equally involved, is more progress than some, perhaps many, would like to see. Nevertheless, it is for real."

Fannie Lou Hamer

On March 14, 1977, Fannie Lou Hamer died penniless in Mound Bayou. Friends made the arrangements for her funeral and raised the funds to pay for it. Her last years were spent at home in Ruleville, where she raised thousands of dollars to feed displaced farm laborers through her Freedom Farm Cooperative and pig bank.

Mrs. Hamer also raised funds for housing and for the day care center that was named for her. She continued as an activist, speaking against the Vietnam War and abuses in the state's poverty and Medicaid programs.

In her final years, Hamer was in pain as she suffered from breast cancer, heart disease, and diabetes. A friend and fellow civil rights activist said she had never totally recovered from the beating she received by a policeman in Winona. "Everyone said she died of diabetes and cancer, but she died from those beatings," Margaret Block said.

At the service, Julian Bond, Stokely Carmichael, Aaron Henry, and Hodding Carter II spoke of her contributions and Andrew Young, the principal speaker, praised Mrs. Hamer as "a woman who literally helped turn this nation around."

Sam Block

Margaret Block's brother, Samuel Block, a pioneer civil rights leader in the modern civil rights movement and early SNCC field secretary who fought for voting rights in the Delta and elsewhere, did not escape the chaos once he left Mississippi.

After moving to California, where he remained a political activist, Block ended up serving time in federal prison at Maxwell Air Force Base in Alabama, his sister said. "Sam had been set up for an embezzlement charge and for running guns to the Contras. My brother was very bright, but not stupid. And he would never have committed such crimes."

Block was in prison for five years until "he finally got out on parole and appeals." His alleged crime took place in California, but the trial ended up in federal court in Oxford, Mississippi, Margaret Block said. "I've never figured out why this happened and I'll never forget at sentencing when the judge told him, 'We finally got your smart ass now. I've waited a long time.'"

The Mississippi Delta civil rights pioneer died on April 13, 2000, in his Los Angeles apartment at the age of 60. "There was never an inquest; no coroner pronounced him dead, and I still have questions," Margaret Block said. "He had not been ill. I do know that someone removed the hard drive to his computer and took his papers. That apparently happened during his funeral."

Block's sister said that she learned from her brother's daughter that the coroner was never called to pronounce her brother dead and that his death certificate was not signed until two weeks later, after an autopsy was performed. "The police and medics called the funeral home and took him there directly. This held up the funeral service for two weeks because the coroner finally was able to do an autopsy. The results were termed inconclusive because his body had been embalmed."

Sam Block was scheduled to keynote a civil rights conference celebrating the 40th anniversary of SNCC at Shaw University in North Carolina. "He did not show up and people began to worry. I don't know exactly what happened next but that his daughter was called. She went to his apartment and found him dead."

Sam Block was an early target, as one of the first early voting rights advocates from Mississippi allowed to move into a SNCC leadership role while the organization picked up speed. In the 1960s, Block served as point man for voter registration effort in Greenwood a key battleground, and headquarters of the white Citizens Councils. In his first six months working Greenwood, the violent response of Council members and others made the job nearly impossible. *Look* magazine reported in 1963 that Block had signed up only five black voters.

James Travis of Greenwood, who was shot in the head and neck as he drove a car with several SNCC colleagues in 1963 — and survived — once called his old friend Block "very smart" and "fearless." Travis died of pancreatic cancer in 2009.

Who Killed Emmett Till?

The Mississippi Delta keeps its own history files. And in the file drawers are the stories of people like Fannie Lou Hamer, Aaron Henry, Amzie Moore, Cleve McDowell, Sam Block and so many others. Learning more about these people means looking through boxes of old newspapers held by libraries, reading some of the few books that have been written about them, and talking to people still living who were around during the 1950s and 1960s. These people and their stories are the stuff of Mississippi's state history and are of critical importance to understanding the history of this country.

All stories are important, but one stands out: In the early morning hours August 28, 1955 two or possibly three white men from the Mississippi Delta kidnapped and killed a 14-year-old black kid who was visiting his mother's relatives in Money.

Emmett Till, born in Chicago's Cook County Hospital in 1941 to Louis and Mamie Till, he should never have been allowed to visit relative in Mississippi. The state was a powder keg after the Supreme Court's Brown v Board of Education ruling; voting rights and school integration were coming to a head.

On May 17, 1954 the US Supreme Court had ordered public schools desegregated and the watershed case overturned the separate-but-equal doctrine. The Warren Court's unanimous (9–0) decision stated that "separate educational facilities are inherently unequal" and paved the way for integration and the modern civil rights movement.

The watershed case overturned the separate-but-equal doctrine, which dated back to the 1896 decision in Plessy versus Ferguson and Southern segregationists vowed to oppose this ruling, labeling the day of issuance as Black Monday. A white supremacist organization, "Citizens Councils," was quickly formed, with its first meeting taking place in the Sunflower County seat of Indianola.

Brown II, issued one year later, on May 31, 1955 decreed that the dismantling of separate school systems for blacks and whites could proceed with "all deliberate speed."

In early May of 1955, just three weeks before Brown II and almost four months before Emmett Louis "Bobo" Till was killed, Reverend George Lee, a grocery owner and NAACP field worker in Belzoni was shot and killed at point blank range while driving in his car after voting. A few weeks later in Brookhaven, Lamar Smith, another black man, was shot and killed in front of the county courthouse, in broad daylight and in front of witnesses, after casting his vote. Both men had been active in voter registration drives and no one was ever arrested in connection with either murder.

Till was just a kid, a black kid from Chicago who had limited ideas about racial politics or an old man called Jim Crow with unspoken rules that varied town by town. Till's mother had given her son some warning, based on her own experiences living in Mississippi as a young girl but her stern talk didn't sink in.

When she learned her son was dead, Mrs. Till Mobley and the NAACP decided the whole world should know what happened to Emmett and held an open-casket funeral in Chicago, allowing a photograph of her son's disfigured face appear in Jet magazine:

"...for over four days, thousands of people saw Emmett's body. Many more blacks across the country who might not have otherwise heard of the case were shocked by pictures that appeared in Jet magazine. These pictures moved blacks in a way that nothing else had. When the *Cleveland Call and Post* polled major black radio preachers around the country, it found that five of every six were preaching about Emmett Till and half of them were demanding that "something be done in Mississippi now," wrote Juan Williams in his classic *Eyes on the Prize: America's Civil Rights Years, 1954-1965*.[134]

Mississippi's largest newspaper, *The Jackson Daily News*, termed the murder "brutal" and "senseless," but complained that the NAACP was arousing "hatred and fear" by calling Till's murder a lynching. Civil Rights activist Rosa Parks of Montgomery, Alabama saw the picture in the newspaper and encouraged by the NAACP decided there would never be a better time to take a stand, something she had been planning to do all along but for which she hadn't set a date. Thus, Emmett Till's lynching is said to have sparked the modern civil rights movement.

The trial was dramatic, with coverage by national and international reporters — a first for such a crime carried out in the United States.

In Belgium, two left-wing newspapers published articles on the acquittal.

Le Peuple, the daily Belgian Socialist newspaper, calling the acquittal "a judicial scandal in the United States."

Le Drapeau Rouge headlines announced "Killing a black person isn't a crime in the home of the Yankees: The white killers of young Emmett Till are acquitted!"

In France, the daily newspaper *Le Monde*, on September 27, ran an article titled, "The Sumner Trial Marks, Perhaps, an Opening of Consciousness."

But on the next day, in Germany, the newspaper *Freies Volk* published an article with the headline, "The Life of a Negro Isn't Worth a Whistle."

As the trial of J.W. Milam and Roy Bryant ended:

"Defense attorney John C. Whitten told the jurors in his closing statement, 'Your fathers will turn over in their graves if [Milam and Bryant are found guilty] and I'm sure that every last Anglo-Saxon one of you has the courage to free these men in the face of that [outside] pressure."

"The jurors listened to him," wrote Juan Williams. "They deliberated for just over an hour, and then returned a 'not guilty' verdict on September 23rd, the 166th anniversary of the signing of the Bill of Rights. The jury foreman later explained, "I feel the state failed to prove the identity of the body."

After the murder trial of Milam and Bryant ended in September, with an all-white 12-man jury finding both men innocent in just 67 minutes, the two men later confessed their crime to a national magazine reporter.

In May of 2004, the U.S. Justice Department reopened the Emmett Till case after a young black filmmaker, Keith A.

Beauchamp, produced a documentary articulating the madness of racism in the South of the 1950s. Then three years passed before a Leflore County Grand Jury decided not to prefer charges against Carolyn Bryant Donham and said no others were involved. The black Mississippi prosecutor wasn't much help, refusing assistance from the FBI.

Once again, the crime is being reconsidered for opening. Meanwhile, few good words are spoken of the prosecutor, Joyce Chiles, by black Delta residents and others who wanted to see resolution. Some believe that she was compromised by local white planters.

It was not until October 7th, 2008, that the Emmett Till Unsolved Civil Rights Crime Act was actually signed into law by President George Bush who seemed to want to leave something positive of his poor civil rights record. This legislation provided the Justice Department with additional money and resources to investigate unsolved murders committed during the Civil Rights era.

While 422 members of Congress voted in favor of the bill, two voted against it, Rep. Ron Paul and Rep. Lynn Westmoreland. In the Senate, it had been blocked by Sen. Tom Coburn who, after much public criticism, finally ended his opposition. On September 24, 2008, the full Senate passed the Till bill by voice vote after Senator Coburn lifted his hold. Putting aside that money is finally available to investigate this cold case and others, it still might fall to the former wife of a dead grocer, Carolyn Bryant Donham, to help bring final resolution to the Emmett Till matter.

Was Bryant's wife involved? Was she with her husband and others on that dark night in 1955 outside of Mose Wright's home? Who else was there? Did she point out young Emmett as the kid who embarrassed her in their small family grocery store?"

Donham was still residing in Greenwood in the fall of 2009. Some who are familiar with Till's murder believe that Donham was probably sitting inside the truck that early August morning in Money, waiting to identify Emmett Till when her husband shined a light in the young man's face, asking her if this was the right person, the young man who'd embarrassed her in his store.

She might tell her story some day, but probably she won't. Unless she finishes writing her own account for an unidentified publishing house as rumor has it. Will Carolyn Bryant Donham's book will be hitting the shelves in 2010?

ON AUGUST 13, 1993, Erle Johnston, former Sovereignty Commission director and the most powerful person to ever hold the position, sat down for an oral history interview with Yasuhiro Katagiri, a Fulbright scholar from Japan studying at the University of Southern Mississippi.[135]

Johnston waxed philosophic of his days growing up in Grenada and about the state spy organization he headed for five years — from 1963 to 1968 — giving a unique look into his own life and into the agency that served as Mississippi's "all-seeing eyes" in the modern Civil Rights Movement, his manner stereotypical of white Southern men involved in some of the cruelest and reprehensible acts against black people.

The honey always drips as stories like Johnston's slip, slide from their mouths. "I remember growing up…in a segregated town. I thought nothing about it. The town built a swimming pool. It was for whites only. Blacks never even tried to get in it."

"The picture show — blacks went upstairs and whites went downstairs. Nobody objected to it. So, we were always under the impression that they were satisfied with the relationship because — and this is the main reason — because never in my town of Grenada where I grew up, did a black family go hungry or a black family needed help that there wasn't white people that did it for them," Johnston said.

The grand idea," Johnston continued, "…was that we could turn the Sovereignty Commission into a big public relations agency…in order to try to project Mississippi outside the state as a good place to be, as a good place to work, as a good place to settle down."

"Of course we recognized that one civil rights murder was worse than a hundred blacks getting Ph.D. degrees, you know. But the idea was that we could try as much as we could to overcome the attitude outside Mississippi that we were a lawless state as far as race was concerned. "We never got anywhere with it."

Johnston blamed the failure on hippies and the summer of 1964 or Freedom Summer, a campaign launched in June to attempt to register as many African American voters as possible in Mississippi.

Until then, black voters were almost always excluded, despite the efforts of black Mississippians like Birdia Keglar, Adlena Hamlett, Sam and Margaret Block, Jimmy Travis, Amzie Moore, Aaron Henry, Dr. T.R.M. Howard, Cleve McDowell, Fannie Lou Hamer and so many others.

The project was organized by the Council of Federated Organizations (COFO), a coalition basically pulled together by Aaron Henry and Amzie Moore from four established civil rights organizations:

The National Association for the Advancement of Colored People (NAACP), the Congress of Racial Equality (CORE), the Southern Christian Leadership Conference (SCLC) and the Student Nonviolent Coordinating Committee (SNCC), with SNCC playing the lead role.

Poor old Johnston probably never knew what hit him that hot Mississippi summer when the project opened its doors.

Besides the white, uppity college students coming into the state, so many others followed along, including famous activist entertainers like Bob Dylan who set up in Drew, where he taught little black kids how to sing folk songs. Or Joan Baez, who considered taping herself to a schoolyard swing set in Granada during an explosive riot — and was forcibly stopped by others who knew she would be killed.

Imagine. "All these invading people from around the country came in and upset Mississippi," Johnston said. "They went around dressed slovenly and long hair and fingernails ... always confronting people and creating riots. The governor had to get the highway patrol increased to take care of [them].

"Had that not happened, Governor Paul Johnson would have had Mississippi sailing right on into the twentieth century."

Sure, Mr. Johnston. Uh, huh.

Epilogue

From time to time the story of Emmett Till comes up, sometimes inspiring musical and theatrical performances, dance and expression through other art forms. This story stirs a range of emotions, from surprise and shock to anger or fear. Typically, it is a short burst — like this summer, when gravesites were robbed in Burr Oaks Cemetery —that dissipates quickly.

Some of us know this story quite well, thanks to the few researchers and storytellers who keep sifting through data and offering their newest explanations. Others have never heard of Emmett Till or Money, Mississippi. Their history teachers never told them about this important 1955 lynching, an event that has tarnished our international reputation for over 50 years — whether or not all U.S. citizens have heard about it or care.

The latest flare-ups in the summer of 2009 — first sparked by grave robberies where Till and his mother are buried, followed by the reported chase of a young black man in the Delta by an armed prosecutor driving a home-made tank, on the anniversary of Till's lynching — seem to be more ludicrous bursts than usual.

When I was living in Mississippi several years ago, Till's body was exhumed and autopsied for the first time. Officials submitted a report to the local black district attorney in Sunflower County who didn't seem to make use of the new information.

Partly because of her inept performance and the lack of concern by others, the Emmett Till case went back into the cold case freezer. At least for a while.

—

I am a white woman from Oregon who is not a lawyer, political science professor or professional investigator. I am not a historian. What's more, the lynching happened when I was just seven years old. But as is the case with so many other people, the story captured my passion the first time I heard it, as a newcomer to the Mississippi Delta. It has never let me go.

The story of "who killed Emmett Till" drove me to find people in the Delta with horrifying stories to share, and soon I was hearing so much more than Till's story. I learned about a compassionate woman with a graceful soul named Fannie Lou Hamer, who discovered quite late in life that she had the right to vote. Hamer was raped and beaten by police officers when she used the white bathroom in a Winona bus station while returning home from advocacy training.

I heard about two grandmothers, an accomplished businesswoman and a dedicated teacher — both voting rights advocates — who were killed when coming home from a civil rights meeting. Because the county sheriff didn't view the deaths of these two black women as significant, he failed to investigate the auto accident that took their lives. Then again, perhaps the sheriff damned well knew what happened to these women — that they likely run off the road, killed and tortured by Klansmen posing as state troopers — a common practice in his territory — and ignored it altogether.

I learned about a black attorney, a highly accomplished man who set state records for African Americans, who was shot to death in his home. After tracking down his autopsy report, I didn't like what I saw and I have questions about his murder, and about the questionable "suicide" of his close friend in Alabama. I learned that in his town of Drew, a bogue exists, Whore's Lake, where the bodies of countless black women were dumped over the years by white Klanswomen, who killed them first.

Damn did I get mad as I kept running into story after story about the civil rights and civil wrongs exercised in Mississippi, finding myself learning about people who were connected in one way or another to so many deaths and other horrific crimes.

Emmett Till wasn't the only young person murdered for being black.

So were:

Charles Lang
Ernest Green
Jo Etha Collier
Florence Smith
James Calhoun

...and hosts of unnamed children, like the grandson of a civil rights advocate who with her grandmother was stoned to death, possibly by city government officials.

My husband, a liberal and kind man, was taken back when he would come home at lunch and see me surrounded by books and papers, sitting at my computer, sometimes playing opera music loudly while working. He would come back for dinner and see me working late into the night, coming upon ...name ... after name ... after name ... after name ...of people killed because of the color of their skin.

Two men, Roy Bryant and J.W. Milam, are dead and won't be able to help solve this cold case. But a third person, Carolyn Bryant Donham, is tucked away in her comfortable, Greenwood home where she refuses to talk about her possible role but might be writing a book about it.

Her lack of cooperation in solving this cold case is nothing but obscene. Who killed Emmett Till? Perhaps this old woman could recall what happened in those early morning hours of Aug. 28, 1955. Donham should cough up some answers before she leaves the planet. Until then, if you're waiting for answers about the

majority of racist crimes that happened in the belly of the beast, Mississippi, don't hold your breath.
I'm breathless.

Afterword

Links

Link to Bibliography: http://klopferbibliography.blogspot.com/

Link to Lists of the Dead: http://themiddleoftheinternet.com/OnlineBooks/Rebels/ListofDead.pdf

Link to Civil Rights Library: http://civilrightsbooks.com/

Questions & Answers

Q. Is the Emmett Till story still important? Do people still care?

A. Emmett Till's murder took place over 54 years ago, back in 1955, and yet we are just beginning to learn the details of the crime. Till was a young man known only by his family and friends, but the truth of his lynching remains an important key to understanding American history. Further, the truth about young Till's murder and the truth about the murders of so many others — including President John F. Kennedy, Rev. Martin Luther King, Jr., and Robert F. Kennedy — is crucial to maintaining our democracy, because in a free government ... truth matters.

In each of these murders, there have been numerous threats to the uncovering and exposure of the truth. These threats have often come from within our own government, through such programs as COINTELPRO, a secretive series of covert, and often illegal, projects conducted by the United States Federal Bureau of Investigation (FBI), officially from 1956 to 1971.

While the FBI's COINTELPRO was aimed at "investigating and disrupting dissident political organizations" around the entire country, Mississippi had its own such secret spy agency, the Mississippi Sovereignty Commission. This Commission spied and disrupted, with the help of the Ku Klux Klan, those people who aided in black voter registration and racial integration.

The Sovereignty Commission was formed only one year after Emmett Till's death, the same year as COINTELPRO, because of the pressure the state was receiving from the federal government. Former FBI and military intelligence agents were hired by Mississippi and used as Commission investigators. Ironically, the very federal government that was applying pressure on Mississippi to change, was also using the FBI and COINTELPRO to disrupt many people and organizations trying to bring positive change to the state, often tagging these people as Communists or simply dangerous.

Thanks to people who care about historical truth, their research on Emmett Till, COINTELPRO and the assassinations of our country's peace-seeking leaders continues to bring out new evidence. And as this truth becomes apparent, it serves to keep us free.

Yes, Emmett Till's story still matters. And as the 83,000 "Emmett Till" entries listed on Google as of 11:34 p.m. September 26, 2009, attest, the Emmett Till story continues to hold an important place in history. The story of 14-year-old Emmett Till remains important and people still care. Thank God.

Q. What kind of a boy was Emmett Till?

"I would say that to me, Emmett was very ordinary. But as I look at today's youth, I realize that Emmett was very extraordinary," his mother once told historian Devery Anderson who interviewed Mrs. Till Mobley in 1996. She described her son as responsible and industrious, a youngster who helped her clean, cook and do laundry, recognizing the importance of his help as a single mother. Anderson's site is at emmetttillmurder.com.

In her book, Emmett's mother gives a further glimpse of her son, however. "Emmet was always so confident about his ability to talk his way through things that you could forget that he still had a problem talking. After he had recovered from polio as quickly as he had done, at such an early age, the doctors figured he could lick this problem [stuttering], too And we did everything we were supposed to do. The speech therapy classes had helped some, but the stutter was still apparent at eleven and then at twelve, in normal conversation, but especially when he got excited."[136] Later, she also terms her son as "meticulous" and "independent."

Young Emmett had just finished the seventh grade at the all-black McCosh Elementary School on Chicago's South Side when he went to Mississippi. He was between five-foot- four and five-foot-five and weighed 160 pounds, was physically stocky and muscular. Various authors write he was self-assured despite a speech defect--a stutter that resulted from a bout with nonparalytic polio at the age of three. Emmett was a smart dresser with a reputation as a prankster and a risk taker.

Q. What happened to Emmett Till's father?

Louis Till, drafted in World War II, was convicted of raping two women and killing a third. He was executed by the U.S. Army, which originally told Till's wife, Mamie, only that he had been killed due to "willful misconduct.

One Chicago woman, J. Marie Green, a military retiree who studied black history and is an independent civil rights researcher, remembers Till's murder and has spent years investigating what happened to his father. She wrote this comment on my blog, www.whokilledemmetttill.com:

"Emmett Till's murder is something one never forgets. I was born and raised in Chicago, and was about five years old when he was killed and remember when it happened and saw the Jet magazine photos, and I was scared to death, shocked really and questioned my mother who was from Greenwood, Mississippi, asking her why would two grown men would kill a child and what is a "wolf whistle", and are these men coming after us? "She assured me that these men where not coming to get us, explained what a "wolf whistle" was and meant in relations to that, and as a side bar note, told me that I ask too many questions. (smile). But every child in our area was afraid for a long time. Over the years I have never forgotten him, and have read just about everything I have come across about him every time his name is mentioned somewhere. Just recently his name came up again, with the incident at Burr Oak Cemetery. Somehow I feel his death is not resolved.

"…Mrs. Till's husband's story is another whole story all by itself. Pvt. Louis Till was part of the 177th Port Company, 397th Battalion — an all-"negro" battalion — which left from a NY port and arrived in France during 1944. He was hanged by execution by the U.S. Army on July 2, 1945. by orders of General Eisenhower. Allegedly for the murder of Anna Zanchi, and the rape of Benni Lucretzia and Frieda Muri who lived in Civitavecchia, Italy, these crime supposedly occurred on June 27, 1944, shortly after he arrived, mind you!

"According to records found at The American Battle Monuments Commission, Pvt. Louis Till is buried in an unmarked, prohibited, isolated area of Oise-Aisne Cemetery in Fere-en-Tardenois, France. The military marked his personnel file and the courts-martial records "secret," hushed it up, sent Mrs. Till a telegram, stating that her husband had died because of "misconduct," and she never knew what happened to him until her son's trial, when the Senators pulled some strings and contacted the military and some Staff Judge Advocate General, crossed out the word "secret" and released the information to them.

"Even after the trial of Emmett, she could never get any answers to what happened to her husband and why he was killed, this is clearly a military "railroad job," and has been hushed up all these years for a reason, but if you would check military history during this period you will see that a lot of black men were mysteriously hung for rape of French women. "They" took racism right on with them and convinced the French that "Negroes" had a problem, too."

Q. Why do people sometimes refer to the University of Mississippi as Ole Miss?

The University got its nickname "Ole Miss" via a contest in 1897. That same year, the student yearbook was being published for the first time. As a way to find a name for the book, a contest was held to solicit suggestions from the student body. Elma Meek, a student at the time, submitted the winning entry of Ole Miss. This name was chosen not only for the yearbook, but also became the name by which the University is now known.

Ole Miss, as used by the University, is not a substitute for "Old Mississippi." Rather, this endearing term stands for the wife of the "Ole Massah" on a plantation (the man who enslaved and mistreated Africans).

U of Miss. publicity agents claim the name is thought of in an affectionate manner, today. To check this out, I walked around the campus one day and asked some of the black students what they thought about this nickname and its history. Most were well aware of the story and several said they were disgusted. "It's just embarrassing," one student said. "I wish the school would change it."

Q. Who is your favorite Mississippi hero?

Reading *The Fire Ever Burning* by Constance Curry and Aaron Henry helped get me started on this journey. Henry was a true hero and someone I would have wanted to know.

Henry was a fierce champion of civil rights, a leader of the Mississippi chapter of the NAACP and a member of the Mississippi House of Representatives. He is still one of the most revered civil rights leaders in Mississippi, at least by many older civil rights advocates who know their state's history.

Henry grew up near Clarksdale, Mississippi, and later earned a degree in political science at Xavier University in New Orleans. During World War II, he served as a staff sergeant with the U.S. Army in the Pacific. After the war, Henry attended pharmacy school, and eventually returned to Clarksdale to open a corner drug store where any important civil rights and government leaders met to unite Mississippi blacks in fighting white supremacy. Sadly, the pharmacy no longer stands in Clarksdale. His home was also demolished in a fire.

There were many personal tragedies in Henry's life as well as successes. In 1961, Henry led a highly successful boycott of stores in the Clarksdale, Mississippi, area that refused to hire black workers and discriminated against black customers. He and six others were arrested for "conspiring to withhold trade."

These charges were eventually reversed on appeal but another charge, of sexual harassment, against Henry, soon followed came soon after. While he was fighting this case, which he eventually won, his pharmacy was firebombed and his wife, Nicole, was fired from her job as a public school teacher. Several years later, Medgar Evers was assassinated in 1963 after taking Henry to the airport.

For Henry, there was no such thing as a small victory and because each victory usually led to an even greater success. "I think," Henry once said, "that every time a man stands for an ideal or speaks out against injustice, he sends out a tiny ripple of hope."

After the passage of the Voting Rights Act in 1965, the number of black voters grew rapidly and as African Americans began to be elected winning elections to various local, county and statewide offices. Henry was elected to serve in the State House of Representatives in 1982, a post he held until 1996 where he continued to fight against racial injustice.

Henry introduced legislation to remove the Confederate battle flag from the state flag and continued to call for the reopening of the murder case for his old friend, Medgar Evers. Aaron Henry suffered a stroke in 1996, and died on May 19, 1997 in Clarksdale, Mississippi, just two months and five days after the murder of his friend, Cleve McDowell.

Q. Can I see a movie about Emmett Till

Yes, thanks to Keith Beauchamp, a young man who saw the photograph of Emmett Till's brutally beaten face that ran on the cover Jet magazine and became a civil rights activist in 2004. Beauchamp directed The Untold Story of Emmett Louis Till that is available on DVD. Till's murder has yet to be solved and Beauchamp said he is committing his energy to solving this and other civil rights cold cases. We owe him our extreme thanks and appreciation for his tenacity, perseverance and dedication to the cause of civil rights.

Q. What's happening these days in Mississippi?

Many activities are going on — some good and some disgusting. Friends of Justice is a nonprofit organization working to uphold due process for all Americans with the goal of building a public consensus behind equal access to justice and respect for human dignity in our criminal justice system, according to Executive Director, Dr. Alan Bean.

Friends of Justice formed in response to the infamous Tulia drug sting of 1999 in which 47 people, 39 of them African Americans, were rounded up based on the false testimony of an undercover agent, he explains.

The unique group emerged as a coalition of defendant's defendants' families and other concerned citizens who believed the defendants were being prosecuted on faulty evidence. "Because of the work of Friends of Justice, the Texas Legislature passed the Tulia Corroboration Bill, which has led to the exoneration of dozens of innocent people by raising the evidentiary standards for undercover testimony."

Learning from their experience in Tulia, Friends of Justice started organizing across Texas, Louisiana, Arkansas and Mississippi.

"We launch narrative-based campaigns around unfolding cases where due process has broken down, and empower affected communities to hold public officials accountable for equal justice. For more on our work, check their blog at http://friendsofjustice.wordpress.com/blog/

A wrongful conviction in a murder trial recently actually brought FOJ to Mississippi. In July 1996, four people were killed execution style at a Montgomery County furniture store: owner Bertha Tardy, bookkeeper Carmen Rigby, and two hired men, Bobo Stewart and Robert Golden. Golden was black, the other three victims were white. Six months later, Curtis Flowers, a young black Winona resident - who had worked three days for Bertha Tardy - was arrested and charged with the brutal murder of four innocent people.

Thirteen years, $300,000 and five trials later, Mr. Flowers remains behind bars and during which the state has been unable to obtain a final conviction.

Dr. Bean's group believes that the state's theory of the murder crime accused of a Winona company's former worker, by Flowers, "... doesn't fit the actual evidence, and the state manufactured phony evidence by manipulating, badgering and bribing witnesses." Details of the Curtis Flowers case are shared at the FOJ website in a story titled, "A brief primer in wrongful conviction. You can find more at www.friendsofjustice.com.

A similar but unrelated ongoing case occurred three years earlier on December 24, 1993 when Scott County Sheriff's Department arrested sisters Gladys and Jamie Scott for an armed robbery they in which they vehemently deny participation in. In 1994 they were convicted after being implicated in the crime by three young black men who confessed to the robbery in exchange of a plea bargain that gave them 10 ten months. The sisters were not offered a plea and went to trial, each receiving two life sentences for a crime that netted 11 eleven dollars where no one was injured.

Don't think these cases happen only in Mississippi. Another comparable case involves an Illinois social justice group seeking 11,000 signatures to present a petition to Illinois Governor Pat Quinn to order DNA testing to exonerate Johnnie Lee Savory.

Convicted of double murder by an all-white jury in 1977 at the age of fourteen, Johnnie Savory served thirty years in prison for a crime he did not commit, the group asserts. Released on parole in 2006, Savory still had not been officially exonerated by fall of 2009. After his release from prison, Johnnie attended a play about Emmett Till and found himself overwhelmed with emotion as he related to the horrible fate of another innocent fourteen-year old child. Johnnie's deep connection to Emmett was cemented when he discovered that they share the same birthday, July 25th.

Johnnie and Emmett's cases both represent a state-sponsored denial of justice and the loss of innocence for children, for communities of color, and for our entire nation, committee members said.

"However, these stories also are a part of a collective story for change, they contribute to the struggle for justice. Emmett's death sparked change in this nation and his mother ensured that his legacy lives on for eternity. While Emmett's voice was silenced, the strength and courage of so many in the civil rights movement allowed for their collective voice to be heard and heeded."

Also happening in Mississippi...

Even though the cold case is very famous, most Mississippi students have never heard of Emmett Till. And they haven't been taught about the 1964 Freedom Summer when 1,000 volunteers swept into the state to register black voters.

Students haven't heard of Fannie Lou Hamer or the story of Mae Bertha Carter, who defied gunfire and the loss of employment to send her children to previously all-white public schools in Drew, eventually winning a legal battle that confirmed their right to be there. "They don't know about ordinary citizens who faced extraordinary odds to bring change," wrote Carmen K. Sisson, Correspondent of The Christian Science Monitor in the October 4, 2009 edition.

"But they're going to know all about it soon. In a groundbreaking reform — believed to be the first in the nation — Mississippi will require civil rights as part of its U.S. history curriculum. McComb schools made that move in 2006; but starting next fall, the stories of the civil rights era will be taught — and tested — in all public schools."

This is going to be tough. But if Mississippi allows outside historians to participate and leaders refused refuse to be compromised, and if truth is the bottom line, the education program could set an example for the rest of this country.

Most states have their own civil rights histories that have not been covered. The stories are hidden and some might quite possibly just as horrid as what happened in Mississippi, especially in the western states where genocide was practiced on Native Americans and on the eastern seaboard where many wealthy families made their fortunes from the slave trade.

Even in my own (current) state of Iowa, the incarceration rate of blacks compared to the incarceration rate of whites is the highest in the nation. There is plenty of history to be researched and acted upon. Good jobs abound for citizen journalists.

Q. Why is it so important to think so much about the past?

I like to remember a quote by Winston Churchill, what he had to say about the importance of knowing our history: "The farther backward you can look, the farther forward you are likely to see."

Q. Is there anything else important to know about all of this?

Unfortunately, there is something else that must be addressed. Old-fashioned Citizens Councils still meet around Mississippi and some politicians openly say it is perfectly acceptable to become members and attend meetings and special events.

When questioned about these organizations and their memberships, they slip slide away, typically answering they don't agree with everything the councils stand for but they "do lots of good things, too."

Q. Where can I find more books and more information about civil rights history in Mississippi?

Go to my blog, www.whokilledemmetttill.com where I've posted my Selected Biography, a link to lists of Mississippi victims of lynching and murders and a link to a growing civil rights library. This book has been recorded as an audio book and has also been published as a print book. Links to these versions are at the Emmett Till website mentioned above.

Acknowledgements

Thank you so much for taking the time to read *Who Killed Emmett Till?*. If you learned something new, please tell your friends about it. The Mississippi Delta is a fascinating place to visit. I've placed a link to photos I took while living there and you can find the link on my website at www.whokilledemmetttill.com

I would be happy to speak to your group about this book and related topics. You can contact me by sending email to sklopfer@whokilledemmetttill.com.

It is not possible to list all of their names here of those who contributed into making this book possible. Particular thanks go to Margaret Block, Dr. L.C. Dorsey, June M. Green and Terry Housholder. Also to Keith Beauchamp, a special person who initiated public interest in Emmett Till and re-opening of this cold case. Keith is now working to have other such civil rights cases explored and resolved. Thanks also to Ron Herd II of W.E. A.L.L. B.E. Radio. Ron stays on top of the civil rights scene and uses his creativity to keep us informed. Fred Klopfer, my husband, always gives his help with mytremendous help when doing the initial research for this book. Most importantly, there are many special people in the Delta who shared their stories and my thanks goes to all of them. Without their help, this book would not have been written. A very special thanks also goes to Jay Mattsson for his kind and clear editing.

About the author

Susan Klopfer is a graduate of Hanover College and holds a master's degree from Indiana Wesleyan University. She has worked as an acquisitions and development editor for Prentice Hall and has won journalism awards from the Missouri Press Associations. Her book *Abort! Retry! Fail!* was named an alternate selection for the Book of the Month Club. She and her husband, Fred, lived on the grounds of Parchman Penitentiary when she completed the initial research for *Who Killed Emmett Till?* with help from Fred and their son, Barry. Susan and Fred now reside in Iowa where they enjoy partaking in the Iowa Caucuses and petting Ralph, Popsicle and Maury, their dog and two cats.

Connect with Me Online:

Website: http://susanklopfer.com

Twitter: http://www.twitter.com/sklopfer

Facebook: http://www.facebook.com/susan.klopfer?ref=profile

LinkedIn: http://www.linkedin.com/in/susanklopfer

MySpace: http://myspace.com/susanklopfer

Blog: http://emmett-till.blogspot.com

Smashwords Profiles: http://www.smashwords.com/profile/view/sklopfer

End Notes

1. Oral history interview with Cleve McDowell by Owens Brooks, Aug 11, 1995. Tougaloo College Archives.

2. David Perdue, "Charles Dickens Home Page," Dickens in America. (Internet Online).

3. James Cobb, "The Most Southern Place on Earth," (New York: Oxford University Press, 1992), 311. Cobb cites David Coh, "Where I was Born and Riased," (Boston: University of Notre Dame Press, 1948),320.

4. John Hebron Moore, "The emergence of the Cotton Kingdom in the Old Southwest: Mississippi, 1770-1860," (Louisiana State University Press, 1988), 127.

5. John Hatch, "Africa Love," (Berkeley, Calif.: 2ndsight Books, 2002). Instructions appear on Hatch's website. He explains that maps show the location because the Sunflower River was the only way to move crops, and that following the Civil War the Corps of Engineers had to dredge it for freight traffic, at least until a railroad was built in the late 1880s.

6. Bradley G. Bond, "Mississippi, A Documentary History," (Jackson: University Press of Mississippi, 2003), 67.

7. Jaime Boler, "Slave Resistance in Natchez, Mississippi (1719-1861)," Mississippi History Now. (Internet Online).

8. Oral history of Dr. L. C. Dorsey, Tougaloo College, Delta Collection.

9. In 1822 the settlement of American colonists along the Liberian shore began and continued until after the US Civil War. Though tracts of land along the coast were "purchased," the indigenous people of Liberia were not happy with the encroachment of the Americans, and waged numerous wars against them. Eventually, the Americans were able to establish themselves, and eclared themselves an independent nation in 1847. The "American Liberians" and the "Congo" descendents from those rescued from slave ships, came to dominate the political and economic life of the country even though they represented a minority. TheAmerican LLiberian grip on power was broken leading to prolonged civil war followed by persistent fighting. Source: Mel Fisher Maritime Heritage Society (Online). See Huffman, Alan. Mississippi in Africa. (New York: Gotham Books, 2004), 49.

10. Interview by author with Ser Seshs Ab Heter of Natchez, coordinator of the Friends of the Forks of the Roads, summer of 2004.

11. Bond, 86.

12. Conversation with Margaret Block, March 25, 2005.

13. John F. Marszalck and Clay Williams, "Mississippi Soldiers in the Citil War," Mississippi History Now, online publication of the Mississippi Historical Society.

14. The primary source material for this sidebar was found on the web page   http://www.usconstitution.net/consttop_slav.html   which

referenced the book *The Origins of American Slavery* by Betty Wood (Hill and Wang, New York, 1997):

15. David M. Oshinsky, "Worse. Than Slavery: Parchman Farm and the Ordeal of Jim Crow Justice," (New York: Simon and Schuster, 1996). Quoted by Johnathan Yardley, "In the Fields of dispair," The Washington Post, March 31, 1996. A review of Oshinsky.

16. Mississippi went through two phases of Reconstruction following the Civil War: Presidential, from 1865 to 1868, and the Congressional Reconstruction, from 1869 to 1875.

17. James Cobb, "The Most Southern Place on Earth," (New York: Oxford University Press, 1992), 88.

18. Nan Elizabeth Woodruff, "American Congo: The African American freedom Struggle in the Delta," (Cambridge: Harvard University Press, 2003), 49.

19. Cobb, 62.

20. "The Threatened Negro Insurrections --Riot at Winona -- The Military Called Out --Thirteen Negroes Reported Killed," The New York Herald, November 29, 1860, Clarksdale Public Library.

21. Earnest McBride, "JSU Lynching Exhibit," Jackson Advocate, Jan. 22-28, 2004.

22. The Bolton location is cited in a Bolton Centennail brochure from the Jan Hilligas COFO collection, Jackson, Miss.

23. Dale Krane and Stephen D. Shaffer, "Mississippi Governmetn and Politics: Modernizers versus Traditionalists," (Lincoln: University of Nebraska Press, 1992).

24. Clyde Woods, "Development Arrested," (London: Verso, 1998) 85.

25. Ibid., 85.

26. Susie James, "The Carrollton Massacre," The Commonwealth, March 12, 1996.

27. Henry Waring Ball, (1858 -1934). Diary, 1884-1928). Mississippi Dept. of Archives and History, Special Collections Section, Manuscript Collection.

28. Leon F. Litwack, "Trouble in Mind," (New York: Vintage Books), 240. According to Litwack, the term Jim Crow got ts start in minstrel shows in the early 1800s. A white minstrel, Thomas "Daddy" Rice, popularized the term, using burned cork to blacken his face. "Wearing ill-fitting, tattered clothing and grinning broadly, Rice danced, sang and portrayed behavior generally ascribed to black characters. Rice called his act "Jump Jim Crow" based on a song and dance routine he had seen in Louisville, performed by an old stableman belonging to a Mr. Crow. By the 1830s, Rice's performances were highly popular, and minstrel shows, one of the most popular forms of white entertainment. "Jim Crow" was in the American vocabulary. Many whites, northern and southern,, used the term in the 1840s in describing separate railroad cars for blacks and whites in the North. By the 1890s, Jim Crow took on new force and meaning to represent the subordination and separation of black people in the South, much of it codified, much of it still enforced by custom and habit."

29. An interesting namesake, since Oliver Cromwell the Englishman "rose from the middle ranks of English society to be Lord Protector of England, Scotland and Ireland, the only non-royal ever to hold that position. He played a leading role in bringing Charles I to trial and to execution; he undertook the most complete and the most brutal military conquest ever undertaken by the English over their neighbours; he championed a degree of religious freedom otherwise unknown in England before the last one hundred years; but the experiment he led collapsed within two years of his death, and his corpse dangled from a gibbet at Tyburn. He was --and remains--one of the most contentious figures in

world history," according to Professor John Morrill, writing for BBC History Online.

30. Woods, 86. Also, Patrick Dickson of the African Studies and Research Center at Cornell University wrote that in Mississippi, in the summer of 1889, Cromwell, a black man, began organizing farmers for the Colored Alliance in Leflore County. "His strategy was to encourage famers to refrain from doing business with local merchants and instead trade with the Southern Farmers' Alliance store in Durant. That the Durant store accepted their business is another example of the type of cooperation between the organizations. Cromwell's activities however threatened to break the economic hold local whites had on the majority black population in that county, and trouble soon arose. After an armed group of Colored Alliance members demonstrated in solidarity with Cromwell, a white posse was formed and a violent attack ensued killing many, including Colored Alliance leaders Adolph Horton, Scott Morris, Jack Dial and J.M. Dial, though Cromwell is believed to have escaped. After the outbreak of violence, the store was instructed to abstain from any further business with the Colored Alliance. This, along with the murder of several Colored Alliance leaders, destroyed the organization in Leflore County."(A Brief History of the Colored Farmer's Alliance through 1891," June 1999, Indigenous People of African and America magazine, online.)

31. Woods, 86.

32. Louis S. Gerteis, "Montgomery, Benjamin Thornton," American National Biography Online, American Council of Learned Societies, (Cambridge: Oxford Universsity Press, 2000),

33. John R. Salter, R. Edwin King, "Jackson, Mississippi: An American Chronicle of Struggle and Schism," (Exposition-Banner), 9.

34. Jeff Jacoby, "An execution, not a lynching," Jewish World Review, May 15, 2001.

35. Ethan Crosby, "Rural Blues: Structure and Development in the Post-Civil War South," (online), cites William Barlow, "Looking Up at Down: the Emergence of Blue Culture," (Philadelphia: Temple University Press, 1989), 27.

36. Ida B. Wells, "The Red Record," (Project Gutenberg), online.

37. Sources: Lerone Bennett, Jr., "A History of Black America," (Chicago: Johnson Publishing, Millennium Edition, 2003; Woods.

38. David M. Oshinsky, "Worse. Than Slavery: Parchman Farm and the Ordeal of Jim Crow Justice (New York: Simon and Schuster, 1996), 85.

39. Ibid, 100.

40. Cobb, 114.

41. Ibid, 115.

42. Ibid, 259. Cobb explains that in later years and because of Eastland's agricultural influence in the U.S. Senate, Sunflower County planters received more than $10.2 million in cotton program payments in 1967 alone, while federal food program expenditures in the county totaled less than 5 percent of the amount. "The face that acreage-reduction payments of farms amounted to a total of twenty-three times greater than the expenditures to combat hunger in a county where 65 percent of the population was living in poverty was difficult to explain away."

43. James W. Silver, "Mississippi: The Closed Society," (New York: Harcourt, Brace and World, 1964), ix.

44. Ann Waldron, "Hodding Carter: The Reconstruction of a Racist," (Chapel Hill: Algonquin Books, 1993), 64.

45. Woodruff, 69.

46. Silver, 83.

47. In 2000, Delta & Pine Land (Mississippi USA) was the world's 9th largest seed corporation with revenues of $301 million. The company was reported to have joint ventures and/or subsidiaries in North America, Brazil, Argentina, China, Mexico,l Paraguay, South Africa and Australia. The USDA and D&PL are co-owners of three patents on the controversial technology that genetically modifies plants to produce sterile seeds, preventing farmers from re-using harvested seed.

48. Woodruff, 23-28.

49. Woodruff, 1.

50. Herbert Shapiro, "White Violence and Black Response From Reconstruction to Montgomery (Amherst: University of Massachusetts Press, 1988), 165. Garvey believed that liberty and democracy could not be acquired without bloodshed: The blood was not to be shed in America, but "one day on the African battlefield" in order to repossess what properly belonged to blacks. Africa had given mankind its civilization, had supplied science, art, and literature to whites, but, the time had come for blacks to take back the power they had once held, Garvey believed. When Blacks ruled, democracy would prevail. The white man had shown he was incapable of ruling, and "he has to step off the stage of action."

51. Interview with Margaret Block, an early member of SNCC. Block and her brother, the late Sam Block, joined the Civil Rights Movement as soon as they were out of high school -- Margaret worked in Charleston (Tallahatchie County) and Sam was a movement leader in Greenwood (LeFlor County). Sam is considered a pioneer for his early voting rights activities he led before SNCC came into the state.

52. Dorsey.

53. Woodruff, 138.

54. Alan Lomax, "The Land Where the Blues Began," (New York: The New Press, 1993), 206-7, 468.

55. Donald Spivey, "Schooling for the New Slavery: Black Industrial Education, 1868-1915," (Westport, CT: Greenwood Press), 74.

56. *The Cleveland Advocate*, July 31, 1920. Cited by Woodruff, 140.

57. John W. Barry, "Rising Tide," (New York: Simon & Schuster, 1997), 334.

58. Mamie Till-Mobley and Christopher Benson, "Death of Innocence," (New York: Random House, 2003), 19.

59. Woodruff, 150.

60. Woods, 152.

61. Woodruff, 154. Cites various newspaper reports including the *Arkansas Gazette*, September 11, 1931, the *Atlanta Constitution*, September 10, 1931, and the *Chicago Whip*, November 3, 1931.

62. Jane Adams, D. Gorton, "Southern Trauma; Revisiting Caste and Class in the Mississippi Delta," American Anthropologist, Vol. 106, Issue 2, 334-345.

63. Hortense Powdermaker, "After Freedom," (New York: Viking Press, 1939), 32, 33, 53, 54, 173, 174, 332, 335, 351.

64. Anthropologist Jane Adams D. Gorton on her website pointed out that both researchers' work had significant impact, but both studies contained flaws that contributed to steereotyping of the white Southern aristocracy that was only myth. She further stated that Dollard's psychologically-based work helped to define the nature of race relations for generations of college students and policy makers in its stereotyping of "poor whites as vicious and unredeemable racists that has been reenacted

in countless films and television shows." In April 1986, a *Washington Post* reporter following up on the Powdermaker's earlier study, asserted that Indianola was still dominated by a "propertied white elite that runs this Mississippi Delta town like an antebellum plantation, ceding power only gradually to the black majority in a manner and at a pace of its own choosing."

65. Woodruff, 157.

66. Woodruff, 156-157. Cites M.S. Stuart to John Ross, January 25, 1934, box G199; Nat Williams et al., WPA, Tunica, Miss., box C386; and Walter White to Harry Hopkins, September 9, 1936, box C386; all in NAACP Papers, group 1.

67. Ibid., 158.

68. Ibid., 177. Cites F. Raymond Daniell, "AAA Piles Misery on Sharecroppers," *New York Times*, April 15, 1935, TCF, 48:0958.

69. William Rauthrauff Amberson Papers. Abstract, Manuscripts Department, Library of the University of North Carolina at Chapel Hill: *Southern Historical Collection*, #3862.

70. Valerie Grim, "Black Farm Families in the Yazoo-Mississippi Delta. A study of the Brooks Farm Community, 1920 to 1970," dissertation submitted to the graduate faculty, Iowa State University, Ames 1990, 47.

71. John Dittmer, "Local People," (Urbana and Chicago: University of Illinois Press, 1955), 15.

72. Ibid., 15.

73. Monica Moorhead, "The Port Chicago Mutiny," *Workers World*, February 23, 1995.

74. Pete Daniel, "Lost in the Revolution: The South in the 1950s," (Urbana: University of North Carolina, 2000).

75. Cobb, 213. Cites *The New York Times*, February 7, 1982; James A. Burran III, "Racial Violence in the South During World War II" (Ph.D. dissertation, University of Tennessee, 1977), 263-65; Williams, "Mississippi and Civil Rights," 54. In some accounts the victim in the case is referred to as Leon McAtee rather than McTatie.

76. Frances Kimbriel Showers, "Memories of Life in Drew," *Recollections*, (compiled for the Drew Centennial, September 23, 1999), 23.

77. Oral history, Amzie Moore, University of Southern Mississippi Libraries and USM Center for Oral History and Cultural Heritage. March 29 and April 13, 1977. Mike Garvey, interviewer.

78. Oral history with Charles Cobb, University of Southern Mississippi Libraries and The Center for Oral History and Cutural Heritage, Oct. 21, 1996. Interviewer, John Rachal.

79. Aaron Henry and Constance Curry, "The Fire Ever Burning," (Jackson University Press of Mississippi, 2000), 3.

80. The mistreatment of black soldiers has been well documented in oral histories, interviews and other research. This writer's own father, a WWII Navy veteran, recalled seeing a white officer with his hands around the neck of a black soldier, beating the soldier's head into a cement wall.

81. Oral history with Aaron Henry for the Lyndon B. Johnson Library, September 12, 1970. Interviewed by T.H. Baker.

82. Myrlie Evers, with William Peters, "For Us, The Living.," (Jackson Univesity Press of Mississippi), 24.

83. Even in 1960, a full sixteen years beyond the Supreme Court's White Primary decision (*Smith v. Allright*), only 28 percent of the southern

African-American electorate were registered to vote. Most were not staying away from the polls out of personal choice.

84. An Oral History with the Honorable Harvey Ross, USM Libraries and Center for Oral History and Cultural Heritage, December 1, 1994. Interviewer, Homer Hill.

85. Anyone can access Mississippi Sovereignty Commission files online by visiting http://mdah.state.ms.us/. Select Archives and Records Services. Then select Digital Archives. Select Sovereignty Commission Online. From there, search by names or search entire files. Note these records have been scanned. Take care to search under a variety of correct and incorrect spellings. Some items have not been entirely indexed, so it is important to be flexible and search for related names and files. I enjoy browsing records to see what I can discover! When these records were first made public, most journalists did not take them very seriously and one reporter wrote they represented the activities of keystone cops. This is not true. There is a wealth of fascinating information and untold stories contained in this online archive.

86. William H. Tucker , "The Funding of Scientific Racism: Wickliffe Draper and the Pioneer Fund," (Urbana and Chicago: University of Illinois Press, 2002).

87. Tucker wrote that "[New York Times reporter] Blackmon was the only national reporter that I know of who seemed interested in Draper...searching for bottom line information, and after looking through the treasure trove of ledgers,invoices and correspondence recording the commission's finances [he reported that that "[R]ecords show large transfers of money by Morgan on behalf of a client who turns out be a wealthy and reclusive New Yorker named Wycliffe Preston Draper. Mr. Draper used his private banker to transfer nearly $215,000 in stock and cash to the Sovereignty Commission for use in its fight against the Civil Rights Act. The entire budget for the effort amounted to about $300,000.Adjusted for inflation, Mr. Draper's contributions would be worth more than $1.1 million today.The Sovereignty Commission files do

more than simply document one man's role. They show that some of the most virulent resistance to civil-rights progress in the 1960s was supported and funded from the North, not just the South. The files also highlight the ethical issues that confront an institution like Morgan Guaranty, the private-banking unit of J. P Morgan & Co.,when it is drawn, even unwittingly, into a client's support for repugnant causes.When Mr. Draper died in 1972, Morgan was an executor of his estate, overseeing distributions totaling about $5 million to two race-oriented foundations. The primary beneficiary was the Pioneer Fund, an organization Mr. Draper helped found and which became known in recent years for funding research cited in "The Bell Curve," a book arguing that blacks are genetically inclined to be less intelligent than whites or Asians. In his will, Mr. Draper instructed that after his death, the Pioneer Fund use Morgan for financial advice; the fund did so for two decades." Records in Sovereignty Commission files under Weyher support this finding.
Also, Blackmon, Douglas A."Silent Partner: How the South's Fight To Uphold Segregation Was Funded Up North,"Institute for the Study of Academic Racism. Also, Douglas A. Blackmon, "Silent Partner: How the South's Fight To Uphold Segregation Was Funded Up North," The *Wall Street Journal*, June 11, 1999.

88. During late 1965, the Internal Revenue Service and the House Committee on Un-American Activities also began to play a significant role in the FBI-coordinated anti-Klan effort. In October the FBI distributed its reports on White Knights finances to the IRS, which had provided Sam Bowers' tax returns to the Bureau earlier in the year. That same month, the House Committee on Un-American Activities began to expose the structure, size and internal documents of Klan groups across the South.In January and February 1966, the Committee interrogated officers of the White Knights, exposing them and the activities of their Klansmen to public scrutiny. Klansmen responded by burning at least one hundred crosses across the State. Gene Roberts, "Violence and Rights in South," New York Times, 9 January 1966, 4.

89. Mississippi Sovereignty Commission report [2-92-0-15-1-1-1] filed under "Birdie Kegler," dated November 21, 1961. As with many Sovereignty Commission reports, the name is mispelled.

90. Mississippi Sovereignty Commission record [4-0-1-68-1-1-1] filed under "Birdie Kegler."

91. An undated news clipping was given to Robert Keglar by the 2004 Leflore County District Attorney. The clipping reported the deaths. "A two-car crash on U.S. 40 about five miles south of Greenwood accounted for the death of two Negro women Tuesday night. The Mississippi Highway Patrol said Birda [sic] Clark Kegler [sic], 57, of Charleston and Adlema [sic] Amlett [sic] of Scobey, were killed in the accident. Admitted to the Greenwood Leflore Hospital for treatment of injuries were Brown Lee Bruce, Jr. of Sidon, who was alone in one of the automobiles, and Jesse J. Brewer and Grafton Gray, Negroes, and Richard L. Simpson, 27, white, of Mass., occupants of the other car. No other details of the accident are available at this time, authorities say.

92. Mark Gado, "Mississippi Madness: The Story of Emmett Till," Court TV Crime Library (online).

93. Interview with Robert Keglar by Susan Klopfer, 2003.

94. David T. Beito and Linda Royster Beito, "Black Maverick," (Urbana and Chicago: University of Illinois Press, 2009), 118.

95. Ibid., 108.

96. Ibid., 112.

97. Simeon Wright, "Simeon's Story," (Chicago: Lawrence Hill Books, 2010), 41.

98. Ibid., 25.

99. Valerie Smith, "*Emmett Till's Ring*," WSQ: Women's Studies Quarterly - Volume 36, Numbers 1 & 2, Spring/Summer 2008, pp. 151-161.

100. Till-Mobley, 186.

101. Wright, 51.

102. The FBI's investigation was opened on May 7, 2004, at the request of the District Attorney in Greenwood, Mississippi, in an effort to determine if other individuals were involved in these crimes. Files from the case, including the FBI's 2006 report and a transcript of the September 1955 trial are online at http://foia.fbi.gov/foiaindex/till.htm

103. David Halberstam, "Tallahatchie County Acquits a Peckerwood," 1956, online.

104. Interviewed by Susan Klopfer, 2004.

105. Till-Mobley, 111.

106. Evers, 552.

107. Interview with Woodrow Jackson, 2005.

108. Roger Ebert, "The Untold Story of Emmett Till," Movie Reviews, The Chicago Sun Times, October 14, 2005 (Online).

109. Waldron, 257.

110. Wright, 59.

111. Letters between the U.S. Justice Department and the FBI found on "American Experience," the Public Broadcasting System (PBS) website (online).

112. Anne Moody, "Coming of Age in Mississippi," (New York: Dell, 1992), 123-124.

113. Till-Mobley, 101.

114. Ibid., 114.

115. Ibid., 120.

116. Till-Mobley, 127.

117. Kwame Alford, "Emmett Till: the Sacrificial Lamb of the Civil Rights Movement, 3rd Revised edition," The Western Journal of Black Studies, Spring, 2001. Cites Clenora Hudson-Weems, in her pioneering book Emmett Till: The Sacrificial Lamb of the Civil Rights Movement.

118. Hank Klibanoff, "L. Ale Wilson: A Reporter Who Refused to Run," Media Studies Journal, Vol. 14, no. 2, Spring/Summer 2000.

119. Mark Gado, "Mississippi Madness: The Story of Emmett Till," TruTV Crime (online).

120. Till-Mobley, 189.

121. The short account presented here of what went on during the trial comes from a variety of sources including the writings of Halberstam, Beito, Till-Mobley and others.

122. Telephone interview with Michael Rosa, 2009.

123. Interview with Rev. Jesse Gresham, 2004.

124. All biographical information about Cleve McDowell was gathered from a Mississippi Legislature Proclamation, Cleve McDowell, 1997, online. Information was also gathered from a sister and a nephew, his former office manager, his minister, papers from the Mississippi

Sovereignty Commission, and from other Mississippians who knew and worked with him. There have been no books written about McDowell and the state archives say they have no records.

125. Interview with guard, 2004.

126. Interview with Dr. John Howard, 2004.

127. Interview with Lucy Boyd.

128. Information regarding Adlena Hamlett and Birdia Keglar has been gleaned through dozens of interviews with family members and friends since 2003 as well as from Sovereignty Commission files. To date, the FBI refuses to see their deaths as worthy of investigation as cold cases.

129. Interview with Zachery-Black, 2010.

130. Telephone interview with Richard Simpson, 2009.

131. From a letter found in the civil rights archives of Tougaloo College. These materials were turned over to the Mississippi State Archives at the William Winters Library. Since the time of their moving, to date, no Tougaloo records have been available to researchers. Archivists say they are "preparing" the documents for further use.

132. Interview with Charles Sudduth.

133. I have not been able, thus far, to learn very much about this murder. I was told that it was klan-related and that "someone went to prison" for a short period of time and then his sentence was restructured and he was let out of prison. Apparently, there are records at the Sunflower Country Courthouse in Indianola.

134. Juan Williams, "Eyes on the Prize: America's Civil Rights Years, 1954-1965," (New York: Penguin, 1988).

135. Oral history with Erle Johnston, a cooperative project of the University of Southern Mississippi Libraries and USM's Center for Oral History and Cultural Heritage. Interview conducted by Yasuhiro Katagiri at Johnston's home in Forrest, Miss. on August 13, 1993.

136. Till-Mobley, 65.Extended

Extended Bibliography

Books

Barry, John W. Rising Tide, New York: Simon & Schuster, 1997.

Beito, David T. and Royster Beito, Linda. Black Maverick, Urbana and Chicago: University of Illinois Press, 2009.

Bennett Jr., Lerone. A History of Black America, Chicago: Johnson Publishing, Millennium Edition, 2003.

Bond, Bradley G. Mississippi, A Documentary History, Jackson: University Press of Mississippi, 2003.

Branch, Taylor. Parting the Waters, New York: Simon & Schuster, 1988.

Cagin, Seth and Philip Dray. We Are Not Afraid, New York: Bantam Books, 1988.

Case, Carroll. The Slaughter: An American Atrocity, FBC, Inc., 1998.

Cobb, James (ed.). The Mississippi Delta and the World; The Memoirs of David L. Cohn, Baton Rouge and London: Louisiana State University Press, 1995.

Cobb, James. The Most Southern Place on Earth, New York: Oxford University Press, 1992.

Cockrell, ed., Monroe F. The Lost Account of the Battle of Corinth, North Carolina: Broadfoot Publishing, 2003.

Cohn, David. Where I was Born and Raised, Boston: University of Notre Dame Press, 1948.

Cohodas, Nadine. The Band Played Dixie, New York: The Free Press, 1997.

Cothren, Paige. The Echo of Silence, First Biltmore Corporation, 2003.

Cutler, James E. Lynch Law, New York: Patterson Smith, 1969.

Delaughter, Bobby. Never Too Late, New York: Scribner, 2001.

Dittmer, John. Local People, Urbana and Chicago: University of Ilinois Press, 1995.

Doyle, William. An American Insurrection, New York: Anchor Books, 2003.

Du Bois, W . E. B. Black Reconstrucion: An Essay Toward a History of the Part Which Black Folk Played in the Attempt to Reconstruct Democracy in America, 1860-1880, South Bend, IN: University of Notre Dame Press, updated Feb. 28, 2005.

Elkins, Stanley M. Slavery and the Formation of Character and Slavery, Chicago: University of Chicago Press, 1968.

Evers, Charles. Have No Fear, New York: John Wiley & Sons, 1997.

Evers, Myrlie with William Peters. For Us, The Living, Jackson: University Press of Mississippi.

Fitzgerald, Michael W. The Union League Movement in the Deep South Politics and Franklin, John Hope and Loren Schweninger.

Runaway Slaves: Rebels on the Plantation, New York: Oxford University Press, 1999.

Germany, Dr. Horace. At Any Cost, Anderson, Indiana: Warner Press, 2000.

Glick, Brian. War at Home: Covert Acions Against U.S. Activists and What We Can Do About It, Cambridge, MA: South End Press, 1989.

Halberstam, David. The Fifies, New York: Villard Books, 1993.

Halberstam, David. The Children, New York: Random House, 1998.

Hatch, John Africa, Love, Berkeley, California: 2ndsight Books, 2002.

Hatch, John. Mississippi Swamp, Berkeley, Calif: 2ndsight Books, 2001.

Hemphill, Marie M. Fevers, foods and faith, Indianola: private press, 1980.

Henry, Aaron and Constance Curry. The Fire Ever Burning, Jackson: University Press of Mississippi, 2000.

Hill, Lance. The Deacons For Defense Chapel Hill: The University of North Carolina Press, 2004.

Holland, Ph.D., Endesha Ida Mae. From the Mississippi Delta, a Memoir, New York: Simon & Schuster, 1997.

Howard, John. Men Like That A Southern Queer History, London: The University of Chicago Press, 1999.

Hudson-Weems, Clenora. Emmett Till: The Sacrificial Lamb in the Modern Civil Rights Movement, Bedford Pub; 3 Revised edition, 2000.

Huffman, Alan. Mississippi in Africa. New York: Gotham Books, 2004.

Libby, David J. Slavery and Frontier Mississippi, 1720-1835, Jackson: University Press of Mississippi, 2004.

Litwack, Leon F. Trouble in Mind, New York: Vintage Books.

Loewen, James W. Lies My Teacher Told Me, New York: Touchstone, 1995.

Lomax, Alan. The Land Where the Blues Began, New York: The New Press, 1993.

Markle, Donald E. Spies and Spymasters ofhe Civil War, New York: Hippocrene Books, 1995.

Massengill, Reed. Portrait of a Racist, New York: St. Martins Press, 1993.

McIlhany II, William H. Klandestine, New Rochele: Arlington House, 1975.

McMillen, Neil R. The Citizens Council, Urbana: University of Illinois Press, 1994.

Mettress, ed., Christopher. The Lynching of Emmett Till: a Documentary Narrative, Charlottesville and London: University of Virginia Press, 2002.

Minor, Bill. Eyes on Mississippi, Jackson: J. Pritchard Morris Books, 2001.

Mitchell, Dennis J. Mississippi Liberal A Biography of Frank E. Smith, Jackson: University Press of Mississippi, 2001.

Mitchell, H.L. Mean Things Happening in This Land: The Life and Times of H.L. Mitchell, Cofounder of the Southern Tenant Farmers' Union, Montclair, New Jersey: Alanheld, Osmun, 1979.

Moody, Anne. Coming of Age in Mississippi, Laurel Leaf: New York, reissue 1997.

Move, J. Todd. Let the People Decide: Black Freedom and White Resistance Movements in Sunfower County, Mississippi,

1945-1986, Chapel Hill: The University of North Carolina Press, 2004.

Nossiter, Adam. Of Long Memory, New York: Da Cappo Press, 1994.

Oshinsky, David M. Worse. Than Slavery: Parchman Farm and the Ordeal of Jim Crow Justice, New York: Simon and Schuster, 1996.

Patterson, James T. Brown v. Board of Education: A Civil Rights Milestone and its Troubled Legacy, New York: Oxford University Press, 2001.

Quarles, Benjamin. The Negro in the Civil War, Boston: Little, Brown and Company, 1953.

Rabinowitz, ed., Howard N. Southern Black Leaders of the Reconstruciton Era, Urbana: University of Illinois Press, 1982.

Ransby, Barbara. Ella Baker & the Black Freedom Movement, Chapel Hill, North Carolina, 2003.

Raphael, Ray. A People's History ofhe American Revolution: How Common People Shaped the Fight for Independence.

Ravage, John W. Black Pioneers - Images of he Black Experience on the North American Frontier, Salt Lake City: The University of Utah Press, 1997.

Reynolds, David S., John Brown Abolitionist, New York: Alfred Knopf, 2005.

Sydnor, Charles Sackett. Slavery in Mississippi, Gloucester, MA.: Peter Smith Publishing, 1933.

Scaturro, Frank J. President Grant Reconsidered, New York: Madison Books, 1999.

Shapiro, Herber. White Violence and Black Response: From Reconstruction to Montgomery. Amherst: University of Massachusetts Press, 1988.

Silver, James W. Mississippi: The Closed Society, New York: Harcourt, Brace and World, 1964.

Silver, James W. Running Scared: Silver in Mississippi, Jackson: University Press of Mississippi, 1984.

Stampp, Kenneth. The Peculiar Institution, New York: Vintage Books, 1956.

Till-Mobley, and Benson, Christopher. Death of Innocence, New York: Random House Publishing Group, 2003.

Tucker, William H. The Funding of Scientific Racism, Urbana: University of Illinois Press, 2002.

Tyson, Timothy B. Radio Free Dixie, Chapel Hill: The University of North Carolina Press, 1999.

Volers, Maryanne. Ghosts of Mississippi, New York: Little, Brown & Company, 1995.

Waldron, Ann. Hodding Carter: The Reconstruction of a Racist, Chapel Hill: Algonquin Books, 1993.

Williams, Juan. Eyes on the Prize: America's Civil Rights Years, 1954-1965, New York: Penguin, 1988.

Willis, John C. Forgotten Time: The Yazoo-Mississippi Delta after the Civil War, Charlottesville: University Press of Virginia, 2000.

Woodruff, Nan. American Congo: The African American Freedom Struggle in the Delta, Cambridge, Mass.: Harvard University Press, 2003.

Woods, Clyde. Development Arrested, London: Verso, 1998.

Wright, Simeon. Simeon's Story, Chicago: Lawrence Hill Books, 2010.

Zinn, Howard. A People's History of the United States: 1492 – Present, New York: Harper Perennial, updated 1995.

Howard Zinn, A People's History of the United States, 1492-Present [New Ed.], New York: Harper Collins,2003.

Zinn, Howard. Voices of a People's History ofhe United States, New York: Seven Stories Press, 2004.

Dissertations

Grim,Valerie. "Black farm families in the Yazoo-Mississippi Delta: A study of the Brooks Farm Community, 1920-1970," Dissertation submitted to the graduate faculty, Iowa State University, Ames, 1990.

Walters, Vernon L. Migration into Mississippi, 1798-1837, M.A. Thesis, Mississippi State College, 1969.

Williams, Jr., James Levin. "Civil War and Reconstruction in the Yazoo Mississippi Delta, 1863-1875 (Mississippi)," Dissertation, 1992, The University of Arizona; Advisor: John V. Mering, Source: DAI, 53, no. 11A, 1992.

Articles

"A Study of the Tenant Systems of Farming in the Yazoo-Mississippi Delta," Bulletin 337, Washington, D.C.: United States Department of Agriculture, 1916.

Adams, Jane D. Gorton. "Southern Trauma; Revisiting Caste and Class in the Mississippi Delta," American Anthropologist, Vol. 106, Issue 2, 334-345.

Alston, Edith. "Review: Subversive Southerner: Anne Braden and the Struggle for Racial Justice in The Cold War South," The Anniston Star, December 1, 2002.

Associated Press. "Civil Rights Attorney Found Dead," Lubbock Avalanche-Journal, March 14, 1997.

Associated Press. "Secret Investigation Unit Disbanded in Mississippi," Washington Star, March 1, 1949.

Begos, Kevin. "Against Their Will," five-part series in Journal Now (online) of the Winston Salem Journal, September 15, 2003.

Blackmon, Douglas A. "New York Millionaire Secretly Sent Cash to Mississippi Via His Morgan Account: Wall Street Gang' Pitches In," The Wall Street Journal, June 11, 1999.

Blackwell, Unita with JoAnne Prichard Morris. "Summer of '64: A Mississippi Freedom Fighter Remembers the Struggle," The Jackson Free Press, July 2004.

Bond, Julian. "Tribute to Fannie Lou Hamer," Delta Democrat-Times, March 16, 1977.

Chaddister, Diane. "Interview with Steven Schwerner," Yellow Springs News, January 13, 2005.

Cunnigen, Donald. "Bringing the Revolution Down Home: The Republic of New Africa in Mississippi, Sociological Specrum, 19: 63-92, 73-5, 1999.

Daniel, F. Raymon. "AAA Piles Misery on Sharecroppers," New York Times, April 15, 1935, TCF, 48:0958.

Drabble, Ph.D., John. "From Vigilante Violence to Revolutionary Terror: FBI Operations against the Ku Klux Klan, 1964-1971," paper, 2003.

Eagles, Charles W. "The Closing of Mississippi Society," Journal of Southern History, May 1, 2001.

Emily Wagster Pettus. "Conservative group to meet with state lawmakers," Associated Press, January 23, 2005.

Emmerich, Wyatt. "Embrace the Uniqueness of the Delta," Delta Magazine, September 2003.

Franklin, Ben A. "Mississippi Funds Fight Rights Bill State Gives $20,000 in Tax Money to Capitol Lobby," The New York Times, November 3, 1963.

Gado, Mark. "Mississippi Madness: The Story of Emmett Till," Court TV Crime Library (online).

Grayson, Crystal. "Abstract: Changing Behaviors/Changing Health Risks: Agricultural Pesticide Education in the Mississippi Delta," Department of Anthropology, The University of Mississippi, (online) May 2002.

Greenberg, Benjamin T. "Don't Thank COINTELPRO. Thank Chaney, Goodman and Schwerner," Hungry Blues blog, June 23, 2004.

Halberstam, David. "Negroes Meet Nightly Despite Tension in the Delta," New York Times, June 29, 1964.

Halberstam, David. "Tallahatchie County Acquits a Peckerwood," 1956, online.

Henry, Aaron E. "Mississippi Delegation," Letter to the editor, New York Review of Books, XI, August 22, 1968.

Homes, William F. "The Leflore County Massacre and the Demise of the Colored Farmers' Aliance," Phylon, September 1973.

Jacoby, Jeff. "An execution, not a lynching," Jewish World Review, May 15, 2001.

James, Susie. "The Carrollton Massacre," The Commonwealth, March 12, 1996.

Kay Mills. "Interview with Unita Blackwell MacArthur Genius Award Caps Creative Political Life," Los Angeles Times, August 2, 1992.

Klibanoff, Hank. "L. Ale Wilson: A Reporter Who Refused to Run," Media Studies Journal, Vol. 14, no. 2, Spring/Summer 2000

Lockett, James D. "The Lynching Massacre of Black and White Soldiers at Fort Pillow, Tennese April 12, 1864," The Western Journal of Black Studies, Volume: 22, Issue: 2, 1998.

Maute, Nikki Davis. "Civil Rights Stories Find Home," Hattiesburg American, Feb. 24, 2005.

Miller, Kelly. "Is Race Prejudice Innate or Acquired?" Journal of Applied Sociology, 1 (July-August, 1927), 520-524.

Minor, Bill. "At least 20 state lawmakers still 'cozying up' to CCC hate group," Special to The Clarion-Ledger, November 14, 2004.

Mitchell, Jerry. "Killen Avoided Conviction in '67 Case," The Clarion-Ledger, January 12, 2006.

Mitchell, Jerry. "The Last Days of Ben Chester White," The Clarion-Ledger, February 23, 2003.

Moorehead, Monica. "The Port Chicago Mutiny," Workers World, February 23, 1995.

"Negroes Pledge Their Loyalty," Cleveland Enterprise, April 10, 1919.

O'Connell, Geoffrey F.X. "The Mystery of the 364th," Gambit Weekly, April 3, 2001.

Optowsky, Stan. "White Citizen's Council Menace To South, North," (reprinted in The Pittsburgh Courier), N.Y. Post Corp., 1957.

Paul, Peraite C. "USDA Undermines Historical Civil Rights Settlement with Black Farmers," The Atlanta Journal-Constitution, September 10, 2004.

Polsgrove, Dr. Carol. "Southern Exposures," The American Prospect, Vol. 12, Issue, April 23, 2000.

Roberts, Gene. "Violence and Rights in South," New York Times, 9 January 1966.

"Roosevelt is Roasted for Negrophile Policy," Atlanta Constitution, January 9, 1903

Saul, Stephanie. "FBI Files Detail 5 Slayings," Newsday, May 9, 2000.

Smith, John Burl. "A Lot to Change," The Dish, Volume 5, Issue 50, December 20, 2002.

Stringfellow, Eric. "McDowell may have been killed by teen client," The Clarion-Ledger, March 15, 1997, 3-B.

"The Fort Pilow Massacre," The New York Herald Tribune, May 2, 1864.

"The Short History of Mississippi's State Penal Systems," Mississippi Law Journal (April 1938), 267-269.

"The Threatened Negro Insurrections – Riot at Winona – The Military Called Out – Thirteen Negroes Reported Killed," The New York Herald, Nov. 29, 1869.

Turner, Rene D. "Reopening of case revives interest in Medgar Evers assassination; Mississippi decision sparks questions about mysteries surrounding death of civil rights hero," Ebony, May 1, 1991.

United Press International. "Meredith Hits Removal Of UM Troops," The Clarion-Ledger, June 13, 1963.

United Press International. "Three Charged in Slaying of Girl, 18," Evening Sentinel of Holland, Mich., May 27, 1971.

Williams, Kam. "An Interview with the Publisher of 'The Slaughter," Black World Today, December 23, 2000.

Yardley, Johnathan. "In the Fields of Despair," Washington Post, March 31, 1996.

Collections, Interviews, Oral Histories

"Bolton Centennial brochure." The Jan Hiligas COFO collection, Jackson, Mississippi.

Fannie Lou Hamer, "To Raise Our Bridges," an autobiography. Published by SNCC. Pages were not numbered and the date was not given in the copy available at Tougaloo College archives.

FBI 2006 Emmett Till report and a transcript of the September 1955 trial, online at http://foia.fbi.gov/foiaindex/till.htm.

"Henry Waring Ball, (1858-1934) Diary, 1884-1928." Mississippi Dept. of Archives & History, Special Collections Section, Manuscript Collection.

Interview with Charles Felder Sudduth Jr., 2004. Conducted at Parchman, Miss.

Interview with Margaret Block, 2005. Conducted in Cleveland, Miss.

Interview with Marvin Flemmons, 2004 and 2005. Conducted in Drew, Miss.

"Interview with Mary Fisher Robinson." Historical Research Project of Coahoma County, Mrs. Donna E. Dance, canvasser for WPA, assignment no. 14, Clarksdale Public Library.

Interview with Woodrow Wilson Jackson, 2003. Conducted in Tutwiler, Miss.

Interviews (2) with Robert Patterson, July 2004.Conducted in Itta Bena, Miss.

Interviews (multiple) with Robert Keglar, 2003, 2004. Conducted in Charleston, Miss.

"Julie Dixon to Harry St. John Dixon, January 29, [1870]." Harry St. John Dixon Papers, Mississippi Department of Archives and History.

Kirsty Powell, "A Report, Mainly on Ruleville Freedom School, Summer Project, 1964," Mississippi Freedom School Curriculum. The document is from: SNCC, The Student Nonviolent Coordinating Committee Papers, 1959-1972 (Sanford, NC: Microfilming Corporation of America, 1982) Reel 68, File 367, Page 0582. The original papers are at the King Library and Archives, The Martin Luther King Jr. Center for Nonviolent Social Change, Atlanta, GA.

Letter dated May 21, 1954, by Walter Sillers to Hon. Eugene Cook. From the Walter Sillers, Jr. papers at the Charles Capps, Jr. archives at Delta State University.

Letter from George F. Maynard to Mrs. Mary Fisher Robinson." Friars Point, Mississippi, September 7, 1929, The Mississippi Room of the Clarksdale Public (Carnegie) Library.

Letter from Judge Luther Manship to J. Edgar Hoover, dated April 27, 1945. Acquired under the Freedom of Information Act.

Letter to Aaron Henry and Rev. Emmet Burns, dated March 20, 1972, from Melvyn R. Leventhal. Part of the Aaron Henry collection.

McDowell, Jennifer. "Black Politics: A study and an Annotated Bibliography of the Mississippi Freedom Democratic Party," 1971.

Office memo to FBI director from SAC, New Orleans, dated December 11, 1947, regarding "Mississippi Bureau of Investigation." Acquired under the Freedom of Information Act.

"Old Citizen." Circa 1939 for the Coahoma County Historical Research Project, No. 2984, Assignment#14. Clarksdale Public Library.

Oral history interview (tape) with Cleve McDowell by Owen Brooks. Tougaloo Archives, August 11, 1995.

Oral history of Dr. L. C. Dorsey. Tougaloo College, Delta Collection.

Oral history with Aaron Henry for the Lyndon B. Johnson Library, September 12 1970, interviewed by T.H. Baker.

Oral history with Amzie Moore, University of Southern Mississippi Libraries and USM's Center for Oral History and Cultural Heritage. March 29 and April 13, 1977. The interviewer was Mike Garvey.

Oral history with Charles Cobb, University of Southern Mississippi Libraries and The Center for Oral History and Cultural Heritage, October 21, 1996. Interviewer, John Rachal.

Oral history with Erle Johnston, a cooperative project of the University of Southern Mississippi Libraries and USM's Center for Oral History and Cultural Heritage. Interview conducted by Yasuhiro Katagiri at Johnston's home in Forest, Miss., on August 13, 1993.

Oral history with Lawrence Guyot, September 7, 1996, interviewed by John Rachel, a cooperative project of USM Libraries and USM's Center for Oral History and Cultural Heritage.

Robinson, Mary Fisher. "Outlaw Days," Historical Research Project of Coahoma County, Assignment #14, July 27, 1936. Clarksdale Public Library.

"Satterfield's (John) Final Report to CCFAF," 65-pages, 15 June 1964, Sovereignty Commission, ID 6-70-0-1-6-1-1. Sovereignty Commission documents. Mississippi Department of Archives and History.

"The Box Project." Report, the Aaron Henry Collection at Tougaloo College.

The Jerry Dallas Delta Cooperative Farm Collection, Delta State University. Manuscript No.: M209, Inclusive Dates: 1936-1987, Bulk Dates: 1936–1987 Biographical/Historical Sketch.

"Wilbur T. Gibson interview." The U. S. Work Progress Administration, Friars Point file, Clarksdale Public Library.

William Ruthrauf Amberson Papers. Abstract. Manuscripts Department, Library of the University of North Carolina at Chapel Hill Southern Historical Collection, #3862.

Index

'

'not guilty', 221
'rednecks', 31

"

"After Freedom: A Cultural Study in the Deep South", 74
"best nonfiction about the South,", 88
"Bye, baby.", 123
"Caste and Class in a Southern Town,", 74
"contraband of war.", 20
"Emmett, Down in My Heart,", 83
"furnish", 77
"I have a Dream", 85
"New Negro,", 53
"no mixing", 82
"Noon on Doomsday,", 84
"Pecking Order,", 117
"racial purity.", 101
"rock of waters.", 146
"Singing River,", 33
"Sumner — a good place to raise a boy.", 146
"the briefcase guy", 181
"the Delta", 8
"the most Southern place on Earth,", 10
"The Plight of the Sharecropper,", 77
"There he is,", 148
"white" restroom, 31
"with all deliberate speed.", 121

1

17th Amendment, 26
1875 campaign, 28
1890 Constitutional Convention Mississippi, 35
1927 flood, 70
1964 Civil Rights Act, 5

1964 convention in Atlantic City, 194

4
45-caliber Colt automatic, 132

7
75-pound cotton gin fan, 132

A
A Red Record, 40
AAA, 77
Abernathy, Rev. Ralph David, 208
abolitionist, 18
Abolitionist, 31
abolitionists, 16
abuse, 28
ACORN, 197
Adams, Arnold, 124
Africa
   continent, 10
Africa Love, 13
Africa, in Mississippi, 15
African Americans in Mississippi, 76
African Congo, 54
Agricultural Adjustment Act, 77
agricultural flood plain, 1
Alabama, 10, 17, 19, 74, 172, 179, 180, 206, 217, 220
Alexander, D. O., 54
all-"negro" battalion, 234
all-black community, 35
alleged "race riots.", 40
Alligator, 15
alluvial soil, 1
all-white grand jury, 147

Alsip, 191
Alsip, Ill., 152
American army, hangings, 90
American Colonization Society, 16
American Congo, 54, *See* Nan Woodruff
American Cotton Oil Trust, 64
American Notes. *See* Charles Dickens
American Revolution, 16
Ames
   Governor Adelbert, 26
Amite County, 91
Anderson, Devery, 232
Anglo-Saxon, 149
antebellum, 5, 10, 39, 255
antebellum mansions, 41
anthropological studies, 74
anthropologist, 75
anti-lynching and anti-poll-tax laws, 144
Appalachian Mountains, 18
Argo, 140
Arkansas, 7, 52, 53, 54, 60, 71, 78, 254
armed whites. *See* Hoop Spur
Army Corps of Engineers, 72
Army War College, 102
Associated Press, 61, 125, 164, 191, 209
Atkins, W.P., 24
August 28, 117
autoworkers, 143

B
Baez, Joan, 224
Balko, Radley, 172

Banister, Guy, 206
Barry, John M., 70
Battle of Shiloh, 19
Bean, Dr. Alan, 238
beaten to death, 53
Beauchamp, Keith, 85, 134, 222
Beck, Glenn, 193
Beito
   David. T., 119, 149, 150, 259, 261
   Linda Royster, 149
Beito, Linda Royster, 119
Belgium, 221
Belzoni, 109, 212, 214
Berkeley, 197
Bible belt, 184
Big Dipper star, 17
Bilbo, Gov. Theodore, 50
Bilbo, Theodore, 100, 103
Bilbo, U.S. Sen. Theodore, 98
Bill of Rights, 221
Black Codes, 25
Black Delta Soldiers, 92
Black gun owners, 53
black labor, 10, 24
black labor insurrections, 17
black labor manipulation, 63
Black Maverick, 119
Black Monday, 219
Black Panther Party, 197
black president, 6
black separatism, 35
black soldiers, 90, 99
Black soldiers, 20, 90
black soldiers, executed, 90
black Union soldiers, 20
black veterans, 50
Black, James, 203

Black, Jr., James, 203
blacklisting, 78
Blackmon, Douglas, 101
Blackwood, Kenneth, 61
Blakely, George, 54
Block
   Margaret, 19, 59, 60, 71, 105, 106, 117, 157, 174, 205, 217, 218, 248, 253
Block, Sam, 19, 217
blog, 6
blues, 28
blues musicians, 39
bluesmen, 31, 72
Bobo. *See* Till, Emmett
boiling, 27
Bolden, R.L., 215
Boler, Jaime, 15
Bolivar, 78
Bolivar County, 26, 34, 44, 52, 59, 71, 73, 93, 97
boll, 130
boll weevil, 43
Bolton, 27
Bond, Bradley G., 13
Bond, Julian, 217
Boston Globe, 88
Box Project, 197
Boyd, Lucy, 199
Bradley, Ed, 134
Brewer, John Noey, 54
Bridges, Hailey Gail, 173
British mills, 5
British West Indies, 17
Bronstein, David, 216
Brooks Farm, 79, 80
Brooks, Palmer Herbert, 79
Brown

John, 18
Brown II, 121
Brown vs. the Topeka, Kansas Board of Education, 49
Brown's raid, 18
Bruce
   U.S. Sen. Blanche K., 26
brutal mistreatment, 24
Bryant
   Carolyn and Roy, 122
Bryant and Milam, 147
Bryant Grocery & Meat Market, 123
Bryant, Carolyn, 131, 144, 157, 174
Bryant, Milam, 147
Bryant, Roy, xii, 110, 123, 131, 145, 155
Bryant,Roy, 153
Bryant's Grocery and Meat Market, 131
Buchanan, Pat, 99
Bumpers, Lillie Mae, 215
Bunch III, Lonnie G., 67
Bureau of Refugees, Freedmen, and Abandoned Lands
   Freedmen's Bureau, 23
burglary, 81
Burke, W.B., 199
Burma, 93
burning at the stake, 27
Burr Oak, 159
Burr Oak Cemetery, 134, 152, 191, 234
Bush, President George, 222
Bush, President George W., 69

C

Caehixia Africana, 14
Caldwell, Charles, 27
Calhoun, James, 215
California Eagle, 124
Camp Shelby, 96
Campbell, Dr. Clarence C., 102
Canada, 10
capitalist economy, 18
Carlton, Frank, 166
Carmichael, Stokely, 217
Carroll County, 93, 213
Carroll, Jill, 118
Carrollton Courthouse Riot, 29
Carrollton Massacre, 29
Carter II, Hodding, 213, 217
Carter Jr., Hodding, 213
Carter, Gov. Jimmy, 215
Carter, Hodding, 49, 100, 103
Carter, Jr
   Hodding, 49, 132, 133, 149, 195, 197
Carter, Mae Bertha, 240
Carter, Philip, 213
Carter,, Hodding, 134
Carthan
   John and Alma, 122
   Mamie Elizabeth. *See* Till Mobley
Carthan, Wiley Nash, 73
casket, 133, 134
casket, Emmett Till, 67
Cassidy Bayou, 139
Caste and Class, 74
caste system, 50
castration, 27, 152
catfish, 9
catfish farm ponds, 9

Catfish Row, 8
cautionary tale, 141
censorship, 64
Chalfant, Kathleen, 83
Chancellor, John, 146
Charleston, 38, 52, 105, 107, 109, 146, 153, 198, 199, 212, 253, 259
Charleston jail, 149
Chatam, District Attorney, 148
Chatham, District Attorney Gerald, 147
chattel enslavement, 17
Chicago, iii, xi, xii, 10, 41, 67, 72, 85, 109, 120, 121, 131, 132, 133, 135, 136, 137, 140, 147, 148, 165, 182, 191, 252, 254, 255, 257, 259, 260
Chicago blues, 72
Chicago Defender, 120
Chicago FBI, 206
Chicago NAACP, 143
Chicago's South Side, 233
Chickasaw Bluffs, 8
Chickasawhay River, 91
childbearing, 14
Chiles, Joyce, 151, 222
Choctaw, 15, 146
Christian Science Monitor, 88
Churchill, Winston, 241
Citizens Councils, 49, 112, 184, 219, 241
Citizens' Councils, 97
City College of Los Angeles, 180
civil rights, 164, 167
Civil Rights Act of 1866, 25
Civil Rights Act of 1964, 101
civil rights cold cases, 3

Civil Rights Movement, 223
Civil War, 5, 6, 7, 10, 11, 16, 18, 20, 24, 25, 28, 29, 30, 35, 37, 87, 93, 100, 106, 247, 248, 249, 252
Civil Works Administration, 76
civil wrongs, 4
Civitavecchia, Italy, 234
Clarion-Ledger, 186
Clarke County, 91
Clarksdale, 13, 15, 39, 52, 54, 60, 61, 63, 89, 92, 95, 97, 98, 118, 214, 236, 249
ClarksdaleWebinfo.com, 214
Cleveland, 59, 64, 71, 89, 93, 94, 105, 154, 157, 173, 197, 207, 208, 254
Cleveland Call and Post, 220
Clines, Francis X., 90
closed society, 51
Coahoma County, 39, 118
Cobb, Charles, 95
Cobb, James C., 10
Coburn, U. S. Senator, 222
Coffeeville, 200
Cohn, David, 8
COINTELPRO, 231
cold cases, 200
Cole, Billy Ray, 133
Coleman, Lindley, 54
collective plantation, 79
Collier
  Jo Etha, 5
Collier, Jo Etha, v, 207
Collier, Joe Etha, 196
Collins, 124
Colonel Draper, 102
Colored Farmers Alliance, 33

Colored Farmers Alliance
  (CFA), 32
Combash, William T., 26
Coming of Age in Mississippi, 136
Communist, 74
community of freed slaves, 35
Confederate battle flag, 237
Confederate States, 19
Congress of Racial Equality
  (CORE), 224
congressional anti-lynching bill,
  53
Constitution, 20
continental glacier, 1
Contras, 217
Cook County, 3
Cook County coroner, 151
Cook County Hospital, 219
Coolidge, Calvin, 62
cooperative farms, 78
Cooperative Farms, 77
Coopwood, Holly Springs
  Mayor, 213
corpse, 133
Coss, Clare, 83
Cossar, Judge George Payne,
  107
cotton, xi, 1, 2, 4, 5, 8, 9, 10, 11,
  13, 14, 17, 18, 24, 34, 40, 52,
  65, 76, 98, 134, 252
cotton fields, 8, 9, 24, 130
cotton gin fan, xii
cotton planters, 49
cotton prices, 28, 34
Cotton prices, 73
cotton-picking wages, 78
Cottonville, 75

Council of Federated
  Organizations (COFO), 224
courtesy titles, 99
courthouse massacre, 29
court-martial discipline, 90
Cox, Earnest Sevier, 101
Creole
  ship, 17
cries of the cotton fields, 29
Cromwell, Oliver
  Miss. populist leader, 32
crop dispute, 54
Crosby, Ethan, 39
Current, Gloster B., 136
Curry, Constance, 236
CWA, 76

D

Dahmer, Vernon, 106
Dailey, Gwen, 205
Daily Worker, 147
Daley, Mayor Richard J., 143
Damer, Dennis, 183
damn Yankee, 161
Daniel, F. Raymond, 69
Daniell, F. Raymmond, 78
Davis
  Jefferson, 19, 20, 35
Davis, Nettie, 114, 162, 165,
  168, 173, 177
Dawson, Congressman William,
  143
De La Beckwith, Bryon, 183
de la Beckwith, Byron, 92
De La Beckwith, Byron, 36
debt peonage, 38
debt-slavery, 55
Deggins

Boat, 19
Delta and Pine Land Company, 52
Delta blues, 10, 39, 72
Delta Blues, 2
Delta Burial Funeral Home, 215
Delta Council, 97
Delta counties, 11
Delta Democrat-Times, 213
Delta planter, 45
Delta Planting Company, 52
Delta Research and Cultural Institute, 15
Delta sharecroppers, 78
Delta State, 135
Delta State Teachers College, 93
Delta State University, 93, 197
Delta-Born Journalist. *See* Ida B. Wells
Democratic National Convention, 31
Democratic National Convention in 1948, 51
Democratic Party, 27
Democratic Party Administrative Committee, 215
Democratic-Conservatives, 28
Denton, Jack, 212
deportation, 16
Detroit, 197
Dial
   Jack & J.M., 33
Dickens, Charles, 8
Diddley, Bo, 130
dietary-deficiency, 14
Diggs, U.S. Rep. Charles, 146
discrimination, 3, 6

disenfranchise, 38
disfranchisement, 35
dismemberment, 27
Dixiecrats, 51
Dixon, Amos, 124
Doar, John, 107
Doddsville, 43
Doddsville plantation, 44
Dogan, Sheriff, 107
Dogget, J.L., 61
Dollard, Prof. John, 74
Donham, Carolyn, 152
Donham, Carolyn Bryant, 222, *See* Carolyn Bryant
Dorsey, Dr. L.C., 15, 62, 89
Douglass, Frederick, 31
Dr. King. Martin Luther, 182
Drake, S.N., 107
Draper, Wycliffe, 101
Dred Scott, 211
Drew, xi, xii, 3, 7, 31, 59, 60, 61, 62, 65, 72, 79, 94, 110, 111, 113, 114, 135, 144, 145, 147, 154, 161, 162, 163, 166, 172, 173, 179, 180, 182, 196, 198, 207, 208, 209, 211, 256
Drew Blues Tradition, 10
Drew Centennial, 94
Drew Colored School, 115
Drew High School, 166, 207
Drew, R.L., 97
Drew's blues alley, 72
due process, 38
Dukes, Jim, 183
Dylan, Bob, 224

E

East Money, 121

Eastland
    U.S. Sen. James O., 43, 44, 45, 98, 99, 100, 103, 203, 252
Eastland Family Lynching, 43
Eastland plantation, 43
Eastland's father, 44
Eastland's uncle, 44
Ebert, Roger, 134
Eddy, Sherman, 78
egrets, 9
Eisenhower, Gen. David, 234
Eisenhower, Gen. Dwight D., 89
Eisenhower, President, 144
Elaine, Arkansas, 53
Eliza Clark School, 98
Ellis, Joe, 99
emancipation, 16
Emancipation Proclamation, 41
Emerson, Ralph Waldo, 18
Emmett Till Memorial Highway, 133
Emmett Till Murder Trial, 145
Emmett Till Unsolved Civil Rights Crime Act, 222
Emmett Till's body, 126, 152
Emmett Till's father, 233
Emmett whistled, 123
Emmett whistled at a dog, 144
England, 5, 8, 17, 41, 90, 97, 250
Engle, C.F., 33
enslaved, 5
enslaved women, 14
enslaved workers, 11
Enumeration Clause
    Constitution, slavery, 20
escape, 39

Escape, 15
ethnographies, 74
eugenics, 101
eugenics movement, 103
Eugenics Research Association, 102
Evans, Judge Gray, 168, 176
Everett, District Atty. George, 210
Evers, Charles, 97, 198
Evers, Medgar, xii, 36, 89, 95, 100, 119, 120, 132, 136, 167, 182, 186
Evers-Williams, Myrlie, 186
Exalted Cyclops, 70
executed, American soldiers, 90
explosion of ammunition, 93
extermination, 27
extreme racism, 43
Eyes on the Prize: America's Civil Rights Years, 1954-1965, 220

F

Fair Employment Practices, 51
family alliances, 63
Family farms, 79
farm labor representation, 77
farming revolution, 98
farm-labor entrapment, 39
father of secession in Mississippi, 19
Faulkner, William, 4
FBI, 3, 91, 92, 105, 107, 110, 117, 123, 131, 132, 136, 147, 151, 173, 174, 178, 181, 186, 200, 202, 204, 205, 206, 207, 222, 231, 258, 260, 262
federal agricultural policies, 76

Federal Bureau of Investigation, 151
federal kidnapping statute, 132
Fère en Tardenois, France, 90
Finch, Gov. Cliff, 215
firecrackers, 123
first statistical record of lynching in the South. *See* Ida B. Wells
fishing, 131
Fleming, Police Chief J.D., 208
Flood Control Act of 1928, 72
flood plains, 10
flooding, 73
floodwalls, 72
floodways, 72
Flowers, Curtis, 238
flying bullets, 60
FOJ, 238
follow the drinking gourd, 17
food/debt dependency, 32
Foote, Shelby, 100
forced caste division, 75
forced separation, 14
foreign labor, 24
Foreman, Percy, 174
France, 221, 234
free state of Tallahatchie County, 118
freed African Americans, 24
freed blacks, 16
Freedman's Bureau, 24
freedmen, 24
Freedmen, 25
Freedmen's Bureau, 23
Freedom Farm Cooperative and pig bank, 217
Freedom Rider, 118
Freedom Riders, 182
Freedom Route, 17
Freedom Summer, 95, 224
Freedom Summer of 1964, 197
Freies Volk, 221
French Senegal, 20
Frick, Wilhelm, 102
Friends of Justice, 238
Friends of the Forks of the Roads, 17
frustration aggression, 75
Fugitive Slave Clause, 21
funeral, Emmett Till, 134

G

Gado, Mark, 109, 147
Garvey movement, 55
Garvey, Marcus, 48, 55
Garveyism, 54, 55
gay men, 184
gays, 102
genocide, 241
George, Donna S., 183
German Prisoner of War, 94
Germany, 221
Gibbs, Phillips, 198
Gill, G. Wray, 206
Glendora, xii, 113, 126
Glover, Danny, 83
Goat Hill, 212
Gooden, James, 70
Google, 232
Gordon, Carrie, 80
Granada, 224
Grant, President Ulysses S., 25
Gray, Grafton, 107, 205
Gray, Victoria, 108
Great Britain, 184
Great Flood, 72

Great Migration, 72
Great Mississippi Swamp, 15
Great White Chief, 42
greed, 45
Green, Ernest, 91
Green, J. Marie, 90, 233
Green, James Earl, 198
Greenville, 30, 43, 49, 50, 65, 70, 103, 133, 174, 197, 198
Greenville camp on the levee, 71
Greenwood, 24, 26, 33, 36, 54, 73, 92, 105, 131, 132, 133, 152, 153, 156, 176, 218, 253, 254, 259, 260
Grenada, 93, 223
Gresham, Delores, 126
Gresham, Rev. Jesse, 163, 179
Grim, Prof. Valerie, 79
Guaranty Trust, 101
Guest, Ada, 139
Guest, Leola, 97
Gulf of Mexico, 10, 72
gun battle, 61
gunfight, 10, 60
gunfire, 53
gunpoint, 39
guns, 178
Gunter, John, 146
gypsies, 102

H

Hackett, H.Y., 97
Halberstam, David, 125, 126, 146
Hall, Robert F., 147
Hamer
   Fannie Lou, xii, 31, 61, 62, 78, 119, 194, 207, 209, 210, 217, 226
Hamlett
   Adlena, 5
Hamlett, Adlena, v, 106, 153, 200
Hamlett, Berry, 203
Hamlett, Lila, 204
Hamlett, Nina, 262
Hamlett,Adlena, 108
Handy
   W. C., 31
hanging, 27
Harlem, 55
Harper's Ferry, 18
Harris, Circuit Clerk Tom, 107
Harris, Mary Jane, 76
Harrison, Sid, 213
Hatch, John, 13
Hattiesburg, 183
Hayne, M.D., Stephen T., 169
Hazlehurst, 122
Head Start, 164, 215
health, 14
Henry
   Aaron, xi, 39, 89, 95, 96, 97, 99, 100, 184, 200, 210, 211, 212, 213, 215, 217, 236, 250, 256
Henry Waring Ball Diary, 30
Henry, Aaron, 216
Herbers, John, 146
Herd II, Ron, 243
Herd, Ronald, 57
Herron, Isom, 216
Heter, Ser Seshs Ab, 17
Higginbottom, Edgar, 212

Higgs, Bill, 118, 184
high school history texts, 88
Highway 61, 94
Hill, Charles, 96
Hinds County, 27
hippies, 224
historical gatekeepers, 4
History in the Classroom Mississippi, 6
history used as a weapon, 88
Hodges, Robert, 132
Holcomb, 213
Hollandale, 214
Holly Grove church, 180
Holly Springs, 40, 41, 213
Holmes, 78
Holmes, Rev. Amos, 97
Holmes, William F., 32
home guard, 93
homosexuality, 183
Hoop Spur, 53
Hoover, J. Edgar, 120
Hoover, Pres. Herbert, 76
Hoover, President Herbert, 71
horse-care program, 2
Horton, Adolph, 33
House of Representatives' Committee on Un-American Activities, 106
House, Son, 39
Howard General Oliver O., 23
Howard, Dr. T.R.M., 119
Howard, Prof. John, 184
Howard, T.R.M., 36, 124
Hubbard, 124
Huff, William Henry, 143
Hughes, Howard, 101

Huie, William Bradford, 150
human burnings, 28
Hunter Bear, 38
Hurley, Ruby, 97
Hurricane Katrina, 69
hypocrisy, 65

I

Illinois Central Terminal, 133
Indianola, 61, 74, 75, 166, 168, 185, 219, 255, 262
indigents, 102
infant mortality, 14
inhalation of the gas fumes, 44
inhumanity of slavery, 8
Inland Steel Container Company, 143
institution of slavery, 8
insurrection, 48
integration, 3
intermarrying, 15
International Congress for the Scientific Investigation of Population Problems, 102
interrogated, 53
Iola
Ida B. Wells, 41
Iowa, 241
Iowa State University, 79
Issaquena, 11, 24, 214
Itta Bena, 15, 54, 152, 154
Ivy, J.P., 42

J

Jackson Advocate, 124, 249
Jackson bus stations, 182
Jackson Clarion-Ledger, 182
Jackson Daily News, 44

Jackson Free Press, 117
Jackson Movement, 37
Jackson State University, 166, 186, 198
Jackson, Rev. Jesse, xii, 95, 182
Jackson, Woodrow, 133, 135
Jackson,Woodrow, 178
Jackson's lunch counter sit-ins, 38
Jacoby, Jacob, 38
James O. Eastland School of Law, 167
Japan, 223
Jefferson, Sam, 54
Jet magazine, 166
Jews, 102
Jim Crow, 29, 51, 77, 91, 249, 250, 252
Jim Crow laws, 31
Jim Crow practices, 29
Jim Crow rules, 115
Jim Crow rules, unwritten, 141
Jim Crow table, 146
Johnson, Derrick, 118
Johnson, Gov. Paul, 224
Johnston, Erle, 223
Jonesboro, Arkansas, 213
jukes, 39
Jury selection, 145

K

Katagiri, Yasuhiro, 223
Katrina, 72
Keglar, 113
  Birdia, 5
Keglar and Hamlett, 201
Keglar, Birdia, v, 106, 107
Keglar, James, 202
Keglar, James "Sonny Boy", 202
Keglar, Robert, 109, 113, 202, 206
Keglar. Robert, 200
Kennedy
  Pres. John F., 182
  Robert F., 182, 206
Kennedy. Robert F., 206
Kent State, 198
Kentucky, 101
Kenya Emergency, 92
Kenyan independence, 92
key Civil War battle, 41
kidnapped Africans, 6
kidnapping, 143
kidnapping, Emmett Till, 131
Kikuyu, 92
King Leopold II, 54
King, Jr.
  Rev. Martin Luther, xii, 50, 85, 94, 162, 174, 182
King, Mary, 59
KKK, 37
Klan, 25, 53, 62, 64, 70, 105, 111, 202, 203, 214, 258
Klansman, 44, 106, 153
Klansmen, 25, 64, 71, 183, 214
Klanswomen, 227
Klopfer, Grace Sophia, v
Knights and Daughters of Tabor, 35
Krane, Dale, 27
Ku Klux Klan, 24, 25, 28, 50, 51, 53, 96, 106, 120, 203, 232
kudzu, 9, 33, 34, 207

L

laborers, 39

laborers lynched, 43
land reform, 74
Lang, Charlie, 91
Larsson, Cloyte, 157
Laughlin, Harry, 102
Laurel, 91
Le Drapeau Rouge, 221
Le Monde, 221
Le Peuple, 221
Lee
    Rev. George, 5
Lee, Rev. George, v, 109, 120
Leflore County, 32, 109, 131, 132, 136, 151, 202, 251, 259
Leflore County Grand Jury, 222
Leflore grand jury, 174
legal age of consent, 184
Legal Defense fund, 92
lens of race, 74
Levee hollers, 29
levees, 72
Lewis, John, 94, 182
Liberia, 16, 103, 248
Liberian colony, 16
Lilly, Prof. J. Robert, 90
Lincoln
    Abraham, 19, 41, 249
Lincoln County, 121
Litwack, Leon, 38
Litwack, Leon F., 31
Loewen, Prof. James, 4, 87
Loggins, 124
Loggins, Henry Lee, 150, 151
Long, Huey, 49
Look magazine, 218
Los Angeles, 218
Lott, U.S. Sen. Trent, 165

Louisiana, 10, 16, 49, 54, 70, 71, 72, 206, 247
Lucretzia, Benni, 234
Lynch Mob, 57
lynched, 91
lynching, xii, 26, 27, 28, 31, 37, 38, 41, 42, 43, 44, 50, 52, 55, 73, 75, 81, 83, 88, 95, 110, 115, 117, 159, 165, 173, 215, 220, 225, 251
Lynching and the Excuse For It Ida B. Wells, 41
lynching mob, 44
lynching photography, 38
lynchings, 109

M

machine gun fire, 59
Maddow, Rachel, 99
Madigan. Illinois Atty. Gen., 191
Mafia, 206
Magnolia state, 49
male slaves, 15
Man Know Thyself, 48
Manchester Union Leader, 5
Manhunt Rumors, 125
Mannie, George, 159
Marcello, Carlos, 206
Marcus Garvey Movement, 47
maroons, 17
Maroons, 13, 15
Marshall, Thurgood, 95
Martin, Wesley P., 54
Marx, Karl, 77
Masonic, 187
mass exodus, 64
Massachusetts, 101
massacre, 29, 60

Mau Mau, 92
Mau Mau Rebellion, 92
Maxwell Air Force Base, 217
McBride, Earnest, 26
McClinton, Eddie, 212
McCosh Elementary School, 233
McDowell
  Cleveland, v, xii, 5, 7, 8, 50, 157, 161, 162, 163, 164, 166, 167, 168, 169, 172, 173, 174, 176, 177, 178, 179, 180, 181, 182, 183, 184, 185, 187, 209, 210, 247, 261, 262
McDowell, Cleveland
  autopsy report, 171
McDowell, Kwasi, 182
McDowell, Sally, 7
McDowell's coffee table, 178
McLaurin, Charles, 185
McTatie, Leon, 93
mechanization, 77
mechanized cotton production, 73
Medal of Honor, 20
Medgar Evers funeral, 38
mêlée, 53
Melton, Beulah, 126
Melton, Clinton, 126
Memphis, 8, 10, 13, 17, 34, 40, 41, 78, 94, 179, 181, 207
Memphis Commercial Appeal, 147
Meredith, James, 48, 50, 166, 181, 184
Meridian, 26
Merigold, 94
midwives, 14, 80

Milam and Bryant, 81, 99, 124, 135, 149, 150, 151, 221
Milam, Bud, 110
Milam, J.W., xii, 110, 122, 131, 145, 154
Milam, Leslie, 124
Milam, Roy, 148
Milam/Bryant Murder Trial, 139
Milam/Bryant trial, 57, 113, 146
military court martial, 90
military districts, 25
Mims, Henry S., 163, 180
Minter City, 32, 33, 144, 196
Minter City Massacre, 32
misfit horses, 2
Mississippi, 10
  belly of the beast, 6
Mississippi Archives, 75
Mississippi Colonization Society, 16
Mississippi Delta, v, xi, 8, 31, 40, 59, 61, 83, 125, 129, 153, 184, 194, 219, 243, 254, 255
Mississippi Department of Corrections, 176
Mississippi Freedom Democratic Party, 108
Mississippi Freedom Labor Union, 78
Mississippi House of Representatives, 236
Mississippi River, 1, 8, 10, 17, 35, 49, 52, 53, 54, 70, 72, 129
Mississippi Valley State University, 15
Mississippi: Conflict and Change, 4, 88
Mississippi: The Closed Society, 50

Mississippi's confederacy, 28
Mississippi's Department of Archives and History, 2
Mississippi's horrifying history, 37
Mitchell, Jerry, 152, 174
Mitchell,Jerry, 189
Mixing, 82
mob, 91
mob crew, 62
Mob Rule, 57
mob, lynch, 37
modern civil rights movement, 6, 37
Modern Civil Rights Movement, 78
Mohead, James, 199
Mohr, Holbrook, 125
Molestation, 181
Money, xi
Money, Miss., 121, 123, 143
Monks, Vicki, 183
Monmouth, 19
Montgomery, 180
   Benjamin, 35
   Isiah, 35
Montgomery bus boycott, 5
Montgomery, Alabama, xii, 163
Moody, Ann, 136
Moon Lake, 215
Moore, Amzi, 16
Moore, Amzie, 89, 94, 95, 97, 100, 132
MOORE, Amzie, 93
Moore, Isaac, 64
Mooty, Rayfield, 143
Mooty, Raymond, 144
Morgan Guaranty, 101

Morgan Guaranty Trust., 5
Morris, Scott, 33
Mound Bayou, 15, 31, 34, 35, 97, 119, 205, 217
Mrs. Till, 68
Muri, Freida, 234
musicians, 72

N

NAACP, xii, 9, 36, 53, 55, 76, 77, 92, 93, 96, 97, 105, 106, 118, 120, 134, 136, 143, 147, 164, 167, 183, 186, 199, 210, 213, 216, 220, 224, 255
Natchez, 17, 19
National Association for the Advancement of Colored People, 164
National Association of Medical Examiners, 172
National Guard, 71
National Intelligencer, 11
National Museum of African American History and Culture, 67, 152
National Public Radio, 183
National Students Association, 96
National Underground Railroad Network to Freedom Program, 17
Native Africa, 16
Native American, 1, 37
Native Americans, 15, 241
Navy, 20, 93
Nazi, 100
Nazi war criminals, 182
NBC news, 146

Neda, 196
New Africa, 15, 98
New Africa Road, 13
New Deal agricultural programs, 76
New Deal relief policies, 76
New Hampshire, 5
New Orleans, 33, 69, 72, 96, 205, 206
New York, 5
New York Age, 124
New York Times, 101
New York Tribune, 44
Niebuhr, Reinhold, 77
Nixon, President Richard, 210
no quarter, 20
noblesse oblige, 43
Normandy, 97
North Carolina, 102
Northern banking interests, 5
Northern hypocrisy, 68
Northern Kentucky University, 90
northern migration, 73
November 1875 elections, 28
Nuremberg war-crimes tribunal, 102

O

Obama, President Barack, 193
Oise-aisne American Cemetery, 89
Oise-Aisne Cemetery, 234
Ole Miss, 49, 50, 235
Operation PUSH, 119
oppression, 64
Oregon, 3
Osborn, Frederick, 102

outside agitators, 9
Owens, Jesse, 50
Oxford, 49
Oxford, Miss., 107

P

Papa Mose. *See* Wright, Moses
Parchman, 2, 74, 112, 135, 172, 245, 249, 252
Parchman Penitentiary, 2, 152, 167, 199, 200, 245
parity, 76
Parker, Jr.
   Wwheeler, 121
Parks
   Rosa, 5
Parks, Rosa, xii, 119
Parks, Wesley, 207, 210
Patterson, Robert 'Tut', 92
Paul, U.S. Rep. Ron, 222
Peabody Hotel, 8
peckerwoods, 126
Pennington, Jesse, 214
peonage, 76, 80
Percy, Leroy, 43, 65
Peterson, Dewey, 118
PFHUA, 53
Philadelphia, 213
Phillips County, Ar, 53
photographs of Till's corpse, 145
Pickens, William, 54
Pillow Academy, 156
Pioneer Fund, 102
plantation, 14
   "ideal", 11
plantation bloc, 64
plantation regulations, 64

plantations, 24
planter/merchant monopolies, 32
Planters, 63
Plessy versus Ferguson, 219
pogrom, 28
Polak, Andrew, 84
polio, 233
poll tax, 107
poll taxes, 107
Pontotoc, 212
poor Delta children, 45
popular insurrection, 18
Populist, 32
populist rebellion, 18
Port Chicago, 92
Porter, Eddie, 71
post-Civil War occupation of the South, 26
postwar militancy, 55
Powdermaker, Prof. Hortense, 74
Powell, Linda, 83
Powell, Sr., Adam Clayton, 55
power of the press, 41
POWs, 94
President Grant, 28
Presidential Reconstruction, 25
prison punishment, 90
Prisoners of War, 20
private, segregated academies, 5
Progressive Farmers and Householders Union of America, 53
Prologue, xi
protest, 26
Providence farm, 79
provisional government, 19

Pulitzer Prize, 195, *See* Hodding Carter, Jr.
Pullen
   Joe, v, 5, 57, 59, 60, 61, 62, 64, 65, 72, 114
punishment, 24, 44, 71

Q

Queens College, 184
Quitman, 91
Quitman, Jofhn Anthony, 19

R

Race Consciousness, 47
race war, 32
racial and ethnic cooperation, 74
racial prejudice, 19
racial understanding, 89
racial violence, 3, 34
racism, 6, 49, 91, 181
racist, 97, 155
racist tyranny, 39
Rankin, U.S. Rep., 92
Rankin, U.S. Rep. John, 99
rape, 31, 41, 64, 99
rape, English civilians, 90
Ray, James Earl, 174
Rayner and Sons mortuary, 152
Reactions, 150
ReasonOnline, 172
Reconstruction, 23, 25, 26, 27, 29, 31, 32, 87, 106, 107, 202, 249, 252, 253
Red Cross, 70
Red Cross food donations, 74
Redeemers, 27
Reed, Willie, 147, 151
refugee camps, 71

Regional Council of Negro
  Leadership, 120
relief programs, 77
repatriation, 16
Republican, 26, 28
Revolutionary War, 16
Riddick, Leroy, 172
right to appeal, 38
ring, 132
River of Death, 1
roasting, 42
Robinson, Capt. Albert, 166
Robinson, Plater, 205
Rocky Ford, 42
Rod Serling Memorial
  Foundation, 84
Roosevelt, Eleanor, 51
Roosevelt, Pres. Franklin D., 76
Roosevelt, Pres. Theodore, 35
Rosa, Michael, 152
Rosedale, 129
Ross
  Isaac Wade, 16
Ross, Judge Harvey, 98
Ruleville, 31, 61, 62, 64, 110,
  111, 113, 150, 154, 157, 198,
  207, 209, 217
runaway African Americans, 15
runaway slaves, 8
Rust College, 41
Rutgers University, 101

S

safe house, 94
safe houses, 17
Salter, John R., 38
San Francisco, 92
Sanders, J.D., 172

Saunders, W.T., 60
Savage, Daisy, 214
Savory, Johnnie, 239
Scarbrough, Tom, 107
school integration, 219
scientific management
  techniques, 52
SCLC, 162
Scott, Gladys and Jamie, 239
SCU, 74
Scurlock, Walter, 3, 110, 187
Scurlock, Walter, 162
Segregated schools, 27
segregation, 98
Serling, Rod, 83
Sexual battery, 64
Shaffer, Stephen D., 27
Share Croppers Union, 74
sharecropping, 55
Sharkey
  Governor William, 24
Shaw University, 218
Shell Mound, 32
Shelton, Sheriff Ike, 120
Shepherd, Charley, 44
Sheridan plantation, 135
shooting, 27, 53
Shorter, Isaac Henderson, 197
shot in cold blood, 53
Showers, Frances Kimbriel, 94
Shubuta Bridge, 91
Shuttlesworth, Rev. Fred, 182
Sidon, 202
Sierra Leone, 16
Sillers, Walter, 73
silver ring, 122, 148
Silver, James W., 49, 51
Silver, Prof. James W., 48

Simeon, Booker, 146
Simmons, Rev. Isaac, 91
Simpson, Richard "Dick", 204
Sisson, Carmen K., 240
Slaughter, Constance, 186
slave patrols, 15
slave rebellion, 18, 19
slave revolt, 16
slave ship, 17
Slave ships, 5
slave trade, 5, 20
slavery, 10
slavery in America, 18
slaves, 102
sleeping car porter unions, 143
Smith
    Lamar, 5
Smith Funeral Home, 215
Smith, Burner, 173
Smith, Flora Jean, 198
Smith, Lamar, v, 120
Smith, Police Chief Burner, 176
Smith, Robert, 147
Smith, U.S. Rep. Frank Ellis, 103
SNCC, 106, 204, 218
socialist, 77
Socialist Party, 77
sociologist, 37, 62
Soltani, Neda, 195
Southern Christian Leadership Conference, 208
Southern Christian Leadership Conference (SCLC), 224
Southern Farmers Alliance, 32
Southern Tenant Farmer's Union, 77
Sovereignty Commission, 3, 101, 107, 112, 162, 165, 176, 182, 183, 184, 197, 198, 199, 206, 207, 212, 215, 216, 223, 232, 257, 259, 262
Soviet Union, 78
Spearman, Papa, 143
squirrel guns, 54
Standard Oil Company, 64
Staple Singers, 145
Stark, Will, 63
state civil rights act, 27
statistics and alleged causes of lynching. *See* Ida B. Wells
statutory age of sexual consent, 185
Steamship Britannia, 8
Steelwater, Eliza, 37
Steelworkers, 143
STFU, 77
Stillman College, 119
stockade, 53
Stratton, Gov. William, 143
Strider, Sheriff H.C., 146
strike, 78
Stringfellow, Eric, 186
Student Nonviolent Coordinating Committee (SNCC), 224
Sturgis, 215
stutter, 233
subjugation, 28
subsidy payments, 77
Sudduth, Charles, 214
Sullivan, John D., 206
Sumner, 57, 81, 117, 125, 127, 139, 145, 146, 199, 212
Sumner's biggest event, 139
Sunflower County, xi, 2, 7, 26, 27, 31, 43, 44, 54, 59, 61, 62,

74, 78, 93, 135, 164, 165, 166, 167, 173, 219, 252
Sunflower River, 13
swamp communities, 15
swamplands, 13, 15, 41
swamps, 61
Swango, Judge, 123
Sykes, Dorothy, 214

T

Taborians, 35
Taken By Force, 91
Tallahatchie, 109
Tallahatchie County, 38, 52, 81, 105, 106, 107, 117, 123, 125, 131, 132, 135, 139, 145, 212, 253, 260
Tallahatchie County Jail, 113
Tallahatchie River, xii, 32, 85, 126, 130, 132, 134, 145, 150
tar-and-featherings, 28
Tardy, Bertha, 238
Taylor, Sidney E., 198
tenants, 77
Tennessee, 10, 13, 53, 71, 256
Tennessee veterans, 24
terrorism, 37, 53
TERRORISM, 26
terrorist, 24
Texas, 206
Texas Southern University, 167
Thar he!, 148
The Box Project, 39
The Christian Science Monitor, 118
the Delta, 8
The Free Speech and Headlight Ida B. Wells, 41
The Lynching of Emmett Till, 112

The Philadelphia Inquirer's, 183
The Twilight Zone, 83
themes surrounding Mississippi's civil rights history, 4
Third Reich, 102
Thompson, U.S. Rep. Benjamin, 117
Thompson, U.S. Representative, 81
three-fifths Constitution, enslavement, 20
Thurgood Marshall School of Law, 167
Till
  Emmett, v, xi, xii, 3, 4, 5, 30, 32, 49, 57, 60, 67, 81, 82, 83, 84, 85, 91, 99, 110, 113, 117, 119, 120, 122, 123, 125, 129, 130, 132, 135, 136, 144, 148, 150, 151, 153, 154, 159, 161, 165, 173, 174, 176, 178, 182, 191, 195, 205, 220, 221, 225, 231, 237, 245, 254, 259, 260, 261, 263
Till Mobley, Mamie, 73, 140, 148, 151, 195
Till, Louis, 89, 90, 122, 233
Till, Mrs., 133, 142
Till,, Louis, 148
Till's grave, 152
Till's mother, 132
Time Bomb: Mississippi Exposed and the Full Story of Emmett Till, 124
Times Picyune, 205
Tombigbee River, 17

torture, 27, 42, 109, 163, 180
tortured, 53
torturing, 44
Tougaloo, 213, 247, 248, 262
Tougaloo College, 4, 38, 87, 211, 215
Trannam, Sumner Night Marshall, 212
Travis, Jams, 218
Treaty of Dancing Rabbit Creek, 15
tributary basin improvements, 72
Truman, Harry, 51
Tucker, Dr. William, 101
Tulane University, 96
Tulia Corroboration Bill, 238
Tulia drug sting, 238
Tunica, 76, 179
Tunica County, 26
Tupelo, 212
Turner
  Nat, 16
Tuskegee Institute, 96
Tutor, Fulton, 212
Tutwiler, 63, 132, 133

U

U.S. Army, 233
U.S. Attorney General, 81
U.S. Commission On Civil Rights, 206
U.S. Department of Justice, 117
U.S. Dept. of Justice, 105
U.S. Justice Department, 107
U.S. marshals, 48
UGR, 17
Uhuru, 17

Underground Railroad, 17
undertaker, 132
UNIA, 55
Union Army, 20
unions, 143
United Press, 146
United States Department of Justice, 151
Universal Negro Improvement Association, 55
University of Alabama, 119
University of Mississippi, 48, 162, 166, 167, 181, 185
University of Mississippi law school, xii
University of Notre Dame. *See* Prof. James W. Silver
unmarked grave, 89
UP wire, 132
UPI, 210

V

Valley State University, 153
Vardaman, James K., 42
vertical integration, 64
veteran black farmers, 52
Vicksburg, 8, 10, 11, 15, 24, 26, 34, 64, 94, 206
Vicksburg Evening Post, 44
Vicksburgnews, 85
Virginia, 16, 18, 79, 102
voter-registration drives, 94
voting irregularities, 107
voting rights, 3, 38
Voting Rights Act, 237

W

W.C. Brooks' plantation, 54

W.E. AL.L. B.E. News Radio, 57
Waldron, Ann, 149
Walker, Landy, 153
Walker, Peter, 154
Waller, Gov. Bill, 209
Walnut Hills, 8
Walters, Sarah, 80
Wash, Howard, 91
Washington County, 214
Washington, Booker T., 35
Washington, D.C., 11, 106, 152
watershed, 10
Watt's burning, 197
Webb, 142
Webb, Juarez, 166, 174, 175
Webb, Juarze, 168
Webster, Daniel, 18
Wells, Ida B., 40
West Point Daily Times Leader, 147
Western Africa, 16
Westmoreland, U.S. Rep. Lynn, 222
Where Rebels Roost, 112
whipped to death, 63, 93
whippings, 28
whistled, 85
White America,", 102
White Citizens Councils, 36, 84
white coalitions, 63
White League, 28
white Populists, 34
white press, 6
White Primaries, 98
White Raiders, 53
white soldiers, 92
white supremacists, 82, 184
white supremacy, 38, 78

white vigilantes, 53
White, Gov. Hugh, 147
White, Walter, 76
white-terrorism group, 93
Whitten, defense attorney, John C., 221
Whore's Lake, 227
Wilkerson, Allen, 207
Wilkin plantation, 93
William "Bill" Loeb III, 5
William F. Winters Archives, 211
William Winters Library, 185
Williams, Juan, 220
Williford, Mayor W.O., 208
Winchell, Walter, 99
Winona, 31, 54, 217, 226, 238, 239, 249
Winstonville, 15
Winters Archives, 215
Winters, Gov. William, 185
Winters, Hal, 54
Without Sanctuary, 38
witnesses, 149
woman's voice, 135
Woodruff, Nan, 54
Woods, Clyde, 28
Works Progress Administration, 76
World War I, 50, 54, 63, 64, 65
World War II, 51, 90, 233
WORLD WAR II, 92
World War II soldiers, 89
WPA, 29, 76, 255
Wright
   Simeon, 123
Wright, Elizabeth, 148
Wright, Mose, 121, 147

Wright, Moses, 132, 143
Wright, Simeon, 121, 135
WWII, 99

X
X, 144
Xavier University, 236

Y
Yale Institute of Human
   Relations, 74
Yalobusha County, 42
Yazoo, 1

Yazoo City, 25
Yazoo Delta, 53
Yazoo Wildlife Refuge, 214
Yazoo-Mississippi Delta, 1, 7, 8,
   10, 23, 74, 255
Young, Andrew, 94, 217

Z
Zachary Black, Nina, 152
Zachary-Black, Nina, 200
Zanchi, Anna, 234
Zinn, Howard, 18

www.ingramcontent.com/pod-product-compliance
Lightning Source LLC
Chambersburg PA
CBHW020744160426
43192CB00006B/242